Question Words

where (from)?		
what?		
when?		
how?		
how much/long?	quanto?	
how many?	quanti/e?	*KWAHN-tee/-tay?*
why?	perché?	*payr-KAY?*
who?	chi?	*kee?*

Useful Words

big, small	grande, piccolo/a	*GRAHN-day,* *PEEK-koh-loh/-lah*
a lot, a little	molto, un po'	*MOHL-toh, oon poh*
enough	abbastanza	*ahb-bahs-TAHN-tsah*
good, bad	buono/a, cattivo/a	*BWOHN-oh/-ah,* *kaht-TEE-voh/-vah*
hot, cold	caldo/a, freddo/a	*KAHL-doh/-dah,* *FRAYD-doh/-dah*
available	libero/a	*LEE-bay-roh/-rah*

Assistance and Communication

Can you help me?	Può aiutarmi?	*pwoh ah-yoo-TAHR-mee?*
Can you recommend ___?	Può consigliare ___?	*pwoh kohn-seel-LYAH-ray ___?*
How much does it cost?	Quanto costa?	*KWAHN-toh KOHS-tah?*
Do you speak English?	Parla inglese?	*PAHR-lah een-GLAY-say?*
I (don't) understand.	(Non) capisco.	*(nohn) kah-PEES-koh*

Italian Dictionary with Phrases for Travelers

A Practical, Hands-On Resource for Actually Using Italian

Elizabeth Bingham, Ph.D.
Author of *Italian Survival Guide*

World Prospect Press
Waverly, Iowa

Publisher's Note

This book is designed to help prepare travelers for their trips abroad. Its purpose is to educate and entertain. It is sold with the understanding that the publisher and author are not giving legal or financial advice. The author and World Prospect Press shall have neither liability nor responsibility to any person or entity with respect to any loss or damage caused, or alleged to be caused, directly or indirectly, by the information contained in this book.

If you do not wish to be bound by the above, you may return this book to the publisher for a full refund.

ISBN-13: 978-0-9703734-7-2
ISBN-10: 0-9703734-7-3

Library of Congress Control Number: 2013944160

World Prospect Press
P.O. Box 253
Waverly, IA 50677
www.worldprospect.com

First Edition
10 9 8 7 6 5 4 3 2 1

Table of Contents

Introduction

Welcome to the *Italian Dictionary with Phrases for Travelers.* This is the book I want in my hands when I am in Italy, trying to communicate, but not fully confident or capable in the language. It's not, technically, a phrasebook, although it does include many vital phrases that you'll use over and over again. Instead of a phrasebook's numerous sections with separate lists of context-specific vocabulary, this book cuts to the chase with the kind of information *I* need when *I'm* traveling, and that I figure other people can use, as well.

Here are both the basic phrases and the extended vocabulary that will help you communicate most things you'll want or need to in Italy. It's not fancy. You won't find complicated structures, the kind of native-sounding accuracy that fills traditional phrasebooks. I don't know about you, but I can never find the phrase I need on-the-spot when I use one of those things. In contrast, this book offers on-the-ground information to get by with. Survival communication. It may not be pretty, but it works pretty well.

To use this book effectively, first look over the pronunciation guide. If you have time and interest, also take a look at the brief grammar summary that follows. Realize, however, that this book does not attempt to teach either grammar or vocabulary. (Please turn to my book *Italian Survival Guide* if you want a broader and more thorough tourist introduction to Italian language and culture.)

Most importantly, familiarize yourself with the incredibly useful phrases found inside the covers of this book. You are likely to use some of these forms—*Do you have X? I would like Y. Where is Z?*—many, many times. The idea behind this dictionary is that you start with a basic pattern from inside the covers and then look up any words you need to plug into that form to communicate what you want to. Searching for the word you want is easy, because the bulk of this book covers two fairly extensive alphabetized dictionaries, not sections of phrases organized by situation. If you want to ask, for example, "Where is a post office?", you find the section labeled "Locating" inside the back cover, see that your key phrase is "Dov'è ___?", easily look up the word for "post office" in the English-Italian dictionary, and soon ask, "Dov'è un ufficio postale, per favore?"

The emphasis in this book is on usefulness and usability. It is deliberately redundant (so you can find information in more than one place), out of order at times (such as English numbers listed together in numerical order rather than alphabetically), and occasionally incomplete (focusing on forms most likely to be used and omitting unlikely ones) in order to be as practical as possible. Usefulness is more important than consistency here.

I hope you find this resource helpful as you venture into Italian. Please notify me of any suggestions for how I can make it even more useful.

Best wishes on your language journey!

Elizabeth

Pronunciation Guide

The pronunciation guide below is just that—a guide—and is not intended to cover all possible pronunciations of letters and letter combinations in Italian. It should enable you to accurately pronounce the words in this book, however, and to take a very good stab at any new words you encounter in Italy.

Read the following tables across like this: "The Italian letter *a* is pronounced like the English sound in *father* and can be found in the words *casa* and *mangia*." American English pronunciation is used in the English examples. Try not to move your lips and tongue when you make the vowel sounds, to keep them "pure."

Italian	English	Example
a	ah (f<u>a</u>ther)	c<u>a</u>s<u>a</u>, m<u>a</u>ngi<u>a</u>
e	ay (l<u>a</u>te)	tr<u>e</u>, s<u>e</u>ra
e	e or eh (l<u>e</u>t)	b<u>e</u>ne, espr<u>e</u>sso
i	ee (b<u>ee</u>)	l<u>i</u>bri, v<u>i</u>n<u>i</u>
o	oh (t<u>o</u>ne)	m<u>o</u>lt<u>o</u>, n<u>o</u>
u	oo (c<u>oo</u>l)	t<u>u</u>tto, sc<u>u</u>si

An *i* followed by another vowel is frequently contracted to make one syllable starting with a "y" sound. You can get this same sound by pronouncing each vowel separately but very quickly.

ia	yah (y̱ada)	pi̱atti, doppi̱a
ie	yay (y̱ea)	grazi̱e, vi̱ene
io	yoh (y̱oyo)	oli̱o, pensi̱one
iu	yoo (y̱ou)	ai̱utare, pi̱ù

When they are in certain combinations, a number of consonants in Italian are pronounced differently than we would expect. In particular, *c*, *ch*, *g*, *gh* and *sc* are all pronounced "differently" when they are followed by *e* or *i*. There are other surprises, as well, as you will see below. These unexpected pronunciations include the following.

ci	ch or chee (ch̲ow or ch̲eese)	c̲iao, arriveder̲ci
ce	chay (ch̲ase)	piac̲ere, c̲ena
chi	kee (key̲)	zucch̲ini, Ch̲ianti

che	kay (<u>c</u>able)	per<u>ch</u>é, mac<u>ch</u>eroni
gi	j or jee (<u>J</u>oe or <u>j</u>eep)	<u>gi</u>orno, <u>gi</u>ta
ge	jay (blue <u>jay</u>)	<u>ge</u>lato, <u>ge</u>neroso
gh	g (<u>g</u>irl)	spa<u>gh</u>etti, <u>gh</u>etto
gli	lly (mi<u>lli</u>on)	fi<u>gli</u>a, consi<u>gli</u>are
gn	ny (can<u>y</u>on)	lasa<u>gn</u>e, <u>gn</u>occhi
qu	kw (<u>qu</u>ick)	<u>qu</u>ando, ac<u>qu</u>a
sce	shay (<u>sh</u>ame)	pe<u>sce</u>, <u>sce</u>ndere
sci	sh or she (<u>sh</u>arp or <u>sh</u>eep)	<u>sci</u>arpa, u<u>sci</u>ta
z, zz	ts (ca<u>ts</u>) ds (be<u>ds</u>)	pi<u>zz</u>a, gra<u>z</u>ie <u>z</u>ero, <u>z</u>abaglione

Be aware that many consonants are "doubled" in Italian. If you see, for example, *tt*, as in *spaghetti*, the *t* sound should be held longer than you would normally say it. Also, *h* is usually silent in Italian words, as in the English words *honest* and *honor*.

Finally, a word of warning about the American *r*. It is much harder and flatter than the *r* in Italian. The Italian *r* is more like a trill. When you speak Italian, try to trill your *r*. If you can't, at least try to soften it (make it sound like the *r* in a British accent, as in "muth-uh" for *mother*).

Grammar Summary

Subjects and Pronouns

Italian has several ways of saying *you*, depending on how many people are being addressed and how formally they are known. There are two singular forms of *you*, a polite form for people you don't know well (*Lei*) and an informal form for people you are close to (*tu*). There are also two forms of plural *you*, and their use depends on whether the relationship is a formal one (*Loro*) or close (*voi*). <u>This dictionary focuses on the most useful form of *you* for visitors to Italy, the formal, singular version, *Lei*.</u> Verb listings for *you* in the dictionaries are usually just for the *Lei* form.

Pronouns	Singular	Plural
1st **Person**	(I) io	(we) noi
2nd **Person**	(you, inf.) tu (you, fml.) Lei	(you, inf.) voi (you, fml.) Loro
3rd **Person**	(he/she) lui/lei	(they) loro

In Italian, you usually leave the subject out, because the verb shows who is being talked about.

Verb Endings

Italian verbs in dictionary form have one of three endings: -are, -ere, or -ire. Verbs ending in –are (such as *parlare*, to speak) follow one pattern, and verbs ending in –ere (*vedere*, to see) or in –ire (*partire*, to leave) follow slightly different patterns that are almost identical to each other, so they will be lumped together here.

	-are	-ere/-ire
(I) io	-o parl<u>o</u>	-o ved<u>o</u>/part<u>o</u>
(you, sing. inf.**) tu**	-i parl<u>i</u>	-i ved<u>i</u>/part<u>i</u>
(you, sing. fml.**) Lei**	-a parl<u>a</u>	-e ved<u>e</u>/part<u>e</u>
(he/she/it) lui/lei	-a parl<u>a</u>	-e ved<u>e</u>/part<u>e</u>
(we) noi	-iamo parl<u>iamo</u>	-iamo ved<u>iamo</u>/part<u>iamo</u>
(you, pl. inf.**) voi**	-ate parl<u>ate</u>	-ete/-ite ved<u>ete</u>, part<u>ite</u>
(you, pl. formal**) Loro**	-ano parl<u>ano</u>	-ono ved<u>ono</u>/part<u>ono</u>
(they) loro	-ano parl<u>ano</u>	-ono ved<u>ono</u>/part<u>ono</u>

Tourists will want to concentrate on I, you (*Lei*) and he/she/it forms, which are gray in these tables. These forms are most useful for visitors to Italy. Most of us can safely ignore the white portions of these verb charts.

Irregular Verbs

Many of the most common verbs are *irregular* and don't follow the standard patterns. Here are the most important ones.

"To be"

There are two different verbs to express *to be* in Italian. The more common one, *essere*, is used most of the time English-speakers would use a form of *to be*. The other verb for *to be* is *stare*, which is used to describe temporary characteristics, the state you are in (I'm sad), or, sometimes, time or location.

As a practical matter, unless you see a form of *stare* listed in a translation (e.g., *sto bene* for "I'm fine"), you will probably want to stick with *essere*.

essere

I am = sono	we are = siamo
you are (sing. inf.) = sei	you are (pl. inf.) = siete
you are (sing. fml.) = è	you are (pl. fml.)=sono
he/she/it is = è	they are = sono

stare

I am = sto	we are = stiamo
you are (sing. inf.)= stai you are (sing. fml.) = sta	you are (pl. inf.) = state you are (pl. fml.) = stanno
he/she/it is = sta	they are = stanno

"To have"

avere

I have = ho	we have = abbiamo
you have (sing. inf.) = hai	you have (pl. inf.) = avete
you have (sing. fml.) = ha	you have (pl. fml.) = hanno
he/she/it has = ha	they have = hanno

Negatives

To make a negative, add the word *non* before the main verb of the sentence.

> <u>Non</u> capisco. (*I don't understand.*)
>
> <u>Non</u> ho niente da dichiarare.
>
> (*I have nothing to declare.*)

How to inflect verbs

If you want to use a verb from the dictionary but it doesn't list the form that you need, you can build it by referring to the verb-ending chart on p. 14. For example, you might want to share that you adore the opera. The verb for adore is *adorare*. To get the I/io form, drop the –are ending and add an –o, resulting in *Adoro l'opera*. And if you *don't* adore the opera, you can say (see Negatives, above), *Non adoro l'opera*.

Warning: Because some verbs are irregular, following the rules may not result in a "perfect" verb form. You will probably still be understood, though, and Italians are very forgiving of imperfect language use by visitors.

Gender and Articles

All Italian nouns are either masculine or feminine, and that difference is reflected in the form of articles that are used with a particular word. Articles are little words like *the* (a definite article) or *a/an* (indefinite articles).

Definite articles (*the*)

before a . . .	Masc. *the*	Fem. *the*
consonant	**il** bagno (the bath) **il** letto (the bed)	**la** camera (the room) **la** madre (the mother)
vowel	**l'**albergo (the hotel) **l'**acquaio (the sink)	**l'**ora (the hour) **l'**amica (the female friend)
z or s + consonant	**lo** zio (the uncle) **lo** stadio (the stadium)	**la** zia (the aunt) **la** stazione (the station)

Indefinite articles (*a/an*)

before a . . .	Masc. *a/an*	Fem. *a/an*
consonant	**un** bagno (a bath) **un** letto (a bed)	**una** camera (a room) **una** madre (a mother)
vowel	**un** albergo (a hotel) **un** acquaio (a sink)	**un'**ora (an hour) **un'**amica (a female friend)
z or s + consonant	**uno** zio (an uncle) **uno** stadio (a stadium)	**una** zia (an aunt) **una** stazione (a station)

Dictionary Detective—Noun Gender

The dictionaries in the back of this book include definite articles (and some indefinite articles) for nouns but usually do not state the gender of the word. It's easy enough to figure out whether a noun is masculine or feminine, though. Starting with singular forms, if the definite article is *la*, it's a feminine word; if the definite article is *il* or *lo*, it's a masculine word. If the definite article is contracted to *l'*, then the gender is indicated in these dictionaries by *m* or *f*.

Plurals

In plural form, both the noun and the definite article change from their singular form.

Gender	Singular	Plural
Masculine	il libro	i libri
	l'anno	gli anni
	lo studente	gli studenti
Feminine	la casa	le case
	l'ora	le ore
	la madre	le madri

Dictionary Detective—Plurals and Singulars

If you see a noun listed with a plural article, you can still identify its gender, *and* you can convert it to a singular form.

Plural Article =	Gender	Converts to Singular
le	feminine	la or l' (before vowel)
i	masculine	il
gli	masculine	l' (before vowel) or lo

Plural Noun Ending	Converts to Singular
-i	-o or -e (fem. must be -e)
-e	-a

Adjective Endings

Adjective endings also differ depending on
whether the noun is masculine or feminine,
whether the noun is singular or plural, and what
ending the base form of the adjective itself has.
Here is a short summary.

Gender	Singular	Plural
Masculine	il passaporto americano	i passaporti americani
	il ristorante nuovo	i ristoranti nuovi
	il libro verde	i libri verdi
Feminine	la camera libera	le camere libere
	la tavola nuova	le tavole nuove
	la carta verde	le carte verdi

Possessives

You can indicate possession by saying that
something is *of* someone, using the word *di*.

È il libro di Maria. *It's the book of Maria.*

You can also indicate possession by using a possessive adjective, usually with the appropriate definite article.

Il Suo passaporto, per favore. *Your passport, please.*

Possessives		Masculine	Feminine
my/mine	sing.	il mio	la mia
	plural	i miei	le mie
your/yours	sing.	il tuo	la tua
(sing. inf.)	plural	i tuoi	le tue
your/yours	sing.	il Suo	la Sua
(sing. fml.)	plural	i Suoi	le Sue
his/her(s)/its	sing.	il suo	la sua
	plural	i suoi	le sue
our/ours	sing.	il nostro	la nostra
	plural	i nostri	le nostre
your/yours	sing.	il vostro	la vostra
(pl. inf.)	plural	i vostri	le vostre
your/yours	sing.	il Loro	la Loro
(pl. fml.)	plural	i Loro	le Loro
their/theirs	sing.	il loro	la loro
	plural	i loro	le loro

English-Italian Dictionary

How to use this dictionary

The purpose of this dictionary is to help you find and pronounce the Italian words you might need to communicate as a visitor in Italy.

English words are listed in bold. Most Italian verbs are listed in infinitive form; you usually need to change them to get the *io* and *Lei* forms. Some verb forms are included, however. Most nouns are listed in singular, but some plurals are included. Many indefinite articles (a/an) are also included, for ease of use.

A

A, a A, a *(ah)*

@-symbol chiocciola, la *(KYOHT-choh-lah)* (press Alt Gr key, right of space bar, with the @, right of the L key) ("at" in e-mail address)

abandon, to abbandonare *(ahb-bahn-doh-NAH-ray)*

able to, to be potere *(poh-TAY-ray)*

   I am able to posso *(POHS-soh)*

   we are able to possiamo *(pohs-SYAH-moh)*

   you are able to può *(pwoh)* (form. sing.)

aboard a bordo *(ah BOHR-doh)*

above sopra *(SOH-prah)*

abroad all'estero *(ahl-LES-tay-roh)*

abuse, to abusare *(ah-boo-ZAH-ray)*

accept, to accetare *(aht-chayt-TAH-ray)*

   Do you accept ___?

   Accettate ___? *(aht-chay-TAH-tay __?)*

acceptance accetazione, l' *f* *(aht-chay-taht-TSYOH-nay)*

access accesso, l' *m* *(aht-CHES-soh)*

accident incidente, l' *m*/un *(een-chee-DEN-tay)*

accommodaton alloggio, l' *m* *(ahl-LOH-joh)*

accompany, to accompagnare *(ahk-kohm-pahn-NYAH-ray)*

account conto, il *(KOHN-toh)*

  my account il mio conto *(eel MEE-oh KOHN-toh)*

  your account il Suo conto *(eel SOO-oh KOHN-toh)*

accountant ragioniere/a, il/la *(rah-joh-NYEH-ray/-rah)*

ache, to dolere *(doh-LAY-ray)*

acquire, to acquistare *(ahk-kwees-TAH-ray)*

adaptor (electrical) spina multipla, la/una *(SPEE- nah MOOL-tee-plah)*, adattatore, l' *m*/un *(ah-daht-tah-TOH-ray)*

address indirizzo, l' *m*/un *(een-dee-REET-tsoh)*

  e-mail address indirizzo di email, l' *m*/un *(een-dee-REET-tsoh dee EE-mayl)*

adjust, to (=to regulate) regolare *(ray-goh-LAH-ray)*

administration amministrazione, l' *f* *(ahm-mee-nees-traht-TSYOH-nay)*

admire, to ammirare *(ahm-mee-RAH-ray)*

admission (price) entrata, l' *f* *(ayn-TRAH-tah)*, ingresso, l' *m* *(een-GRES-soh)*, prezzo d'ingresso, il *(PRET-tsoh deen-GRES-soh)*

  free admission ingresso gratuito, l' *m* *(een-GRES-soh grah-TOO-ee-toh)*

admittance ingresso, l' *m* *(een-GRES-soh)*

  admittance ticket biglietto, il/un *(beel-LYAYT-toh)* (i biglietti)

  free admittance ingresso gratuito, l' *m* *(een-GRES-soh grah-TOO-ee-toh)*

admitted ammessi *(ahm-MES-see)*

adore, to adorare *(ah-doh-RAH-ray)*

ADSL ADSL, a type of broad-band DSL communication *(ah-dee-ess-EL-lay)*

adult adulto/a, l'/l' *m*/*f* un/un' *(ah-DOOL-toh/-tah)*

  adults adulti/adulte, gli/le *(ah-DOOL-tee/-tay)*

advance, in in anticipo *(een ahn-TEE-chee-poh)*

advertisement annuncio, l' *m*/un *(ahn-NOON-choh)*

Africa Africa, l' *f* *(AHF-ree-kah)*

after dopo *(DOH-poh)*

after-dinner drink digestivo, il/un *(dee-jays-TEE-voh)*

afternoon pomeriggio, il *(poh-may-REED-joh)*

  afternoon snack merenda, la/una *(may-REN-day)*

in the afternoon del
pomeriggio *(dayl poh-may-REED-joh)*

this afternoon oggi
pomeriggio *(OHD-jee poh-may-REED-joh)*

yesterday afternoon ieri
pomeriggio *(YEH-ree poh-may-REED-joh)*

afternoon snack merenda,
la/una *(may-REN-day)*

aftershave dopobarba, il/un
(doh-poh-BAHR-bah)

again di nuovo *(dee NWOH-voh)*

against contro *(KOHN-troh)*

age età, l' *f* /un' *(ay-TAH)*

aged stagionato/a *(stah-joh-NAH-toh/-tah)*

aggressive aggressivo/a *(ahg-grays-SEE-voh/-vah)*

agnostic agnostico/a *(ahn-NYOHS-tee-koh/-kah)*

ago fa *(fah)*

agree, I d'accordo *(dahk-KOHR-doh)*

agreement accordo, l' *m* /un
(ahk-KOHR-doh)

agriculture agricoltura, l' *f* *(ah-gree-kohl-TOO-rah)*

ahead avanti *(ah-VAHN-tee)*

air aria, l' *f* *(AHR-yah)*

air conditioning aria
condizionata, l' *f* *(AHR-yah kohn-deet-tsyoh-NAH-tah)*

airline company compagnia
aerea, la/una *(kohm-pahn-NYEE-ah ah-EH-ray-ah)*, linea aerea, la *(LEE-nay-ah ah-EH-ray-ah)*

airmail, by per via aerea
(payr VEE-ah ah-EH-ray-ah)

airplane aeroplano, l' *m* /un
(ah-ay-roh-PLAH-noh), aereo, l'
m /un *(ah-EH-ray-oh)*

airport aeroporto, l' *m* /un
(ah-ay-roh-POHR-toh)

air sickness mal di aereo, il
(mahl dee ah-EH-ray-oh)

aisle corridoio, il/un *(kohr-ree-DOH-yoh)*

alarm allarme, l' *m* /un *(ahl-LAHR-may)*

alarm clock sveglia, la/una
(ZVAYL-lyah)

alcohol alcolico, l' *m* *(ahl-KOH-lee-koh)*

alcoholic (drink) alcolico/a
(ahl-KOH-lee-koh/-kah)

all tutto/a (sing.) *(TOOT-toh/-tah)*,
tutti/e (pl.) *(TOOT-tee/-tay)*

That's all È tutto *(eh TOOT-toh)*

allergic (to) allergico/a (a)
(ahl-LEHR-jee-koh/-kah [ah])

allergy allergia, l' *f* /un' *(ahl-layr-JEE-ah)* (le allergie)

allow, to permettere *(payr-MAYT-tay-ray)*

almond mandorla, la/una
(MAHN-dohr-lah) (le mandorle)

alone solo/a *(SOH-loh/-lah)*

alphabet alfabeto, l' *m* *(ahl-fah-BAY-toh)*

already già *(jah)*

also anche *(AHN-kay)*

altar altare, l' *m* /un *(ahl-TAH-ray)*

always sempre *(SEM-pray)*

a.m. di mattina *(dee maht-TEE-nah)*

am, I sono *(SOH-noh)*

amaro amaro, l' *m*/un *(ah-MAH-roh)*

ambassador ambasciatore/-trice, l'/l' *m*/*f* un/un' *(ahm-bahsh-shah-TOH-ray/-TREE-chay)*

ambulance ambulanza, l' *f* /un' *(ahm-boo-LAHN-tsah)*

America America, l' *f* *(ah-MAY-ree-kah)*

amount quantità, la/una *(kwahn-tee-TAH)*

anchovies acciughe, le *(aht-CHOO-gay)*

ancient antico/a *(ahn-TEE-koh/-kah)*

and e *(ay)*

anesthetic anestetico, l' *m*/un *(ah-nays-TEH-tee-koh)*

animal animale, l' *m*/un *(ah-nee-MAH-lay)* (gli animali)

ankle caviglia, la/una *(kah-VEEL-lyah)* (le caviglie)

annoy, to annoiare *(ahn-noh-YAH-ray)*

annual annuale *(ah-noo-AH-lay)*

annul annulla *(ahn-NOOL-lah)*

another (one) un altro/un' altra *(oon AHL-troh/oon AHL-trah)*

answer riposta, la/una *(ree-POHS-tah)* (le riposte)

answer, to rispondere *(rees-POHN-day-ray)*

ant formica, la/una *(fohr-MEE-kah)* (le formiche)

antacid antiacido, l' *m*/un *(ahn-TYAH-chee-doh)*

antibiotic antibiotico, l' *m* /un *(ahn-tee-bee-OH-tee-koh)* (gli antibiotici)

antifreeze anticongelante, l' *m* /un *(ahn-tee-kohn-jay-LAHN-tay)*

antihistamine antistaminico, l' *m*/un *(ahn-tees-tah-MEE-nee-koh)* (gli antistaminici)

anti-inflammatories antinfiammatori, gli *(ahn-teen-fyahm-mah-TOH-ree)*

antique pezzo d'antiquariato, il/un *(PET-tsoh dahn-tee-kwah-RYAH-toh)*

anxious ansioso/a *(ahn-SYOH-soh/-ah)*

anything qualcosa *(kwahl-KOH-sah)*

apartment appartamento, l' *m* /un *(ahp-pahr-tah-MAYN-toh)*

appendix appendice, l' *f*/un' *(ahp-payn-DEE-chay)*

appetite appetito, l' *m* /un *(ahp-pay-TEE-toh)*

appetizer antipasto, l' *m*/un *(ahn-tee-PAHS-toh)* (gli antipasti)

apple mela, la/una *(MAY-lah)* (le mele)

  apple juice succo di mela, il/un *(SOOK-koh dee MAY-lah)*

appointment (with) appuntamento (con), l' *m* /un *(ahp-poon-tah-MAYN-toh [kohn])* (gli appuntamenti)

approach approdo, l' *m* /un *(ahp-PROH-doh)*

apricot albicocca, l' *f* /un' *(ahl-bee-KOHK-kah)* (le albicocche)

April aprile *(ah-PREE-lay)*

archeological archeologico/a *(ahr-kay-oh-LOH-jee-koh/-kah)*

architect architetto, l' *m* /un *(ahr-kee-TAYT-toh)*

architecture architettura, l' *f* *(ahr-kee-tayt-TOO-rah)*

are see *to be*

  we are siamo *(SYAH-moh)*

  you are è *(eh)*

area code prefisso, il/un *(pray-FEES-soh)*

arm braccio, il/un *(BRAHT-choh)* (le braccia)

arrange, to organizzare *(ohr-gah-need-DZAH-ray)*, ordinare *(ohr-dee-NAH-ray)*

arrival arrivo, l' *m* /un *(ahr-REE-voh)* (gli arrivi)

arrive, to arrivare *(ahr-reev-VAH-ray)*

  he/she/it arrives arriva *(ahr-REE-vah)*

  I arrive arrivo *(ahr-REE-voh)*

  you arrive arriva *(ahr-REE-vah)* (form. sing.)

art arte, l' *f* *(AHR-tay)*

  art gallery galleria d'arte, la/una *(gahl-lay-REE-ah DAHR-tay)*

artichoke carciofo, il/un *(kahr-CHOH-foh)* (i carciofi)

artist artista, l'/l' *m/f* un/un' *(ahr-TEES-tah)* (gli artisti/le artiste)

arts, the lettere, le *(LET-tay-ray)*

arugula rucola, la *(ROO-koh-lah)*

ashtray portacenere, il/un *(pohr-tah-CHAY-nay-ray)*

Asia Asia, l' *f* *(AHZ-yah)*

ask, to chiedere *(KYEH-day-ray)*

asparagus asparagi, gli *(ahs-PAH-rah-jee)*

aspirin aspirina, l' *f* *(ahs-pee-REE-nah)*

assist, to assistere *(ahs-SEES-tay-ray)*

assistance assistenza, l' *f* *(ahs-sees-TEN-tsah)*

asthma asma, l' *f* *(AHZ-mah)*

asthmatic asmatico/a *(ahz-MAH-tee-koh/-kah)*

at (time) a *(ah)*, alle/all' *(AHL-lay/ahl)*

atheist ateo/a *(AH-tay-oh/-ah)*

ATM bancomat, il/un *(BAHN-koh-maht)*

  ATM card carta bancomat, la/una *(KAHR-tah BAHN-koh-maht)*

@-symbol chiocciola, la *(KYOHT-choh-lah)* (press Alt Gr key, right of space bar, with @, right of L key), ("at" in e-mail address)

attack, to aggredire *(ahg-gray-DEE-ray)*

attention! attenzione! *(aht-tayn-TSYOH-nay)*

audio set auricolare, l' *m* /un *(ow-ree-koh-LAH-ray)*

August agosto *(ah-GOHS-toh)*

aunt zia, la/una *(TSEE-ah)*

Australia Australia, l' *f (ows-TRAHL-yah)*

Austria Austria, l' *f (OWS-tree-ah)*

automatic automatico/a *(ow-toh-MAH-tee-koh/-kah)*

automatic transmission cambio automatico, il *(KAHM-byoh ow-toh-MAH-tee-koh)*

autumn autunno, l' *m (aw-TOON-noh)*

available libero/a *(LEE-bay-roh/-rah)*, disponibile *(dees-poh-NEE-bee-lay)*

Is ___ available? c'è ___ (=there is/is there) *(cheh)*

Are ___ available? ci sono ___ (=there are/are there) *(chee SOH-noh)*

avenue viale, il/un *(vee-AH-lay)*

avoid, to evitare *(ay-vee-TAH-ray)*

away, far lontano/a *(lohn-TAH-noh/-nah)*

awful orrendo/a *(ohr-REN-doh/-dah)*

B

B, b B, b *(bee)*

baby bambino/a, il/la un/una *(bahm-BEE-noh/-nah)* (i bambini /le bambine)

baby changing room bagno con fasciatoio, il/un *(BAHN-nyoh kohn fahsh-shah-TOH-yoh)*

baby food cibo da bebè, il *(CHEE-boh dah bay-BEH)*

baby powder borotalco, il *(boh-roh-TAHL-koh)*

babysitter babysitter, il/la un/una *(BAY-bee-see-ter)*

babysitting service servizio di babysitter, il/un *(sayr-VEET-tsyoh dee BAY-bee-see-ter)*

baby wipes salviettine detergenti per bambini, le *(sahl-vyayt-TEE-nay day-tayr-JAYN-tee payr bahm-BEE-nee)*

back (body) dorso, il *(DOHR-soh)*, schiena, la *(SKYEH-nah)*

backpack zaino, lo/uno *(DZAH-ee-noh)* (gli zaini)

backward indietro *(een-DYEH-troh)*

bacon pancetta, la *(pahn-CHAYT-tah)*

bad brutto/a *(BROOT-toh/-tah)*, cattivo/a *(kaht-TEE-voh/-vah)*

bag (suitcase) valigia, la/una *(vah-LEEJ-jah)*, bagaglio, il/un *(bah-GAHL-lyoh)*; (small bag) busta, la/una *(BOOS-tah)*; (small bag) sacchetto, il/un *(sahk-KAYT-toh)*; (purse) borsa, la/una *(BOHR-sah)*

baggage bagaglio, il *(bah-GAHL-lyoh)*

my baggage il mio bagaglio *(eel MEE-oh bah-GAHL-lyoh)*

your baggage il suo bagaglio *(eel SOO-oh bah-GAHL-lyoh)*

baggage claim ritiro bagagli, il *(ree-TEE-roh bah-GAHL-lyee)*

baggage deposit, il deposito bagagli *(day-POH-zee-toh bah-GAHL-lyee)*

bakery panetteria, la/una *(pah-nayt-tay-REE-ah)*, panificio, il/un *(pah-nee-FEE-choh)*

balcony balcone, il/un *(bahl-KOH-nay)*

ball (sports) palla, la/una *(PAHL-lah)*; (soccer, basketball) pallone, il/un *(pahl-LOH-nay)*; (dance) ballo, il/un *(BAHL-loh)*

ballet balletto, il/un *(bahl-LAYT-toh)*

ballpoint pen penna a sfera, la/una *(PAYN-nah a SFEH-rah)*

banana banana, la/una *(bah-NAH-nah)* (le banane)

band (music) gruppo, il/un *(GROOP-poh)*

bandage fascia, la/una *(FAHSH-shah)* (le fasce)

band-aid cerotto, il/un *(chay-ROHT-toh)* (i cerotti)

B and B pensione, la/una *(payn-SYOH-nay)*

bank banca, la/una *(BAHN-kah)*

bar (cafe) bar, il/un *(bahr)*; (nightclub) locale, il/un *(loh-KAH-lay)*

barber barbiere, il/un *(bahr-BYEH-ray)*

bargain (buon) affare, l' *m* /un *([bwohn] ahf-FAH-ray)*

baroque barocco/a *(bah-ROHK-koh/-kah)*

basket cestino, il/un *(chays-TEE-noh)*

bath bagno, il/un *(BAHN-nyoh)*

bath in hallway bagno esterno, il/un *(BAHN-nyoh ays-TEHR-noh)*

bathing suit costume da bagno, il/un *(kohs-TOO-may dah BAHN-nyoh)*

bathing trunks costume da bagno, il/un *(kohs-TOO-may dah BAHN-nyoh)*

bathroom toilette, la/una *(twah-LET)*, toeletta, la/una *(toh-ay-LET-tah)*, gabinetto, il/un *(gah-bee-NAYT-toh)*, WC, il/un *(vee-CHEE)*, bagno, il/un *(BAHN-nyoh)*

battery pila, la/una *(PEE-lah)*; (for car) batteria, la/una *(baht-tay-REE-ah)*

be, to essere *(ES-say-ray)*
   I am sono *(SOH-noh)*
   he/she/it is è *(eh)*
   they are sono *(SOH-noh)*
   we are siamo *(SYAH-moh)*
   you are è *(eh)* (form. sing.); sei *(SEH-ee)* (inf. sing.)

be, to (health) stare *(STAH-ray)*
   I am sto *(stoh)*
   he/she/it is stah *(stah)*
   they are stanno *(STAHN-noh)*
   you are sta *(stah)* (form. sing.)

beach spiaggia, la/una *(SPYAHD-jah)*

baroque barocco/a *(bah-ROHK-koh/-kah)* — (see above)

beans, dried fagioli, i *(fahd-JOH-lee)*

beans, green fagiolini *(fahd-joh-LEE-nee)*

beautiful bello/a *(BEL-loh/-lah)*

  most beautiful bellissimo/a *(bayl-LEES-see-moh/-mah)*

beauty salon parrucchiere, il/un *(pahr-rook-KYEH-ray)*

because perché *(payr-KAY)*

become, to divenire *(dee-vay-NEE-ray)*, diventare *(dee-vayn-TAH-ray)*

bed letto, il/un *(LET-toh)* (i letti)

  double bed letto matrimoniale, il/un *(LET-toh mah-tree-mohn-NYAH-lay)*

  with a double bed con letto matrimoniale *(kohn LET-toh mah-tree-mohn-NYAH-lay)*

  with twin beds a due letti *(ah DOO-ay LET-tee)*

bedding coperte e lenzuola, le *(koh-PEHR-tay ay layn-TSWOH-lah)*

bedroom camera da letto, la/una *(KAH-may-rah dah LET-toh)*

bee ape, l' *f* /un' *(AH-pay)* (le api)

beef manzo, il *(MAHN-dzoh)*

beef broth brodo di manzo, il/un *(BROH-doh dee MAHN-dzoh)*

beer birra, la/una *(BEER-rah)*

  draft beer birra a la spina, la/una *(BEER-rah ah lah SPEE-nah)*

beet barbabietola, la/una *(bahr-bah-BYEH-toh-lah)* (le barbabietole)

before prima di *(PREE-mah dee)*

beggar mendicante, il/la un/una *(mayn-dee-KAHN-tay)*

begin, to cominciare *(koh-meen-CHAH-ray)*

beginning origine, l' *f* *(oh-REE-jee-nay)*

behind indietro *(een-DYEH-troh)*, dietro *(DYEH-troh)*

beige beige *(bayzh)*

Belgium Belgio, il *(BEL-joh)*

believe, to credere *(KRAY-day-ray)*

  I believe credo *(KRAY-doh)*

  we belive crediamo *(kray-DYAH-moh)*

below sotto *(SOHT-toh)*

belt cintura, la/una *(cheen-TOO-rah)* (le cinture)

bench banco, il/un *(BAHN-koh)*

Berlin Berlino *(bayr-LEE-noh)*

Bern Berna *(BEHR-nah)*

best migliore *(meel-LYOH-ray)*

better migliore *(meel-LYOH-ray)*

between tra *(trah)*

beverage bevanda, la/una *(bay-VAHN-dah)* (le bevande); bibita, la/una *(BEE-bee-tah)* (le bibite)

Bible bibbia, la/una *(BEEB-byah)*

bicycle bicicletta, la/una *(bee-chee-KLAYT-tah)* *(see bike)*

big grande *(GRAHN-day)*

bike bicicletta, la/una *(bee-chee-KLAYT-tah)* (le biciclette)

  bike chain catena di bicicletta, la/una *(kah-TAY-nah dee bee-chee-KLAYT-tah)*

  bike lock lucchetto, il/un *(look-KAYT-toh)*

bike parking posteggio per le biciclette, il/un *(pohs-TAYD-joh payr lay bee-chee-KLAYT-tay)*

bike path ciclopista, la/una *(chee-kloh-PEES-tah)* (le ciclopiste)

bike pump pompa della bicicletta, la/una *(POHM-pah DAYL-lah bee-chee-KLAYT-tah)*

bill (expense) conto, il/un *(KOHN-toh)*

binoculars binocolo, il/un *(bee-NOH-koh-loh)*

bird uccello, l' *m* /un *(oot-CHEL-loh)* (gli uccelli) (Warning: also slang for penis.)

birthday compleanno, il/un *(kohm-play-AHN-noh)*

bite, to mordere *(MOHR-day-ray)*

The dog bit me. Il cane mi morse. *(eel KAH-nay mee MOHR-say.)*

bitter amaro/a *(ah-MAH-roh/-rah)*

black nero/a *(NAY-roh/-rah)*

blanket coperta, la/una *(koh-PEHR-tah)* (le coperti)

blind cieco/a *(CHEH-koh/-kah)*

blister vescica, la/una *(vaysh-SHEE-kah)* (le vesciche)

blond biondo/a *(BYOHN-doh/-dah)*

blood sangue, il *(SAHN-gway)*

  blood pressure pressione del sangue, la *(prays-SYOH-nay dayl SAHN-gway)*

  blood type gruppo sanguigno, il *(GROOP-poh sahn-GWEEN-nyoh)*

blouse camicetta, la/una *(kah-mee-CHAYT-tah)* (le camicette)

blown glass vetro soffiato, il *(VAY-troh sohf-FYAH-toh)*

blue blu *(bloo)*

  light blue azzurro/a *(ahd-DZOOR-roh/-rah)*

blueberry mirtillo, il/un *(meer-TEEL-loh)* (i mirtilli)

board, to salire *(sah-LEE-ray)*

  I board salgo *(SAHL-goh)*

  we board saliamo *(sahl-YAH-moh)*

  you board (form. sing.) sale *(SAH-lay)*

board, on a bordo *(ah BOHR-doh)*

boarding pass carta d'imbarco, la/una *(KAHR-tah deem-BAHR-koh)*

boat nave, la/una *(NAH-vay)*, barca, la/una *(BAHR-kah)*

  boat trip gita in barca, la/una *(JEE-tah een BAHR-kah)*

body corpo, il/un *(KOHR-poh)*

boil, to bollire *(bohl-LEE-ray)*

boiled bollito/a *(bohl-LEE-toh/-tah)*

bone osso, l' *m* /un *(OHS-soh)* (gli ossi)

book libro, il/un *(LEE-broh)* (i libri)

book, to prenotare *(pray-noh-TAH-ray)*

booked full completo/a *(kohm-PLEH-toh/-tah)*

bookstore libreria, la/una *(lee-bray-REE-ah)*

boot stivale, lo/uno *(stee-VAH-lay)* (gli stivali)

boring noioso/a *(noh-YOH-soh/-sah)*

borrow, to prendere in prestito *(PREN-day-ray een PRES-tee-toh)*

bottle bottiglia, la/una *(boht-TEEL-lyah)* (le bottiglie)

bottle opener apribottiglie, l' *m* /un *(ah-pree-boht-TEEL-lyay)*

bowl piatto fondo, il/un *(PYAHT-toh FOHN-doh)*

box scatola, la/una *(SKAH-toh-lah)*

boy ragazzo, il/un *(rah-GAHT-tsoh)* (i ragazzi)

boyfriend ragazzo, il/un *(rah-GAHT-tsoh)*

bra reggiseno, il/un *(rayj-jee-SAY-noh)*

braces (dental) apparecchio, l' *m* /un *(ahp-pah-RAYK-kyoh)*

brake freno, il/un *(FRAY-noh)*

brandy cognac, il/un *(koh-NYAHK)*

brave coraggioso/a *(koh-rahd-JOH-soh/-sah)*

bread pane, il *(PAH-nay)*

rye bread pane di segala, il/un *(PAH-nay dee SAY-gah-lah)*

whole-grain bread pane integrale, il/un *(PAH-nay ee-tay-GRAH-lay)*

break, to rompere *(ROHM-pay-ray)*

breakfast colazione, la/una *(koh-laht-TSYOH-nay)*

breast petto, il *(PET-toh)*, seno, il *(SAY-noh)*

breathe, to respirare *(rays-pee-RAH-ray)*

brewery fabbrica di birra, la/una *(FAHB-bree-kah dee BEER-rah)*

bribe, to corrompere *(kohr-ROHM-pay-ray)*

bridge ponte, il/un *(POHN-tay)*

briefcase valigetta, la/una *(vah-lee-JAYT-tah)*

bright luminoso/a *(loo-mee-NOH-soh/-sah)*

brilliant brillante *(breel-LAHN-tay)*

bring, to portare *(pohr-TAH-ray)*

broadband broadband *(BROHD-band)*, banda larga, la *(BAHN-dah LAHR-gah)*

broiled cotto/a a fuoco vivo *(KOHT-toh/tah ah FWOH-koh VEE-voh)*

broken rotto/a *(ROHT-toh/-tah)*

broken down guastato/a *(gwahs-TAH-toh/-tah)*

bronchitis bronchite, la *(brohn-KEE-tay)*

broth brodo, il/un *(BROH-doh)*

brother fratello, il/un *(frah-TEL-loh)* (i fratelli)

brother-in-law cognato, il/un *(kohn-NYAH-toh)*

brown marrone *(mahr-ROH-nay)*

bruise livido, il/un *(LEE-vee-doh)* (i lividi)

Brussels Bruxelles *(brew-SEL)*

bucket secchio, il/un *(SAYK-kyoh)*

Buddhist buddista, il/la *(bood-DEES-tah)*

budget bilancio, il/un *(bee-LAHN-choh)*

buffet (meal) pasto freddo, il/un *(PAHS-toh FRAYD-doh)*

bug insetto, l' *m*/un *(een-SET-toh)* (gli insetti)

build, to costruire *(kohs-troo-EE-ray)*

building edificio, l' *m*/un *(ay-dee-FEE-choh)*

burger hamburger, l' *m*/un *(ahm-BOOR-gayr)*

burn, to bruciare *(broo-CHAH-ray)*, ardere *(AHR-day-ray)*

"burn", to (e.g., CD) masterizzare *(mahs-tay-reet-TSAH-ray)*

bus (within city) autobus, l' *m*/un *(OW-toh-boos)*; (town-to-town) pullman, il/un *(POOL-mahn)*

by bus con l'autobus *(kohn LOW-toh-boos)*

bus line linea, la/una *(LEE-nay-ah)*

bus station stazione d'autobus, la/una *(staht-TSYOH-nay DOW-toh-boos)*

bus stop fermata (dell'autobus), la/una *(fayr-MAH-tah [dayl-LOW-toh-boos])*

business affari, gli *(ahf-FAH-ree)*; (field of study) commercio, il *(kohm-MEHR-choh)*

on business per affari *(payr ahf-FAH-ray)*

business card biglietto da visita, il/un *(beel-LYAYT-toh dah VEE-zee-tah)*

business class classe business, la *(KLAHS-say BEEZ-nays)*

businessman uomo d'affari, l' *m*/un *(WOH-moh dahf-FAH-ray)*

business trip viaggio d'affari, il/un *(vee-AHD-joh dahf-FAH-ree)*

businesswoman imprenditrice, l' *f*/un' *(eem-prayn-dee-TREE-chay)*, donna d'affari, la/una *(DOHN-nah dahf-FAH-ray)*

busker musicista di strada, il/la un/una *(moo-zee-CHEES-tah dee STRAH-dah)*

bus station stazione d'autobus, la/una *(staht-TSYOH-nay DOW-toh-boos)*

bus stop fermata (dell'autobus), la/una *(fayr-MAH-tah [dayl-LOW-toh-boos])*

the next bus stop la prossima fermata *(lah PROHS-see-mah fayr-MAH-tah)*

busy occupato/a *(ohk-koo-PAH-toh/-tah)*

but ma *(mah)*

butcher's shop macelleria, la/una *(mah-chayl-lay-REE-ah)*

butter burro, il *(BOOR-roh)*

butterfly farfalla, la/una *(fahr-FAHL-lah)* (le farfalle)

button bottone, il/un *(boht-TOH-nay)* (i bottoni), tasto (=key) *(TAHS-toh)* (i tasti)

buy, to acquistare *(ahk-kwees-TAH-ray)*, comprare *(kohm-PRAH-ray)*

by the slice (pizza) all'taglio *(ahl-TAHL-lyoh)*

'bye Ciao! *(chow)*

byzantine bizantino/a *(beed-dzahn-TEE-noh/-nah)*

C

C, c C, c *(chee)*

cab taxi, il/un *(TAHK-see)*, tassì, il/un *(tahs-SEE)*

cabbage cavolo, il/un *(KAH-voh-loh)*

cabin cabina, la/una *(kah-BEE-nah)*

cable cavo, il/un *(KAH-voh)*

  cable car funivia, la/una *(foo-nee-VEE-ah)*

cafè bar, il/un *(bahr)* (i bar)

caffeine caffeina, la *(kahf-fay-EE-nah)*

cake torta, la/una *(TOHR-tah)* (le torte)

  cake shop pasticceria, la/una *(pahs-teet-chay-REE-ah)*

calculate, to calcolare *(kahl-koh-LAH-ray)*

calculator calcolatrice, la/una *(kahl-koh-lah-TREE-chay)*

calendar calendario, il/un *(kah-layn-DAH-ryoh)*

call, to chiamare *(kyah-MAH-ray)*

  Can you call ___ for me? Può chiamarmi ___? *(pwoh kyah-MAHR-mee __?)*

  Call ___! Chiami ___! *(KYAH-mee)*

  Call a doctor! Chiami un medico! *(KYAH-mee oon MEH-dee-koh)*

  Call an ambulance! Chiami un'ambulanza! *(KYAH-mee oon ahm-boo-LAHN-tsah)*

  Call the police! Chiami la polizia! *(KYAH-mee lah poh-leet-TSEE-ah)*

I am called ___. (=My name is ___.) Mi chiamo ___. *(mee KYAH-moh __)*

camera macchina fotografica, la/una *(MAH-kee-nah foh-toh-GRAH-fee-kah)*

  camera shop negozio di fotocine, il/un *(nay-GOHT-tsyoh dee foh-toh-CHEE-nay)*

  digital camera macchina fotografica digitale, la/una *(MAH-kee-nah foh-toh-GRAH-fee-kah dee-jee-TAH-lay)*

  disposable camera macchina fotografica usa-e-getta, la/una *(MAH-kee-nah foh-toh-GRAH-fee-kah oo-zah-ay-JET-tah)*

  underwater camera macchina fotografica subacquea, la/una *(MAH-kee-nah foh-toh-GRAH-fee-kah soo-BAHK-kway-ah)*

camp, to campeggiare *(kahm-payd-JAH-ray)*

camper (vehicle) roulotte, la/una *(roo-LOHT)*

camp ground campeggio, il/un *(kahm-PAYD-joh)*

camping store negozio da campeggio, il/un *(nay-GOHT-tsyoh dah kahm-PAYD-joh)*

can (=be able to) potere *(poh-TAY-ray)*

  I can posso *(POH-soh)*

we can possiamo (pohs-SYAH-moh)

you can/can you? può (form. sing.) (pwoh)

can (tin) scatola, la/una (SKAH-toh-lah)

can opener apriscatole, l' m /un (ah-prees-KAH-toh-lay)

Canada Canada, il (kah-nah-DAH)

cancel, to cancellare (kahn-chayl-LAH-ray)

cancel (ATM prompt) cancella (kahn-CHEL-lah)

cancelled cancellato/a (kahn-chayl-LAH-toh/tah)

cancer cancro, il (KAHN-kroh)

candle candela, la/una (kahn-DAY-lah) (le candele)

candy caramella, la/una (kah-rah-MEL-lah), dolciumi, i (dohl-CHOO-mee)

cane bastone, il/un (bahs-TOH-nay)

cantaloupe melone, il/un (may-LOH-nay) (i meloni)

cappuccino cappuccino, il/un (kahp-poot-CHEE-noh)

car auto, l' m/un (OW-toh), macchina, la/una (MAHK-kee-nah), veicolo, il/un (vay-EE-koh-loh), (on train) carrozza, la/una (kahr-ROHT-tsah)

car key chiave della macchina, la/una (KYAH-vay DAYL-lah MAHK-kee-nah)

car registration bollo di circolazione, il (BOHL-loh dee cheer-koh-lah-TSYOH-nay)

car rental autonoleggio, l' m /un (ow-toh-noh-LAYD-joh)

car sickness mal di macchina, il (mahl dee MAHK-kee-nah)

car title libretto di circolazione, il (lee-BRAYT-toh dee cheer-koh-lah-TSYOH-nay)

a car with automatic transmission una macchina automatica (OO-nah MAH-kee-nah ow-toh-MAH-tee-kah)

a car with manual transmission una macchina manuale (OO-nah MAH-kee-nah mah-noo-AH-lay)

carafe caraffa, la/una (kah-RAHF-fah)

carbonated gassato/a (gahs-SAH-toh/-tah), frizzante (freed-ZAHN-tay)

cards carte, le (KAHR-tay)

careful! attento! (aht-TEN-toh), attenzione! (aht-tayn-TSYOH-nay)

Carnevale mask maschera di Carnevale, la/una (MAHS-kay-rah dee kahr-nay-VAH-lay)

carpenter carpentiere, il/un (kahr-payn-TYEH-ray)

carrot carota, la/una (kah-ROH-tah) (le carote)

carry, to portare (pohr-TAH-ray)

carry-on luggage bagaglio a mano, il (bah-GAHL-lyoh ah MAH-noh)

carton scatola, la/una *(SKAH-toh-lah)*

cash, to riscuotere *(rees-KWOH-tay-ray)*

cash a check, to riscuotere un assegno *(rees-KWOH-tay-ray oon ahs-SAYN-nyoh)*

cash contante, i *(kohn-TAHN-tay)*, soldi, i *(SOHL-dee)*

(pay) with cash in contanti *(een kohn-TAHN-tee)*

cash card carta bancomat, la/una *(KAHR-tah BAHN-koh-maht)*

cash machine bancomat, il/un *(BAHN-koh-maht)*

cash register cassa, la/una *(KAHS-sah)*

cashew noce di acagiù, la/una *(NOH-chay dee ah-kah-JOO)*

cashier cassiere/a, il/la un/una *(kahs-SYEH-ray/-rah)*

casino casinò, il/un *(kah-zee-NOH)*

castle castello, il/un *(kahs-TEL-loh)*

cat gatto, il/un *(GAHT-toh)* (i gatti)

catalog catalogo, il/un *(kah-TAH-loh-goh)*

cathedral duomo, il/un *(DWOH-moh)*, cattedrale, la/una *(kaht-tay-DRAH-lay)*

Catholic cattolico/a *(kah-TOH-lee-koh/-kah)*

cauliflower cavolfiore, il *(kah-vohl-FYOH-ray)*

cause, to causare *(kow-ZAH-ray)*

cave grotta, la/una *(GROHT-tah)*

caviar caviale, il/un *(kah-VYAH-lay)*

cavity cavità, la/una *(kah-vee-TAH)*

CD CD, il/un *(chee-DEE)*

ceiling soffitto, il/un *(sohf-FEET-toh)*

celebrate, to celebrare *(chay-lay-BRAH-ray)*

celebration celebrazione, la/una *(chay-lay-braht-TSYOH-nay)*

cell phone (telefono) cellulare, il/un *([tel-EH-foh-noh] chayl-loo-LAH-ray)*, telefonino, il/un *(tay-lay-foh-NEE-noh)*

cell phone number numero di celluare, il/un *(NOO-may-roh dee chayl-loo-LAH-ray)*

prepaid cell phone cellulare prepagato, il/un *(chayl-loo-LAH-ray pray-pah-GAH-toh)*

cent centesimo, il/un *(chen-TEH-zee-moh)*

center centro, il *(CHEN-troh)*

center of town centro, il *(CHEN-troh)*

centimeter centimetro, il/un *(chen-TEE-may-troh)* (i centimetri)

central heating riscaldamento centrale, il *(rees-kahl-dah-MAYN-toh chayn-TRAH-lay)*

ceramics ceramiche, le *(chay-RAH-mee-kay)*

cereal cereale, il/un *(chay-ray-AH-lay)* (i cereali)

certainly certo *(CHEHR-toh)*

certificate certificato, il/un *(chayr-tee-fee-KAH-toh)*

chain catena, la/una *(kah-TAY-nah)* (le catene)

snow chains catene da neve, le *(kah-TAY-nay dah NAY-vay)*

chair sedia, la/una *(SED-yah)*

chairlift seggiovia, la/una *(sayd-joh-VEE-ah)*

wheelchair sedia a rotelle, la/una *(SED-yah ah roh-TEL-lay)*

chairlift seggiovia, la/una *(sayd-joh-VEE-ah)*

champagne champagne, il/un *(shahm-PAHN-nyay)*

chance fortuna, la *(fohr-TOO-nah)*

change (coins) moneta, la *(moh-NAY-tah)*, spiccioli, gli *(SPEET-choh-lee)*, (money back) resto, il *(RES-toh)*

my change il mio resto *(eel MEE-oh RES-toh)*

change, to cambiare *(kahm-BYAH-ray)*

change money, to cambiare denaro *(kahm-BYAH-ray day-NAH-roh)*

charger (phone) caricabatterie, il/un *(kah-ree-kah-baht-tay-REE-ay)*

charming affascinante *(ahf-fahsh-shee-NAHN-tay)*

cheap economico/a *(ay-koh-NOH-mee-koh/-kah)*

cheaper più economico/a *(pyoo ay-koh-NOH-mee-koh/-kah)*

check, to controllare *(kohn-trohl-LAH-ray)*

Can you check ___? Può controllare ___? *(pwoh kohn-trohl-LAH-ray ___?)*

I'll check (with) ___. Controllo (con) ___. *(kohn-TROHL-loh [kohn] ___)*

check (bill) conto, il/un *(KOHN-toh)*, (e.g., traveler's) assegno, l' *m* /un *(ahs-SAYN-nyoh)*

check, please! Il conto, per piacere! *(eel KOHN-toh, payr pyah-CHAY-ray)*

check-in (hotel) registrazione, la *(ray-jees-traht-TSYOH-nay)*; (airport) accetazione, l' *f* *(aht-chayt-taht-TSYOH-nay)*

checkroom guardaroba, la/una *(gwahr-dah-ROH-bah)*

cheers! salute! *(sah-LOO-tay)*

cheese formaggio, il/un *(fohr-MAHD-joh)* (i formaggi)

chef cuoco/a, il/la un/una *(KWOH-koh/-ah)*

cherry ciliegia, la/una *(chee-LYED-jah)* (le ciliegie)

chest torace, il *(toh-RAH-chay)*, petto, il *(PET-toh)*

chewing gum gomma da masticare, la *(GOHM-mah dah mahs-tee-KAH-ray)*

chicken pollo, il/un *(POHL-loh)*

chicken broth brodo di pollo, il/un *(BROH-doh dee POHL-loh)*

chickpeas ceci, i *(CHAY-chee)*

child bambino/a, il/la un/una *(bahm-BEE-noh/-nah)* (i bambini/le bambine)

for a child/child's per bambini *(payr bahm-BEE-nee)*

child discount sconto per bambini, lo/uno *(SKOHN-toh payr bahm-BEE-nee)*

child's menu menù per bambini, il/un *(may-NOO payr bahm-BEE-nee)*

child seat seggiolino per bambini, il/un *(sayd-joh-LEE-noh payr bahm-BEE-nee)*

children bambini, i *(bahm-BEE-nee)*

children's menu menù per bambini, il/un *(may-NOO payr bahm-BEE-nee)*

chili pepper peperoncino, il/un *(pay-pay-rohn-CHEE-noh)*

chili sauce salsa di peperoncino rosso, la *(SAHL-sah dee pay-pay-rohn-CHEE-noh ROHS-soh)*

chiropractor chiropratico/a, il/la un/una *(kee-roh-PRAH-tee-koh/-kah)*

chocolate cioccolato, il *(chohk-koh-LAH-toh)*

cholesterol colesterolo, il *(koh-lays-tay-ROH-loh)*

cholesterol-free senza colesterolo *(SEN-tsah koh-lays-tay-ROH-loh)*

choose, to scegliere *(SHAY-lyay-ray)*

Christian cristiano/a *(krees-TYAH-noh/-nah)*

Christmas Natale, il *(nah-TAH-lay)*

church chiesa, la/una *(KYAY-zah)*

cigar sigaro, il/un *(SEE-gah-roh)* (i sigari)

cigarette sigaretta, la/una *(see-gah-RAYT-tah)* (le sigarette)

cigarette lighter accendino, l' *m* /un *(aht-chayn-DEE-noh)*

circus circo, il/un *(CHEER-koh)*

citizenship cittadinanza, la *(cheet-tah-dee-NAHN-tsah)*

city città, la/una *(cheet-TAH)*

class classe, la/una *(KLAHS-say)*

economy class classe turistica, la *(KLAHS-say too-REES-tee-kah)*

first-class di prima classe *(dee PREE-mah KLAHS-say)*

second-class di seconda classe *(dee say-KOHN-dah KLAHS-say)*

class (course) corso, il/un *(KOHR-soh)* (i corsi)

cooking class corso di cucina, il/un *(KOHR-soh dee koo-CHEE-nah)*

language class corso di lingua, il/un *(KOHR-soh dee LEEN-gwah)*

classical classico/a *(KLAHS-see-koh/-kah)*

clean pulito/a *(poo-LEE-toh/-tah)*

clean, to pulire *(poo-LEE-ray)*

clear chiaro/a *(KYAH-roh/-rah)*

clear annulla (e.g., ATM) *(ahn-NOOL-lah)*

client cliente, il/la un/una *(klee-EN-tay)*

cliff scogliera, la/una *(skohl-LYEH-rah)*

climb, to scalare *(skah-LAH-ray)*

cloakroom guardaroba, la/una *(gwahr-dah-ROH-bah)*

clock orologio, l' *m*/un *(oh-roh-LOH-joh)*

close, to chiudere *(KYOO-day-ray)*

When does it close? A che ora chiude? *(ah kay OH-rah KYOO-day?)*

closed (to be) chiuso/a *(KYOO-soh/-ah)*

closing day giorno di chiusura *(JOHR-noh dee kyoo-SOO-rah)*

close by vicino/a *(vee-CHEE-noh/-nah)*

clothes abbigliamento, l' *m* *(ahb-beel-lyah-MAYN-toh)*

clothes line corda del bucato, la/una *(KOHR-dah dayl boo-KAH-toh)*

clothing abbigliamento, l' *m* *(ahb-beel-lyah-MAYN-toh)*

clothing store negozio di abbigliamento, il/un *(nay-GOHT-tsyoh dee ahb-beel-lyah-MAYN-toh)*

cloud nuvola, la/una *(NOO-voh-lah)*

cloudy nuvoloso/a *(noo-voh-LOH-soh/-sah)*

club club, il/un *(kloob)*

coach (=bus) pullman, il/un *(POOL-mahn)*

coast costa, la *(KOHS-tah)*

coastline linea costiera, la *(LEE-nay-ah kohs-TYEH-rah)*

coat cappotto, il/un *(kahp-POHT-toh)*

cockroach scarafaggio, lo/uno *(skah-rah-FAHD-joh)* (gli scarafaggi)

cocktail aperitivo, l' *m*/un *(ah-pay-ree-TEE-voh)*, cocktail, il/un *(KOHK-tay-eel)*

cocoa cacao, il *(kah-KAH-oh)*

codeine codeina, la *(koh-day-EE-nah)*

coffee caffè, il/un *(kahf-FEH)*

coin moneta, la/una *(moh-NAY-tah)* (le monete)

some coins della moneta *(DAYL-lah moh-NAY-tah)*

cold (temp.) freddo/a *(FRAYD-doh/-dah)*

cold (illness) raffreddore, il *(rahf-frayd-DOH-ray)*

to have a cold essere raffreddato/a *(ES-say-ray rahf-frayd-DAH-toh/-tah)*

I have a cold sono raffreddato/a *(SOH-noh rahf-frayd-DAH-toh/-tah)*

cold cuts salumi, i *(sah-LOO-mee)*, affettato, l' *m* *(ahf-fayt-TAH-toh)*

colleague collega, il/la un/una *(kohl-LEH-gah)*

my colleague il mio collega *(eel MEE-oh kohl-LEH-gah)*, la mia collega *(lah MEE-ah kohl-LEH-gah)*

collect, to (=pick up) ritirare *(ree-tee-RAH-ray)*

collect call chiamata a carico del destinatario, la/una *(kyah-MAH-tah ah KAH-ree-koh dayl days-tee-nah-TAH-ryoh)*

color colore, il/un *(koh-LOH-ray)*

comb pettine, il/un *(PET-tee-nay)*

combined (as in the bill) unico/a *(OO-nee-koh/-kah)*

come, to venire *(vay-NEE-ray)*

Come in. Avanti. *(ah-VAHN-tee)*

come back, to tornare *(tohr-NAH-ray)*

Come back later. Torni più tardi. *(TOHR-nee pyoo TAHR-dee)*

I'm come back. Torno. *(TOHR-noh)*

comedy commedia comica, la/una *(kohm-MEH-dyah KOH-mee-kah)*

comfortable comodo/a *(KOH-moh-doh/-dah)*

commission commissione, la/una *(kohm-mees-SYOH-nay)*

common comune *(koh-MOO-nay)*

communicate, to comunicare *(koh-moo-nee-KAH-ray)*

communion comunione, la *(koh-moo-NYOH-nay)*

companion compagno/a, il/la un/una *(kohm-PAHN-nyoh/-nyah)*

company (business) azienda, l' f/un' *(ahd-DZYEN-dah)*; ditta, la/una *(DEET-tah)*

compass bussola, la/una *(BOO-soh-lah)*

complain, to lamentarsi *(lah-mayn-TAHR-see)*

complimentary (free) gratuito/a *(grah-TOO-ee-toh/-tah)*

compose, to comporre *(kohm-POHR-ray)*

compute, to calcolare *(kahl-koh-LAH-ray)*

computer computer, il/un *(kom-PYOO-ter)*

computer game gioco elettronico, il/un *(JOH-koh ay-layt-TROH-nee-koh)*

computer programmer programmatore/trice di computer, il/la un/una *(proh-grahm-mah-TOH-ray/-TREE-chay dee kum-PYOO-tur)*

concert concerto, il/un *(kohn-CHEHR-toh)* (i concerti)

conclude, to concludere *(kohn-KLOO-day-ray)*

conditioner (hair) balsamo per capelli, il *(BAHL-sah-moh payr kah-PAYL-lee)*

condom preservativo, il/un *(pray-sayr-vah-TEE-voh)* (i preservativi)

cone cono, il/un *(KOH-noh)* (i coni); cornetto, il/un *(kohr-NAYT-toh)* (i cornetti)

conference conferenza, la/una *(kohn-fay-REN-tsah)*

confession (church) confessione, la/una *(kohn-fays-SYOH-nay)*

confirm, to confermare *(kohn-fayr-MAH-ray)*

confirmation conferma, la *(kohn-FAYR-mah)*

confuse, to confondere *(kohn-FOHN-day-ray)*

congratulations! congratulazioni! *(kohn-graht-too-laht-TSYOH-nee)*

connect, to collegare *(kohl-lay-GAH-ray)*, collegarsi *(kohl-lay-GAHR-see)*

connection collegamento, il/un *(kohl-lay-gah-MAYN-toh)*, (transportation) coincidenza, la/una *(koh-een-chee-DEN-tsah)*; (Internet) connessione Internet, la/una *(kohn-nays-SYOH-nay EEN-tayr-net)*

constipation stitichezza, la *(stee-tee-KAYT-tsah)*

consulate consolato, il *(kohn-soh-LAH-toh)*

consume, to consumare *(kohn-soo-MAH-ray)*

contact lenses lenti a contatto, le *(LEN-tee ah kohn-TAHT-toh)*

contain, to contenere *(kohn-tay-NAY-ray)*

  It contains ___. Contiene ___. *(kohn-TYEH-nay)*

content contento/a *(kohn-TEN-toh/-tah)*

continue (ATM) esegui *(ay-SAY-gwee)*

continuous hours (no pause) orario continuato, l' *m (oh-RAHR-yoh kohn-tee-noo-AH-toh)*

contraceptive contraccettivo, il/un *(kohn-traht-chayt-TEE-voh)* (i contraccettivi)

contradict, to contraddire *(kohn-trahd-DEE-ray)*

convenience store negozio di alimentari, l' *m/un (nay-GOHT-syoh dee ah-lee-mayn-TAH-ree)*

convert, to convertire *(kohn-vayr-TEE-ray)*

convince, to convincere *(kohn-VEEN-chay-ray)*

cook (person) cuoco/a, il/la un/una *(KWOH-koh/-ah)*

cook, to cuocere *(KWOH-chay-ray)*, cucinare *(koo-chee-NAH-ray)*

cooked cotto/a *(KOHT-toh/-tah)*

cookie biscotto, il/un *(bees-KOHT-toh)* (i biscotti)

cooking cucinare *(koo-chee-NAH-ray)*

cool fresco/a *(FRAY-skoh/-skah)*

copy copia, la/una *(KOH-pyah)*

corkscrew cavatappi, il/un *(kah-vah-TAHP-pee)*

corn mais, il *(MAH-ees)*

  corn flakes fiocchi di mais, i *(FYOHK-kee dee MAH-ees)*

corner angolo, l' *m/un (AHN-goh-loh)*

  at/on the corner all'angolo *(ahl LAHN-goh-loh)*

correct giusto/a *(JOO-stoh/-stah)*

correct, to correggere *(kohr-RED-jay-ray)*

correspond, to corrispondere *(kohr-rees-POHN-day-ray)*

corridor corridoio, il *(kohr-ree-DOH-yoh)*

corrupt corrotto/a *(kohr-ROHT-toh/-tah)*

corrupt, to corrompere *(kohr-ROHM-pay-ray)*

cost, to costare *(koh-STAH-ray)*

  it costs costa *(KOHS-tah)*

How much does it cost? Quanto costa? *(KWAHN-toh KOHS-tah?)*

cot culla, la/una *(KOOL-lah)*

cotton cotone, il *(koh-TOH-nay)*

cotton ball batuffolo di cotone, il/un *(bah-TOOF-foh-loh dee koh-TOH-nay)* (i batuffoli)

cough tosse, la/una *(TOHS-say)*

cough drop pasticca per la tosse, la/una *(pahs-TEEK-kah payr lah TOHS-say)*

cough syrup sciroppo per la tosse, lo/uno *(shee-ROHP-poh payr lah TOHS-say)*

could see *potere*

I could potrei *(poh-TREH-ee)*

you could potrebbe (form. sing.) *(poh-TREB-bee)*

count, to contare *(kohn-TAH-ray)*

counter sportello, lo *(spohr-TEL-loh)*, bancone, il *(bahn-KOH-nay)*

country (nation) paese, il/un *(pah-AY-zay)* (i paesi)

country(side) campagna, la *(kahm-PAHN-nyah)*

course (food) piatto, il/un *(PYAH-toh)* (i piatti); (route) corsa, la/una *(KOHR-sah)*; (class) corso, il/un *(KOHR-soh)* (i corsi)

court (sports) campo, il/un *(KAHM-poh)*

cousin cugino/a, il/la un/una *(koo-JEE-noh/-nah)*

cover, to coprire *(koh-PREE-ray)*

cover charge (prezzo del) coperto, il/un *([PRET-tsoh dayl] koh-PEHR-toh)*

covering copertura, la/una *(koh-payr-TOO-rah)*

cow mucca, la/una *(MOOK-kah)* (le mucche)

crab granchio, il/un *(GRAHNK-yoh)* (i granchi)

cramp crampo, il/un *(KRAHM-poh)* (i crampi)

crazy pazzo/a *(PAHTS-soh/-sah)*

cream crema, la *(KREH-mah)*, panna, la *(PAHN-nah)*

cream cheese formaggio fresco, il *(fohr-MAHD-joh FRAYS-koh)*

create, to formare *(fohr-MAH-ray)*

credit card carta di credito, la/una *(KAHR-tah dee KRAY-dee-toh)*

Croatia Croazia, il *(kroh-AHT-tsyah)*

croissant cornetto, il/un *(kohr-NAYT-toh)* (i cornetti)

crossroads incrocio, l' *m*/un *(een-KROHT-choh)*

crown corona, la/una *(koh-ROH-nah)*

cross croce, la/una *(KROH-chay)*

crutch stampella, la/una *(stahm-PEL-lah)* (le stampelle)

cry, to (weep) piangere *(PYAHN-jay-ray)*

cucumber cetriolo, il/un *(chay-tree-OH-loh)* (i cetrioli)

cuisine cucina, la *(koo-CHEE-nah)*

cup (drink) tazza, la/una *(TAHT-tsah)* (le tazze); (ice cream) coppa, la/una *(KOHP-pah)* (le coppe)

currency valuta, la *(vah-LOO-tah)*

  currency exchange office cambio, il/un *(KAHM-byoh)*, ufficio di cambio, l' *m*/un *(oof-FEE-choh dee KAHM-byoh)*

current (electrical) corrente, la *(kohr-REN-tay)*

curry (spice) curry, il *(KOOR-ree)*

customs dogana, la *(doh-GAH-nah)*

  customs declaration dichiarazione, la *(dee-kyah-raht-TSYOH-nay)*

cut, to tagliare *(tahl-LYAH-ray)*

cutlery posate, le *(poh-SAH-tay)*

cycle, to andare in bicicletta *(ahn-DAH-ray een bee-chee-KLAYT-tah)*

cyclist ciclista, il/la un/una *(chee-KLEES-tah)*

D

D, d D, d *(dee)*

dad papà, il/un *(pah-PAH)*

daily giornalmente *(johr-nahl-MAYN-tay)*, al giorno *(ahl JOHR-noh)*

  daily special (food) piatto del giorno, il/un *(PYAHT-toh dayl JOHR-noh)*

dairy product latticino, il *(laht-tee-CHEE-noh)* (i latticini)

damage danno, il *(DAHN-noh)*

damaged danneggiato/a *(dahn-nayd-JAH-toh/-tah)*

dance, to ballare *(bahl-LAH-ray)*

dance ballo, il/un *(BAHL-loh)*

danger pericolo, il/un *(pay-REE-koh-loh)*

  danger of death pericolo di morte, il/un *(pay-REE-koh-loh dee MOHR-tay)*

dangerous pericoloso/a *(pay-ree-koh-LOH-soh/-sah)*

dark scuro/a *(SKOO-roh/-rah)*

darling caro/a *(KAH-roh/-rah)*

date (day) data, la/una *(DAH-tah)*, (appointment) appuntamento, l' *m*/un *(ahp-poon-tah-MAYN-toh)*

  date of birth data di nascita, la *(DAH-tah dee NAHSH-shee-tah)*

daughter figlia, la/una *(FEEL-lyah)* (le figlie)

  my daughter mia figlia *(MEE-ah FEEL-lyah)*

daughter-in-law nuora, la *(NWOH-rah)*

dawn alba, l' *f (AHL-bah)*

day giorno, il/un *(JOHR-noh)* (i giorni)

  day after tomorrow dopodomani *(doh-poh-doh-MAH-nee)*

  day before yesterday altro ieri *(AHL-troh YEH-ree)*

  day trip escursione in giornata, l' *f*/un' *(ays-koor-SYOH-nay een johr-NAH-tah)*

dead morto/a *(MOHR-toh/-tah)*

deaf sordo/a *(SOHR-doh/-dah)*

debit card carta di debito, la/una *(KAHR-tah dee DAY-bee-toh)*

decaf decaffeinato/a *(day-kahf-fay-ee-NAH-toh/-tah)*

deceased deceduto/a *(day-chay-DOO-toh/-tah)*

December dicembre *(dee-CHEM-bray)*

decide, to decidere *(day-CHEE-day-ray)*

I decide decido *(day-CHEE-doh)*

declare, to dichiarare *(dee-kyah-RAH-ray)*

I have nothing to declare.

Non ho niente da dichiarare. *(nohn oh NYEN-tay day dee-kyah-RAH-ray)*

I have something to declare.

Ho della cose da dichiarare. *(oh DAYL-lah KOH-say dah dee-kyah-RAH-ray)*

decongestant decongestionante, il/un *(day-kohn-jay-styoh-NAHN-tay)*

deep profondo/a *(proh-FOHN-doh/-dah)*

defective difettoso/a *(dee-fayt-TOH-soh/-sah)*

delay ritardo, il/un *(ree-TAHR-doh)*

delayed in ritardo *(een ree-TAHR-doh)*

deli salumeria, la/una *(sah-loo-may-REE-ah)*

delicious delizioso/a *(day-leet-TSYOH-soh/-sah)*

Denmark Danimarca, la *(dah-nee-MAHR-kah)*

dental floss filo dentario, il *(FEE-loh dayn-TAHR-yoh)*

dentist dentista, il/la un/una *(dayn-TEES-tah)*

dentures dentiera, la *(dayn-TYEH-rah)*

design disegno, il/un *(dee-SAYN-nyoh)*

deodorant deodorante, il/un *(day-oh-doh-RAHN-tay)*

depart, to partire *(pahr-TEE-ray)*

he/she/it departs parte *(PAHR-tay)*

I depart parto *(PAHR-toh)*

you depart parte (form. sing.) *(PAHR-tay)*

department store grande magazzino, il/un *(GRAHN-day mah-gahd-DZEE-noh)*

departure partenza, la *(pahr-TEN-tsah)*

depend, to dipendere *(dee-PEN-day-ray)*

deposit (refundable) caparra, la/una *(kah-PAHR-rah)*, (bank) deposito, il/un *(day-POH-zee-toh)*

security deposit cauzione, la/una *(kowt-TSYOH-nay)*, caparra, la/una *(kah-PAHR-rah)*

deposit, to depositare *(day-poh-zee-TAH-ray)*

depressed depresso/a *(day-PRES-soh/-sah)*

descend, to scendere *(SHAYN-day-ray)*

I descend scendo *(SHAYN-doh)*

we descend scendiamo *(shayn-DYAH-moh)*

you descend (form. sing.) scende *(SHAYN-day)*

dessert dolce, il/un *(DOHL-chay)* (i dolci)

destination destinazione, la/una *(days-tee-naht-TSYOH-nay)*

detest, to detestare *(day-tays-TAH-ray)*

diabetes diabete, il *(dee-ah-BEH-tay)*

diabetic diabetico/a *(dee-ah-BEH-tee-koh/-kah)*

dial a number, to fare un numero *(FAH-ray oon NOO-may-roh)*

dial tone segnale acustico, il/un *(sayn-NYAH-lay ah-KOOS-tee-koh)*

diaper pannolino, il/un *(pahn-noh-LEE-noh)* (i pannolini)

disposable diapers pannolini usa-e-getta, i *(pahn-noh-LEE-nee oo-zah-ay-JET-tah)*

diarrhea diarrea, la *(dee-ahr-REH-ah)*

dictionary vocabolario, il/un *(voh-kah-boh-LAHR-yoh)*

die, to morire *(moh-REE-ray)*

diesel gasolio, il *(gah-ZOH-lyoh)*, blugasolio, il *(bloo-gah-ZOH-lyoh)*, diesel, il *(DEE-zul)*

diet dietetico/a *(dee-ay-TEH-tee-koh/-kah)*

diet dieta, la/una *(DYEH-tah)*

special diet dieta speciale, la/una *(DYEH-tah spay-CHAH-lay)*

different (from) diverso/a (da) *(dee-VEHR-soh/-sah [dah])*, differente (da) *(deef-fay-REN-tay [dah])*

difficult difficile *(deef-FEE-chee-lay)*

digital digitale *(dee-jee-TAH-lay)*

digital photos foto digitali, i *(FOH-toh dee-jee-TAH-lee)*

dining car (train) vagone ristorante, il/un *(vah-GOH-nay rees-toh-RAHN-tay)*, carrozza ristorante, la/una *(kahr-ROHT-tsah rees-toh-RAHN-tay)*

dinner cena, la/una *(CHAY-nah)*

direct diretto/a *(dee-RET-toh/-tah)*

a direct route un itinerario diretto *(oon ee-tee-nay-RAH-ryoh dee-RET-toh)*

direct dial telefono diretto, il *(tay-LEH-foh-noh dee-RET-toh)*

direction direzione, la *(dee-rayt-TSYOH-nay)*, (instructions) indicazioni, le *(een-dee-kaht-TSYOH-nee)*

director (film) regista, il/la un/una *(ray-JEES-tah)*

dirty sporco/a *(SPOHR-koh/-kah)*

disabled person disabile, il/la *(dees-AH-bee-lay)*

disappear, to svanire *(svah-NEE-ray)*

disco discoteca, la/una *(dees-koh-TEH-kah)*

discount sconto, lo/uno *(SKOHN-toh)*

Is there a discount for ___? C'è uno sconto per ___? *(cheh OO-noh SKOHN-toh payr ___?)*

discrimination discriminazione, la *(dees-kree-mee-nah-TSYOH-nay)*

discuss, to discutere *(dees-KOO-tay-ray)*

disease malattia, la/una *(mah-laht-TEE-ah)*

disgust, to disgustare *(deez-goos-TAH-ray)*

dish piatto, il/un *(PYAH-toh)* (i piatti)

disk (computer) dischetto, il/un *(dees-KAYT-toh)*

disposable usa-e-getta *(oo-zah-ay-JET-tah)*

divide, to dividere *(dee-VEE-day-ray)*

diving (sea) immersioni, le *(eem-mayr-SYOH-nee)*

divorced divorziato/a *(dee-vohr-TSYAH-toh/-tah)*

dizziness capogiro, il *(kah-poh-JEE-roh)*

dizzy stordito/a *(stohr-DEE-toh/-tah)*

do, to fare *(FAH-ray)*

  he/she/it does fa *(fa)*

  I do faccio *(FAHT-choh)*

  we do facciamo *(faht-CHAH-moh)*

  you do fa (form. sing.) *(fah)*

doctor medico/a, il/la un/una *(MEH-dee-koh/-kah)*

dog cane, il/un *(KAH-nay)* (i cani)

  guide dog cane guida, il/un *(KAH-nay GWEE-dah)*

doll bambola, la/una *(BAHM-boh-lah)* (le bambole)

dollar dollaro, il/un *(DOHL-lah-roh)*

domestic domestico/a *(doh-MES-tee-koh/-kah)*

don't *non* + conjugated verb (e.g., I don't understand. = Non capisco.)

door porta, la/una *(POHR-tah)*

dot punto, il/un *(POON-toh)* (i punti)

double doppio/a *(DOHP-pyoh/-pyah)*

  double bed letto matrimoniale, il/un *(LET-toh mah-tree-mohn-NYAH-lay)*

  double room camera doppia, la/una *(KAH-may-rah DOHP-pyah)*

down giù *(joo)*

download, to scaricare *(skah-ree-KAH-ray)*

downpayment caparra, la *(kah-PAHR-rah)*

downtown centro città, il *(CHEN-troh cheet-TAH)*

dozen dozzina, la/una *(dohd-DZEE-nah)*

draft beer birra a la spina, la/una *(BEER-rah ah lah SPEE-nah)*

drama dramma, il/un *(DRAHM-mah)*

draw, to disegnare *(dee-sayn-NYAH-ray)*

drawing disegno, il/un *(dee-SAYN-nyoh)*

dress vestito, il/un *(vays-TEE-toh)*

dressing condimento, il/un *(kohn-dee-MAYN-toh)*

  dressing on the side il condimento a parte *(eel kohn-dee-MAYN-toh ah PAHR-tay)*

dried secco/a *(SAYK-koh/-kah)*

dried beans fagioli, i *(fahd-JOH-lee)*

drink bevanda, la/una *(bay-VAHN-dah)* (le bevande), bibita, la/una *(BEE-bee-tah)* (le bibite)

drinks list lista delle bevande, la *(LEES-tah DAYL-lah bay-VAHN-day)*

drink, to bere *(BAY-ray)*

　I drink bevo *(BAY-voh)*

　you drink beve (form. sing.) *(BAY-vay)*

　safe to drink potabile *(poh-TAH-bee-lay)*

　not safe to drink non potabile *(nohn poh-TAH-bee-lay)*

drive, to (e.g., a car) guidare *(gwee-DAH-ray)*

　he/she/it drives guida *(GWEE-dah)*

　I drive guido *(GWEE-doh)*

　we drive guidiamo *(gwee-DYAH-moh)*

　you drive guida (form. sing.) *(GWEE-dah)*

driver's license patente (di guida), la *(pah-TEN-tay [dee GWEE-dah])*

drug medicina, la/una *(may-dee-CHEE-nah)* (le medicine), farmaco, il/un *(FAHR-mah-koh)* (i farmaci)

drugstore (medicine) farmacia, la/una *(fahr-mah-CHEE-ah)*, (sundry items) negozio di generi vari, il/un *(nay-GOHT-tsyoh dee JEN-ay-ree VAH-ree)*

drunk (inebriated) ubriaco/a *(oo-bree-AH-koh/-kah)*

dry secco/a *(SAYK-koh/-kah)*

　dry cleaner lavasecco, il/un *(lay-vah-SAYK-koh)*

　dry cleaning lavaggio a secco, il *(lah-VAHD-joh ah SAYK-koh)*

dry, to asciugare *(ahsh-shoo-GAH-ray)*

DSL ADSL, a type of broadband DSL communication *(ah-dee-ess-EL-lay)*

dubbed (film) doppiato/a *(dohp-PYAH-toh/-tah)*

duck anatra, l' *f*/un' *(AH-nah-trah)* (le anatre)

dumpling gnocco di pasta, lo/uno *(NYOHK-koh dee PAH-stah)* (gli gnocchi)

duration durata, la *(doo-RAH-tah)*

during durante *(doo-RAHN-tay)*

DVD DVD, il *(dee-voo-DEE)*

E

E, e E, e *(ay)*

each ciascuno/a *(chahs-KOO-noh/-nah)*

ear orecchio, l' *m* *(oh-RAYK-kyoh)* (gli orecchie)

early presto *(PRES-toh)*

earphone auricolare, l' *m*/un *(ow-ree-koh-LAH-ray)*

earplugs tappi per le orecchie, i *(TAHP-pee payr lay oh-RAYK-kyay)*

earrings orecchini, gli *(oh-rayk-KEE-nee)*

Earth Terra, la *(TEHR-rah)*

earthquake terremoto, il/un *(tayr-ray-MOH-toh)*

east est *(est)*

  to the east all'est *(ahl-EST)*

Easter Pasqua, la *(PAHS-kwah)*

easy facile *(FAH-chee-lay)*

eat, to mangiare *(mahn-JAH-ray)*

  he/she/it eats mangia *(MAHN-jah)*

  I eat mangio *(MAHN-joh)*

  I don't eat ___. Non mangio ___. *(nohn MAHN-joh ___)*

  we eat mangiamo *(mahn-JAH-moh)*

  you eat mangia (form. sing.) *(MAHN-jah)*

economy class classe turistica, la *(KLAHS-say too-REES-tee-kah)*

eczema eczema, l' *m (ayk-DZEH-mah)*

education istruzione, l' *f (ees-troot-TSYOH-nay)*

egg uovo, l' *m/*un *(WOH-voh)* (le uova)

eggplant melanzana, la/una *(may-lahn-DZAH-nah)* (le melanzane)

eight otto *(OHT-toh)*

eighteen diciotto *(dee-CHOHT-toh)*

eight hundred ottocento *(oht-toh-CHEN-toh)*

eighty ottanta *(oht-TAHN-tah)*

  eighty-one ottantuno *(oht-tahn-TOO-noh)*

  eighty-two ottantadue *(oht-tahn-tah-DOO-ay)*

eighty-three ottantatré *(oht-tahn-tah-TRAY)*

eighty-four ottantaquattro *(oht-tahn-tah-KWAHT-troh)*

eighty-five ottantacinque *(oht-tahn-tah-CHEEN-kway)*

eighty-six ottantasei *(oht-tahn-tah-SEH-ee)*

eighty-seven ottantasette *(oht-tahn-tah-SET-tay)*

eighty-eight ottantotto *(oht-tahn-TOHT-toh)*

eighty-nine ottantanove *(oht-tahn-tah-NOH-vay)*

elbow gomito, il *(GOH-mee-toh)*

electrician elettricista, l'/l' *m/f* un/una *(ay-layt-tree-CHEE-stah)*

electricity corrente, la *(kohr-REN-tay)*

electronic elettronico/a *(ay-layt-TROH-nee-koh/kah)*

elevator ascensore, l' *m/*un *(ahsh-shayn-SOH-ray)*

eleven undici *(OON-dee-chee)*

e-mail e-mail, l' *m/*un *(EE-mayl)*

  e-mail address indirizzo di email, l' *m/*un *(een-dee-REET-tsoh dee EE-mayl)*

embarrassed imbarazzato/a *(eem-bah-raht-TSAH-toh/-tah)*

embassy ambasciata, l' *f (ahm-bahsh-SHAH-tah)*

embroidery ricamo, il *(ree-KAH-moh)*

emergency emergenza, l' *f/*un' *(ay-mayr-JEN-tsah)*

employ, to impiegare *(eem-pyay-GAH-ray)*

employee impiegato/a, l'/l' *m*/*f (eem-pyay-GAH-toh/-tah)*

employer datore/datrice di lavoro, il/la *(dah-TOH-ray/dah-TREE-chay dee lah-VOH-roh)*

empty vuoto/a *(VWOH-toh/-tah)*

end fine, la/una *(FEE-nay)*

end, to finire *(fee-NEE-ray)*

engine motore, il/un *(moh-TOH-ray)*

engineer ingegnere, l' *m*/un *(een-jayn-NYEH-ray)*

engineering ingegneria, l' *f (een-jayn-nyay-REE-ah)*

England Inghilterra, l' *f (een-geel-TEH-rah)*

English inglese *(een-GLAY-say)*

in English in inglese *(een een-GLAY-say)*

engraving incisione, l' *f (een-chee-ZYOH-nay)*

enjoy, to godere *(goh-DAY-ray)*

Do you enjoy ___? Gode ___? (form. sing.) *(GOH-day ___?)*

I enjoy ___ Godo ___ *(GOH-doh ___)*

enjoy oneself, to divertirsi *(dee-vayr-TEER-see)*

enough abbastanza *(ahb-bahs-TAHN-tsah)*, basta *(BAHS-tah)*

enter, to entrare *(ayn-TRAH-ray)*

entrance ingresso, l' *m (een-GRES-soh)*, entrata, l' *f (ayn-TRAH-tah)*

entry entrata, l' *f (ayn-TRAH-tah)*

envelope busta, la/una *(BOOS-tah)* (le buste)

padded envelope busta imbottita, la/una *(BOOS-tah eem-boht-TEE-tah)*

epilepsy epilessia, l' *f (ay-pee-lays-SEE-ah)*

epileptic epilettico/a *(ay-pee-LET-tee-koh/-kah)*

equal uguale *(oo-GWAH-lay)*

equipment attrezzatura, l' *f (aht-trayt-tsah-TOO-rah)*

error errore, l' *m*/un *(ayr-ROH-ray)*

escalator scala mobile, la/una *(SKAH-lah MOH-bee-lay)*

espresso espresso, l' *m*/un *(ays-PRES-soh)*

etching acquaforte, l' *f* /un' *(ahk-kwah-FOHR-tay)*

euro euro, l' *m*/un *(AY-oo-roh)*

Europe Europa, l' *f (ay-oo-ROH-pah)*

European europeo/a *(ay-oo-roh-PEH-oh/-ah)*

evening sera, la/una *(SAY-rah)*

in the evening di sera *(dee SAY-rah)*

this evening stasera *(stah-SAY-rah)*

tomorrow evening domani sera *(doh-MAH-nee SAY-rah)*

yesterday evening ieri sera *(YEH-ree SAY-rah)*

everything tutto/a *(TOOT-toh/-tah)*

examine, to esaminare *(ay-zah-mee-NAH-ray)*

example esempio, l' *m*/un *(ay-ZEM-pyoh)*

excellent ottimo/a *(OHT-tee-moh/-mah)*

exceptional eccezionale *(ayt-chayt-tsyoh-NAH-lay)*

exchange, to cambiare *(kahm-BYAH-ray)*

exchange cambio, il/un *(KAHM-byoh)*

exchange office ufficio di cambio, l' *m*/un *(oof-FEE-choh dee KAHM-byoh)*

exchange rate tasso di cambio, il *(TAHS-soh dee KAHM-byoh)*

exclude, to escludere *(ays-KLOO-day-ray)*

excluded escluso/a *(ays-KLOO-zoh/-zah)*

excursion escursione, l' *f*/un' *(ays-koor-SYOH-nay)*

excuse me (mi) scusi *([mee] SKOO-zee)*, (="May I get past") permesso? *(payr-MAYS-soh?)*

execute, to (=to carry out) eseguire *(ay-zay-GWEE-ray)*

exhibition esposizione, l' *f*/un' *(ay-spoh-zeet-TSYOH-nay)*

exhibition hall salone d'esposizione, il/un *(sah-LOH-nay day-spoh-zeet-TSYOH-nay)*

exit uscita, l' *f*/un' *(oosh-SHEE-tah)*

exit, to uscire *(oosh-SHEE-ray)*

expect, to aspettere *(ahs-payt-TAH-ray)*

I'm expecting ___. Aspetto ___. *(ahs-PET-toh ___)*

expensive caro/a *(KAH-roh/-rah)*

experience esperienza, l' *f* /un' *(ays-pay-RYEN-tsah)*

expiration scadenza, la *(skah-DEN-tsah)*

expired scaduto/a *(skah-DOO-toh/-tah)*

express espresso/a *(ays-PRES-soh/-sah)*

express highway (toll road) autostrada, l' *f*/un' *(ow-tohs-TRAH-dah)*; (non-toll road) Superstrada, la/una *(soo-payr-STRAH-dah)* or S.G.C. *(ES-say jee chee)*

express mail posta prioritaria, la *(POHS-tah pree-oh-ree-TAHR-yah)*

international express mail EMS

extended stay soggiorno lungo, il/un *(sohd-JOHR-noh LOON-goh)* (i soggiorni lunghi)

extra supplemento/a *(soo-play-MAYN-toh/-tah)*

eye occhio, l' *m*/un *(OHK-kyoh)* (gli occhi)

eye drops collirio, il/un *(kohl-LEE-ryoh)* (i colliri)

eyeglasses occhiali, gli *(ohk-KYAH-lee)*

F

F, f F, f *(AYF-fay)*

fabric stoffa, la/una *(STOHF-fah)*

face viso, il/un *(VEE-zoh)*, faccia, la/una *(FAHT-chah)*

Facebook, on su Facebook *(soo FAYS-book)*

facial tissues fazzoletti di carta, i *(faht-tsoh-LAYT-tee dee KAHR-tah)*

fact, in infatti *(een-FAHT-tee)*

factory fabbrica, la/una *(FAHB-bree-kah)*

factory worker operaio/a, l'/l' *m/f (oh-pay-RAH-yoh/-yah)*

fail, to fallire *(fahl-LEE-ray)*

faint, to svenire *(zvay-NEE-ray)*

fall (season) autunno, l' *m (aw-TOON-noh)*

fall, to cadere *(kah-DAY-ray)*

falsify, to falsificare *(fahl-see-fee-KAH-ray)*

family famiglia, la/una *(fah-MEEL-lyah)* (le famiglie)

with (a) family con famiglia *(kohn fah-MEEL-lyah)*

family discount sconto per famiglia, lo/uno *(SKOHN-toh payr fah-MEEL-lyah)*

family name cognome, il/un *(kohn-NYOH-may)*

famous famoso/a *(fah-MOH-soh/-sah)*

fan ventilatore, il/un *(vayn-tee-lah-TOH-ray)*

far (away) lontano *(lohn-TAH-noh)*

fare tariffa, la *(tah-REEF-fah)*

farm fattoria, la/una *(faht-toh-REE-ah)*

farm stay agriturismo, l' *m (ah-gree-too-REEZ-moh)*

farmer agricoltore/agricoltrice, l'/l' *m/f (ah-gree-kohl-TOH-ray/ah-gree-kohl-TREE-chay)*

fashion moda, la *(MOH-dah)*

fast veloce *(vay-LOH-chay)*

fat grasso/a *(GRAHS-soh/-sah)*

father padre, il/un *(PAH-dray)*

father-in-law suocero, il *(SWOH-chay-roh)*

Father's Day festa del papà, la *(FES-tah dayl pah-PAH)*

faucet rubinetto, il/un *(roo-bee-NAYT-toh)*

fault (responsibility) colpa, la *(KOHL-pah)*

favorite preferito/a *(pray-fay-REE-toh/-tah)*

fax fax, il/un *(fahks)*

fax number numero di fax, il/un *(NOO-may-roh dee fahks)*

February febbraio *(fayb-BRAH-yoh)*

fee compenso, il *(kohm-PEN-soh)*

feel sentire *(sayn-TEE-ray)*

fence recinto, il/un *(ray-CHEEN-toh)*

ferry traghetto, il/un *(trah-GAYT-toh)* (i traghetti)

festival festa, la/una *(FES-tah)*

fever febbre, la/una *(FEB-bray)*

few pochi/e *(POH-kee/-kay)*

fewer meno *(MAY-noh)*

fiance(e) fidanzato/a, il/la *(fee-dahn-TSAH-toh/-tah)*

fiction narrativa, la *(nahr-rah-TEE-vah)*

fifteen quindici *(KWEEN-dee-chee)*

fifth quinto/a, il/la *(KWEEN-toh/-tah)*

fifty cinquanta *(cheen-KWAHN-tah)*

fifty-one cinquantuno *(cheen-kwahn-TOO-noh)*

fifty-two cinquantadue *(cheen-kwahn-tah-DOO-ay)*

fifty-three cinquantatré *(cheen-kwahn-tah-TRAY)*

fifty-four cinquantaquattro *(cheen-kwahn-tah-KWAHT-troh)*

fifty-five cinquantacinque *(cheen-kwahn-tah-CHEEN-kway)*

fifty-six cinquantasei *(cheen-kwahn-tah-SEH-ee)*

fifty-seven cinquantasette *(cheen-kwahn-tah-SET-tay)*

fifty-eight cinquantotto *(cheen-kwahn-TOHT-toh)*

fifty-nine cinquantanove *(cheen-kwahn-tah-NOH-vay)*

fig fico, il/un *(FEE-koh)* (i fichi)

filling (dental) otturazione, l' *f* /un' *(oht-too-raht-TSYOH-nay)*

fill up the tank Il pieno, per favore *(eel PYEH-noh, payr fah-VOH-ray)*

film (movie) film, il/un *(feelm)*

film, roll of rullino, il/un *(rool-LEE-noh)*, rollino, il/un *(rohl-LEE-noh)*

to develop a roll of film sviluppare un rollino *(zvee-loop-PAH-ray oon rohl-LEE-noh)*

find, to trovare *(troh-VAH-ray)*

I find trovo *(TROH-voh)*

you find trova (form. sing.) *(TROH-vah)*

fine (penalty) multa, la/una *(MOOL-tah)*

finger dito, il/un *(DEE-toh)* (le dita)

finished finito/a *(fee-NEE-toh/-tah)*

fire fuoco, il/un *(FWOH-koh)*

fire! Al fuoco! *(ahl FWOH-koh)*

firemen pompieri, i *(pohm-PYEH-ree)*

first primo/a *(PREE-moh/-mah)*

first-aid pronto soccorso *(PROHN-toh sohk-KOHR-soh)*

first-aid kit cassetta di pronto soccorso, la *(kahs-SAYT-tah dee PROHN-toh sohk-KOHR-soh)*

first-class di prima classe *(dee PREE-mah KLAHS-say)*

the first ___ il/la primo/a ___ *(eel/lah PREE-moh/-mah)*

fish pesce, il/un *(PAYSH-shay)* (i pesci)

fish shop pescheria, la/una *(pays-kay-REE-ah)*

fishing pesca, la *(PAYS-kah)*

five cinque *(CHEEN-kway)*

five hundred cinquecento *(cheen-kway-CHEN-toh)*

fix, to aggiustare *(ahd-joos-TAH-ray)*

fixed-price meal menù a prezzo fisso, il/un *(may-NOO ah PRET-tsoh FEES-soh)*

flag bandiera, la/una *(bahn-DYEH-rah)*

flash (camera) flash, il *(flesh)*

flash drive chiavetta USB, la/una *(kyah-VAYT-tah oo-ES-say-bee)*

flashlight torcia elettrica, la/una *(TOHR-chah ay-LET-tree-kah)*

flat (surface) piatto/a *(PYAHT-toh/-tah)*

flat tire gomma bucata, la/una *(GOHM-mah boo-KAH-tah)*

flea pulce, la/una *(POOL-chay)* (le pulci)

flight volo, il/un *(VOH-loh)* (i voli)

the first flight il primo volo *(eel PREE-moh VOH-loh)*

the flight to ___ il volo per ___ *(eel VOH-loh payr ___)*

the last flight l'ultimo volo *(LOOL-tee-moh VOH-loh)*

the next flight il prossimo volo *(eel PROH-see-moh VOH-loh)*

flip chart lavagna con fogli, la/una *(lah-VAHN-nyah kohn FOHL-lyee)*

flood inondazione, l' *f* /un' *(een-ohn-daht-TSYOH-nay)*

floor (of room) pavimento, il *(pah-vee-MAYN-toh)*, (story of building) piano, il *(PYAH-noh)*

Florence Firenze *(fee-REN-tsay)*

florist fioraio, il/la *(fyoh-RAH-yoh/-yah)*

flour farina, la *(fah-REE-nah)*

flower fiore, il/un *(FYOH-ray)* (i fiori)

flu influenza, l' *f* *(een-floo-EN-tsah)*

fly mosca, la/una *(MOHS-kah)* (le mosche)

fog nebbia, la *(NAYB-byah)*

foggy nebbioso/a *(nayb-BYOH-soh/-sah)*

fold, to piegare *(pyay-GAH-ray)*

follow, to seguire *(say-GWEE-ray)*

food vitto, il *(VEE-toh)*, cibo, il *(CHEE-boh)*

food poisoning intossicazione alimentare, l' *f* *(een-tohs-see-kaht-TSYOH-nay ah-lee-mayn-TAH-ray)*

traditional food cucina tradizionale, la *(koo-CHEE-nah trah-deet-tsyoh-NAH-lay)*

foot piede, il *(PYEH-day)* (i piedi)

on foot a piedi *(ah PYEH-dee)*

for per *(payr)*

forbid, to vietare *(vyay-TAH-ray)*

forbidden vietato/a *(vyay-TAH-toh/-tah)*, proibito/a *(proh-ee-BEE-toh/-tah)*, divieto *(dee-VYEH-toh)*

foreign straniero/a *(strah-NYEH-roh/-rah)*

forest foresta, la/una *(fohr-RES-tah)* (le foreste)

forever per sempre *(payr SEM-pray)*

forge, to (e.g., checks) falsicare *(fahl-see-fee-KAH-ray)*

forget, to dimenticare *(dee-mayn-tee-KAH-ray)*

forgive, to perdonare *(payr-doh-NAH-ray)*

fork forchetta, la/una *(fohr-KAYT-tah)* (le forchette)

form (paperwork) modulo, il/un *(MOH-doo-loh)* (i moduli)

form, to (=to create) formare *(fohr-MAH-ray)*

formula, milk (baby) latte in polvere *(LAHT-tay een POHL-vay-ray)*

fortress fortezza, la/una *(fohr-TAYT-tsah)*

forty quaranta *(kwah-RAHN-tah)*

forty-one quarantuno *(kwah-rahn-TOO-noh)*

forty-two quarantadue *(kwah-rahn-tah-DOO-ay)*

forty-three quarantatré *(kwah-rahn-tah-TRAY)*

forty-four quarantaquattro *(kwah-rahn-tah-KWAHT-troh)*

forty-five quarantacinque *(kwah-rah-tah-CHEEN-kway)*

forty-six quarantasei *(kwah-rahn-tah-SEH-ee)*

forty-seven quarantasette *(kwah-rahn-tah-SET-tay)*

forty-eight quarantotto *(kwah-rahn-TOHT-toh)*

forty-nine quarantanove *(kwah-rahn-tah-NOH-vay)*

forward avanti *(ah-VAHN-tee)*

foul fallo, il/un *(FAHL-loh)*

fountain fontana, la/una *(fohn-TAH-nah)*

four quattro *(KWAHT-troh)*

four-wheel drive fuoristrada, il *(fwoh-ree-STRAH-dah)*

four hundred quattrocento *(kwaht-troh-CHEN-toh)*

fourteen quattordici *(kwaht-TOHR-dee-chee)*

fourth quarto/a, il/la *(KWAHR-toh/-tah)*

one-/a fourth un quarto *(oon KWAHR-toh)*

three-fourths tre quarti *(tray KWAHR-tee)*

four-wheel drive fuoristrada, il *(fwoh-ree-STRAH-dah)*

fowl pollame, il *(pohl-LAH-may)*

fragile fragile *(FRAH-jee-lay)*

France Francia, la *(FRAHN-chah)*

free (no cost) gratuito/a *(grah-TOO-ee-toh/-tah)*, gratis *(GRAH-tees)*; (available) libero/a *(LEE-bay-roh/-rah)*

free-range ruspante *(roos-PAHN-tay)*

freeze, to congelare *(kohn-jay-LAH-ray)*

it's freezing Si gela. *(see JAY-lah)*

French fries patate fritte, le *(pah-TAH-tay FREET-tay)*, patatine, le *(pah-tah-TEE-nay)*

fresh fresco/a *(FRAY-skoh/-skah)*

Friday venerdì *(vay-nayr-DEE)*

fried fritto/a *(FREET-toh/-tah)*

friend (male) amico, l' *m (ah-MEE-koh)* (gli amici); (female) amica, l' *f (ah-MEE-kah)* (le amiche)

my friend il mio amico *(eel MEE-oh ah-MEE-koh)*, la mia amica *(lah MEE-ah ah-MEE-kah)*

from da *(dah)*

from. . . until/to da. . . a *(dah. . . ah)*

front of, in davanti (a) *(dah-VAHN-tee [ah])*

frozen congelato/a *(kohn-jay-LAH-toh/-tah)*

fruit frutta, la *(FROOT-tah)*

fruit juice succo di frutta, il/un *(SOOK-koh dee FROO-tah)*, (fresh) spremuta, la/una *(spray-MOO-tah)*

fry, to friggere *(FREED-jay-ray)*

frying pan padella, la/una *(pah-DEL-lah)*

full (hotel, restaurant) completo/a *(kohm-PLEH-toh/-tah:,* (from food) pieno/a *(PYEH-noh/-nah)*, sazio/a *(SAHT-tsyoh/-tsyah)*

full-bodied corposo/a *(kohr-POH-soh/-sah)*

full-time a tempo pieno *(ah TEM-poh PYEH-noh)*

fun divertimento, il *(dee-vayr-tee-MAYN-toh)*

to have fun divertirsi *(dee-vayr-TEER-see)*

function, to funzionare *(foon-tsyoh-NAH-ray)*

it doesn't function/work non funziona *(nohn foon-TSYOH-nah)*

funeral funerale, il/un *(foo-nay-RAH-lay)*

funny divertente *(dee-vayr-TEN-tay)*

furnished ammobiliato/a *(ahm-moh-bee-LYAH-toh/-tah)*

furniture mobili, i *(MOH-bee-lee)*

future futuro, il *(foo-TOO-roh)*

G

G, g G, g *(jee)*

game (sports) partita, la/una *(pahr-TEE-tah)* (le partite)

game, wild selvaggina, la *(sayl-vahd-JEE-nah)*

garage garage, il/un *(gah-RAHZH)*

garbage spazzatura, la *(spaht-tsah-TOO-rah)*

garden giardino, il/un *(jahr-DEE-noh)*

gardening giardinaggio, il *(jahr-dee-NAHD-joh)*

garlic aglio, l' *m (AHL-yoh)*

gas (cooking) gas, il *(gahs)*

gasoline benzina, la *(bayn-DZEE-nah)*

leaded gasoline benzina con piombo, la *(bayn-DZEE-nah kohn PYOHM-boh)*

unleaded gasoline benzina senza piombo, la *(bayn-DZEE-nah SEN-tsah PYOHM-boh)*

to get gasoline fare la benzina *(FAH-ray lah bayn-DZEE-nah)*

gas station stazione di servizio, la/una *(stah-TSYOH-nay dee sayr-VEET-tsyoh)*, benzinaio, il *(bayn-dzee-NAH-yoh)*

gate cancello, il/un *(kahn-CHEL-loh)*

gay gay *(GAY-ee)*

gears cambio, il *(KAHM-byoh)*

gelatin gelatina, la *(jay-lah-TEE-nah)*

general generale *(jay-nay-RAH-lay)*

Genoa Genova *(JEN-oh-vah)*

gentlemen's room signori *(seen-NYOH-ree)*

Germany Germania, la *(jayr-MAHN-yah)*

get, to ottenere *(oht-tay-NAY-ray)*

I get ___. ottengo *(oht-TAYN-goh)*

You get ___. ottiene (form. sing.) *(oht-TYEH-nay)*

How did you get ___? Come ha ottenuto ___? *(KOH-may ah oht-tay-NOO-toh ___?)*

get off, to scendere *(SHAYN-day-ray)*

I get off here. Scendo qui. *(SHAYN-doh kwee)*

I get off at ___. Scendo a ___. *(SHAYN-doh ah ___)*

get on, to (to board) salire *(sah-LEE-ray)*

gift regalo, il/un *(ray-GAH-loh)* (i regali)

gift shop negozio di regali, il/un *(nay-GOHT-tsyoh dee ray-GAH-lee)*

ginger zenzero, lo *(DZAYN-dzay-roh)*

girl ragazza, la/una *(rah-GAHT-tsah)* (le ragazze)

girlfriend ragazza, la *(rah-GAHT-tsah)*

give, to dare *(DAH-ray)*

Can you give me ___? Può darmi ___? *(pwoh DAHR-me ___?)*

I give do *(doh)*

we give diamo *(DYAH-moh)*

you give da (form. sing.) (dah)

give in, to cedere *(CHEH-day-ray)*

glass (drinking) bicchiere, il/un *(beek-KYEH-ray)*, (substance) vetro, il *(VAY-troh)*

blown glass vetro soffiato, il *(VAY-troh sohf-FYAH-toh)*

glasses occhiali, gli *(ohk-KYAH-lee)*

glassware aricoli di vetro, gli *(ahr-TEE-koh-lee dee VAY-troh)*

glove guanto, il/un *(GWAHN-toh)* (i guanti)

glue colla, la *(KOHL-lah)*

gluten glutine, il *(GLOO-tee-nay)*

gluten-free senza glutine *(SEN-tsah GLOO-tee-nay)*

go, to andare *(ahn-DAH-ray)*; "to go" (food)= d'asporto *(dahs-POHR-toh)*

go! vada *(VAH-dah)*

go away! Se ne vada! *(say nay VAH-dah)*, Vai via! *(VAH-ee VEE-ah)*

he/she/it goes va *(vah)*

I go vado *(VAH-doh)*

Let's go! andiamo *(ahn-DYAH-moh)*

they go vanno *(VAHN-noh)*

we go andiamo *(ahn-DYAH-moh)*

you go va (form. sing.) *(vah)*

go down, to (descend) scendere *(SHAYN-day-ray)*

I go down scendo *(SHAYN-doh)*

we go down scendiamo *(shayn-DYAH-moh)*

you go down scende (form. sing.) *(SHAYN-day)*

go out with, to uscire con *(oosh-SHEE-ray kohn)*

go up, to (ascend) salire *(sah-LEE-ray)*

I go up salgo *(SAHL-goh)*

we go up saliamo *(sah-LYAH-moh)*

you go up sale (form. sing.) *(SAH-lay)*

goal gol, il/un *(gohl)*

goat capra, la/una *(KAH-prah)* (le capre)

God dio, il *(DEE-oh)*

god-awful orrendo/a *(ohr-REN-doh/-dah)*

gold oro, l' *m (OH-roh)*

golden (color) dorato/a *(doh-RAH-toh)*

golf golf, il *(gohlf)*

golf ball palla da golf, la/una *(PAH-lah dah gohlf)* (le palle)

golf course campo da golf, il/un *(KAHM-poh dah gohlf)*

good buono/a *(BWOHN-oh/-ah)*

goodbye arrivederci *(ahr-ree-vay-DAYR-chee)*

good day! Buon giorno! *(bwohn JOHR-noh)*

good evening! Buona sera! *(BWOHN-ah SAY-rah)*

good morning! Buon giorno! *(bwohn JOHR-noh)*

good night! Buona notte! *(BWOHN-ah NOHT-tay)*

Gothic gotico/a *(GOH-tee-koh/-kah)*

government governo, il *(goh-VEHR-noh)*

gram grammo, il/un *(GRAHM-moh)* (i grammi)

100 grams un etto *(oon ET-toh)*

200 grams due etti *(DOO-ay ET-tee)*

grandchild nipote, il/la *(nee-POH-tay)*

grandchildren nipoti (di nonni), i *(nee-POH-tee [dee NOHN-nee])*

granddaughter nipote, la (di nonni) *(nee-POH-tay [dee NOHN-nee])*

grandfather nonno, il *(NOHN-noh)* (i nonni)

grandmother nonna, la *(NOHN-nah)* (le nonne)

grandparents nonni, i *(NOHN-nee)*

grandson nipote, il (di nonni) *(nee-POH-tay [dee NOHN-nee])*

grapes uva, l' *f (OO-vah)*

grape harvest vendemmia *(vayn-DAYM-myah)*

grapefruit pompelmo, il/un *(pohm-PEL-moh)* (i pompelmi)

grapes uva, l' *f (OO-vah)*

grappa grappa, la *(GRAHP-pah)*

grass erba, l' *f (EHR-bah)*

grave (cemetery) tomba, la/una *(TOHM-bah)*

gray grigio/a *(GREE-joh/-jah)*

great ottimo/a *(OHT-tee-moh/-mah)*

green verde *(VAYR-day)*

green beans fagiolini, i *(fahd-joh-LEE-nee)*

grilled alla griglia *(AHL-lah GREEL-lyah)*, ai ferri *(AH-ee FEHR-ree)*

grocery store drogheria, la/una *(droh-gay-REE-ah)*, negozio di alimentari, il/un *(nay-GOHT-tsyoh dee ah-lee-mayn-TAH-ree)*

group gruppo, il/un *(GROOP-poh)* (i gruppi)

  in a group in gruppo *(een GROOP-poh)*

grow, to crescere *(KRAYSH-shay-ray)*

guarantee garanzia, la/una *(gah-rahn-TSEE-ah)*

guarantee, to garantire *(gah-rahn-TEE-ray)*

guesthouse pensione, la/una *(payn-SYOH-nay)* (le pensioni)

guide guida, la/una *(GWEE-dah)*

  audio guide guida audio, la/una *(GWEE-dah OWD-yoh)*

guide, to guidare *(gwee-DAH-ray)*

guidebook guida (turistica), la/una *(GWEE-dah [too-REES-tee-kah])*

guide dog cane guida, il/un *(KAH-nay GWEE-dah)*

guided tour visita guidata, la/una *(VEE-zee-tah gwee-DAH-tah)*

guilty colpevole *(kohl-PAY-voh-lay)*

guitar chitarra, la/una *(kee-TAHR-rah)*

gum (chewing) gomma da masticare, la *(GOHM-mah dah mahs-tee-KAH-ray)*

gums gengive, le *(jen-JEE-vay)*

gym palestra, la/una *(pah-LES-trah)*

gymnastics ginnastica, la *(jeen-NAHS-tee-kah)*

gynecologist ginocologo/a, il/la *(jee-nay-KOH-loh-goh/-gah)*

H

H, h H, h *(AHK-kah)*

hail grandine, la *(GRAHN-dee-nay)*

haircut taglio, il/un *(TAHL-lyoh)*

hairdresser parrucchiere/a, il/la un/una *(pahr-rook-KYEH-ray/-rah)*

hair dryer asciugacapelli, l' *m*/un *(ahsh-shoo-gah-kah-PAYL-lee)*

halal halal *(ah-LAHL)*

half mezzo/a *(MED-dzoh/-dzah)*

  half hour mezz'ora *(mayd-DZOH-rah)*

ham prosciutto, il *(prohsh-SHOOT-toh)*

hamburger hamburger, l' *m*/un *(ahm-BOOR-gayr)*

hammer martello, il/un *(mahr-TEL-loh)*

hammock amaca, l' *f*/un' *(ah-MAH-kah)* (le amache)

hand mano, la *(MAH-noh)* (le mani)

handbag borsetta, la/una *(bohr-SAYT-tah)*

handball pallamuro, la *(pahl-lah-MOO-roh)*

handkerchief fazzoletto, il/un *(faht-tsoh-LAYT-toh)*

handlebars manubrio, il *(mah-NOO-bryoh)*

handmade fatto/a a mano *(FAHT-toh/-tah ah MAH-noh)*

handsome bello/a *(BEL-loh/-lah)*

hang, to pendere *(PEN-day-ray)*

hang up, to (phone) riagganciare *(ree-ahg-gahn-CHAH-ray)*

happy felice *(fay-LEE-chay)*

harassment molestia, la *(moh-LEST-yah)*

harbor porto, il *(POHR-toh)*

hard (substance) duro/a *(DOO-roh/-rah)*, (difficult) difficile *(deef-FEE-chee-lay)*

hard drive hard disk, l' *m*/un *(hahd deesk)*, disco rigido, il/un *(DEES-koh REE-jee-doh)*

    portable hard drive hard disk portatile, l' *m*/un *(hahd deesk pohr-TAH-tee-lay)*

hardware (computer) hardware, l' *m (HAHD-weh-ah)*

hardware store ferramenta, la/una *(fayr-rah-MAYN-tah)*

hat cappello, il/un *(kahp-PEL-loh)* (i cappelli)

hate, to detestare *(day-tays-TAH-ray)*

have, to avere *(ah-VAY-ray)*

    Do you have ___? Ha ___? (form. sing.) *(ah ___?)*

he/she/it has ha *(ah)*

I have ho *(oh)*

they have hanno *(AHN-noh)*

we have abbiamo *(ahb-BYAH-moh)*

you have ha (form. sing.) *(ah)*

have to, to (=must) dovere *(doy-VAY-ray)*

I have to devo *(DAY-voy)*

you have to deve (form. sing.) *(DAY-vay)*

hay fever febbre da fieno, la *(FEB-bray dah FYEH-noh)*, raffreddore da fieno, il *(rahf-frayd-DOH-ray dah FYEH-noh)*

hazelnut nocciola, la/una *(noht-CHOH-lah)* (le nocciole)

he lui *(LOO-ee)*

head testa, la *(TES-tah)*

headache mal di testa, il/un *(mahl dee TES-tah)*

headlight faro, il *(FAH-roh)* (i fari), fanale, il *(fah-NAH-lay)*

headphones cuffia, la/una *(KOOF-fyah)*

heal, to guarire *(gwah-REE-ray)*

health, to your (toast) Salute! *(sah-LOO-tay)*

hear, to sentire *(sayn-TEE-ray)*, udire *(oo-DEE-ray)*

hearing aid apparecchio acustico, l' *m*/un *(ahp-pah-RAYK-kyoh ah-KOOS-tee-koh)*

heart cuore, il *(KWOH-ray)*

heart condition disturbi cardiaci, i *(dees-TOOR-bee kahr-DEE-ah-chee)*

heat calore, il *(kah-LOH-ray)*

heat, to riscaldare *(rees-kahl-DAH-ray)*

heat up, to scaldare *(skahl-DAH-ray)*

heated scaldato/a *(skahl-DAH-toh/-tah)*

re-heated riscaldato/a *(rees-kahl-DAH-toh/-tah)*

heater stufa, la/una *(STOO-fah)*

heating riscaldamento, il *(rees-kahl-dah-MAYN-toh)*

central heating riscaldamento centrale, il *(rees-kahl-dah-MAYN-toh chayn-TRAH-lay)*

heavy pesante *(pay-SAHN-tay)*

height altezza, l' *f (ahl-TAYT-tsah)*

hello buon giorno *(bwohn JOHR-noh)*, ciao *(chow)*

helmet casco, il/un *(KAHS-koh)* (i caschi)

help, to aiutare *(ah-yoo-TAH-ray)*

help! aiuto! *(ah-YOO-toh)*

he/she/it helps aiuta *(ah-YOO-tah)*

I help aiuto *(ah-YOO-toh)*

they help aiutano *(ah-yoo-TAH-noh)*

you help (form. sing.) aiuta *(ah-YOO-tah)*

Can you help me? Mi può aiutare? (form. sing.) *(mee pwoh ah-yoo-TAH-ray?)*

May I help you? mi dica (lit: tell me) *(mee DEE-kah?)*

hepatitis epatite, l' *f (ay-pah-TEE-tay)*

her (object) lei *(LEH-ee)*

herbalist erborista, l'/l' *m/f (ayr-boh-REES-tah)*

herbs erbe, le *(EHR-bay)*

here qui *(kwee)*

here it is/you are ecco *(EK-koh)*

her(s) (possessive) suo/a *(SOO-oh/-ah)*

herring aringa, l' *f/un' (ah-REEN-gah)* (le aringhe)

hi ciao *(chow)*

high alto/a *(AHL-toh/-tah)*

high blood pressure pressione alta, la *(prays-SYOH-nay AHL-tah)*

high school scuola superiore, la/una *(SKWOH-lah soo-pay-RYOH-ray)*

highway autostrada, l' *f/un' (ow-tohs-TRAH-dah)* (le autostrade)

hike escursione a piedi, l' *f/un' (ays-koor-SYOH-nay ah PYEH-dee)*

hiking escursionismo a piedi, l' *m (ays-koor-syoh-NEES-moh ah PYEH-dee)*

hiking boots scarponi, gli *(skahr-POH-nay)*

hiking route itinerario escursionistico, l' *m (ee-tee-nay-RAH-ryoh ays-koor-syoh-NEES-tee-koh)*

hill collina, la/una *(kohl-LEE-nah)* (le colline)

him lui *(LOO-ee)*

Hindu indù *(een-DOO)*

his suo/a *(SOO-oh/-ah)*

historical storico/a *(STOH-ree-koh/-kah)*

  historical center centro storico, il *(CHEN-troh STOH-ree-koh)*

history storia, la *(STOHR-yah)*

hitchhike fare l'autostop *(FAH-ray low-tohs-TOP)*

hobby passsatempo, il *(pahs-sah-TEM-poh)* (i passatempi)

hockey hockey, il *(HOH-kee)*

holiday festivo, il/un *(fays-TEE-voh)*, giorno festivo, il/un *(JOHR-noh fays-TEE-voh)*

Holy Week settimana santa, la *(sayt-tee-MAH-nah SAHN-tah)*

home casa, la/una *(KAH-sah)*

homeless senzatetto *(sayn-tsah-TAYT-toh)*

homemade fatto in casa *(FAHT-toh een KAH-sah)*

homemaker casalingo/a, il/la *(kah-sah-LEEN-goh/–gah)*

homeopathy omeopatia, l' *f* *(oh-may-oh-pah-TEE-ah)*

homosexual omosessuale, l'/l' *m/f* *(oh-moh-says-soo-AH-lay)*

honey miele, il *(MYEH-lay)*

  honeymoon luna di miele, la/una *(LOO-nah dee MYEH-lay)*

horse cavallo, il/un *(kah-VAHL-loh)* (i cavalli)

  horse riding andare a cavallo *(ahn-DAH-ray ah kah-VAHL-loh)*

horseradish rafano, il *(RAH-fah-noh)*

hospital ospedale, l' *m*/un *(ohs-pay-DAH-lay)*

hospitality ospitalità, l' *f* *(ohs-pee-tah-lee-TAH)*

hostel ostello, l' *m*/un *(ohs-TEL-loh)*

  youth hostel ostello della gioventù, l' *m* *(ohs-TEL-loh DAYL-lah joh-vayn-TOO)*

hot caldo/a *(KAHL-doh/-dah)*

  hot chocolate cioccolata calda, la/una *(choh-koh-LAH-tah KAHL-dah)*

  hot dog hot dog, l' *m*/un *(HOT-dog)*

  hot tea tè caldo, il/un *(tay KAHL-doh)*

  hot water acqua calda, l' *f* *(AHK-kwah KAHL-dah)*

hotel albergo, l' *m*/un *(ahl-BEHR-goh)* (gli alberghi)

  budget hotel locanda, la/una *(loh-KAHN-dah)*

hour ora, l' *f*/un' *(OH-rah)* (le ore)

hourly all'ora *(ahl-LOH-rah)*

hours of business orario di apertura, l' *m* *(oh-RAHR-yoh dee ah-payr-TOO-rah)*

house casa, la/una *(KAH-sah)* (le case)

  housewife casalinga, la *(kah-sah-LEEN-gah)*

  house wine vino della casa, il *(VEE-noh DAYL-lah KAH-sah)*

how come *(KOH-may)*

How are you? Come sta? *(KOH-may stah?)*

How's it going? Come va? *(KOH-may vah?)*

how long quanto *(KWAHN-toh)*; (=how long will something take) quanto dura *(KWAHN-toh DOO-rah)*

how many quanti *(KWAHN-tee)*, quante (fem.) *(KWAHN-tay)*

how much quanto *(KWAHN-toh)*

hug, to abbracciare *(ahb-braht-CHAH-ray)*

huge enorme *(ay-NOHR-may)*

humanities lettere, le *(LET-tay-ray)*

hundred cento *(CHEN-toh)*

hunger fame, la *(FAH-may)*

to "have" hunger (=to be hungry) avere fame *(ah-VAY-ray FAH-may)*

I'm hungry. Ho fame. *(oh FAH-may)*

Are you hungry? Ha fame? (form. sing.) *(ah FAH-may?)*

hunting caccia, la *(KAHT-chah)*

hurry fretta, la *(FRAYT-tah)*

to "have" hurry (=to be in a hurry) avere fretta *(ah-VAY-ray FRAYT-tah)*

I'm in a hurry. Ho fretta. *(oh FRAYT-tah)*

hurt dolore, il *(doh-LOH-ray)*

hurt, to fare male *(FAH-ray MAH-lay)*

(to me) it hurts here mi fa male qui *(mee fah MAH-lay kwee)*

husband marito, il *(mah-REE-toh)*

my husband mio marito *(MEE-oh mah-REE-toh)*

hut rifugio, il/un *(ree-FOO-joh)*

hydrofoil aliscafo, l' *m*/un *(ah-lees-KAH-foh)*

I

I, i I, i *(ee)*

I io *(yoh)*

I'm Sono ___. *(SOH-noh)*

ice ghiaccio, il *(GYAHT-choh)*

ice cream gelato, il *(jay-LAH-toh)*

ice cream parlor gelateria, la *(jay-lah-tay-REE-ah)*

ice cubes cubetti di ghiaccio, i *(koo-BAYT-tee dee GYAHT-choh)*

ice hockey hockey su ghiaccio, il *(HOH-kee soo GYAHT-choh)*

ID documento d'identità, il *(doh-koo-MAYN-toh dee-dayn-tee-TAH)*

identification documento d'identità, il *(doh-koo-MAYN-toh dee-dayn-tee-TAH)*

identity card carta d'identità, la/una *(KAHR-tah dee-dayn-tee-TAH)*

idiot idiota, l'/l' *m/f* *(ee-DYOH-tah)*

if se *(say)*

ill malato/a *(mah-LAH-toh/-tah)*

illegal illegale *(eel-lay-GAH-lay)*

I'm ___. Sono ___. *(SOH-noh)*

I'm fine Sto bene. *(stoh BEH-nay)*

immediately subito *(SOO-bee-toh)*

immigration immigrazione, l' *f (eem-mee-graht-TSYOH-nay)*

impose, to imporre *(eem-POHR-ray)*

impossible impossibile *(eem-pohs-SEE-bee-lay)*

important importante *(eem-pohr-TAHN-tay)*

in in *(een)*, (length of time) fra *(frah)*

include, to includere *(een-KLOO-day-ray)*

included incluse *(een-KLOO-day)*, incluso/a *(een-KLOO-soh/-sah)*, compreso/a *(kohm-PRAY-soh/-sah)*

increase, to crescere *(KRAYSH-shay-ray)*

incredible incredibile *(een-kray-DEE-bee-lay)*

indigestion indigestione, l' *f (een-dee-jays-TYOH-nay)*

industry industria, l' *f (een-DOOS-tryah)*

inebriated ubriaco/a *(oo-bree-AH-koh/-kah)*

in fact infatti *(een-FAHT-tee)*

infection infezione, l' *m (een-fayt-TSYOH-nay)*

inflammation infiammazione, l' *f (een-fyahm-maht-TSYOH-nay)*

influenza influenza, l' *f (een-floo-EN-tsah)*

inform, to informare *(een-fohr-MAH-ray)*

information informazioni, le *(een-fohr-maht-TSYOH-nee)*

ingredient ingrediente, l' *m (een-gray-DYEN-tay)* (gli ingredienti)

inhaler inalatore, l' *m (ee-nah-lah-TOH-ray)*

injection iniezione, l' *f/un' (een-yet-TSYOH-nay)*

injury ferita, la/una *(fay-REE-tah)*

inn locanda, la/una *(loh-KAHN-dah)*

innertube camera d'aria, la *(KAH-may-rah DAHR-yah)*

innocent innocente *(een-noh-CHEN-tay)*

insect insetto, l' *m/un (een-SET-toh)* (gli insetti)

inside dentro *(DAYN-troh)*

installation installazione, l' *f (eens-tahl-laht-TSYOH-nay)*

instructor istruttore/istruttrice, l'/l' *m/f (ees-troot-TOH-ray/-TREET-chay)*, maestro/a, il/la *(mah-ES-troh/-trah)*

insurance assicurazione, l' *f (ahs-see-koo-raht-TSYOH-nay)*

insured assicurato/a *(ahs-see-koo-RAH-toh/-tah)*

interest interesse, l' *m/un (een-tay-RES-say)* (gli interessi)

interesting interessante *(een-tay-rays-SAHN-tay)*

intermission intervallo, l' *m/un (een-tayr-VAHL-loh)*

international internazionale *(een-tayr-naht-tsyoh-NAH-lay)*

international express mail
EMS

international phone card
scheda telefonica
internazionale, la/una *(SKEH-dah tay-lay-FOH-nee-kah een-tayr-naht-tsyoh-NAH-lay)*

Internet Internet, l' *m (EEN-tayr-net)*

connect to the Internet, to
collegarsi a Internet *(koh-lay-GAHR-see ah EEN-tayr-net)*

Internet access accesso a
Internet, l' *m (aht-CHES-soh ah EEN-tayr-net)*

Internet address indirizzo
Internet, l' *m/*un *(een-dee-REET-tsoh EEN-tayr-net)*

Internet cafè Internet point, l'
*m/*un *(EEN-tayr-net poynt)*, sala
d'Internet, la/una *(SAH-lah DEEN-tayr-net)*, sito Internet, il/un *(SEE-toh EEN-tayr-net)*

Internet connection
connessione Internet, la/una
(kohn-nays-SYOH-nay EEN-tayr-net),
collegamento a Internet *(koh-lay-gah-MAYN-toh ah EEN-tayr-net)*

Internet point punto
d'Internet, il/un *(POON-toh DEEN-tayr-net)*

Internet site Internet point, l'
*m/*un *(EEN-tayr-net poynt)*, sala
d'Internet, la/una *(SAH-lah DEEN-tayr-net)*, sito Internet, il/un *(SEE-toh EEN-tayr-net)*

on the Internet su Internet
(soo EEN-tayr-net), in rete *(een RAY-tay)*

**use/access the Internet,
to** usare Internet *(oo-ZAH-ray EEN-tayr-net)*

Wi-Fi Wi-Fi *(wy-fy)*

interpreter interprete, l' *m/f*
un/un' *(een-TEHR-pray-tay)*

intersection incrocio, l' *m/*un
(een-KROH-choh)

interstate highway (toll
road) autostrada, l' *f (ow-tohs-TRAH-dah)*; (non-toll road)
superstrada, la *(soo-payr-STRAH-dah)* or S.G.C. *(ES-say jee chee)* (non-toll road)

interview (paper/radio/TV)
intervista, l' *f/*un' *(een-tayr-VEES-tah)*, (e.g., for job)
colloquio, il/un *(kohl-LOH-kwyoh)*

invite, to invitare *(een-vee-TAH-ray)*

iPod iPod, l' *m/*un *(EYE-pod)*

Ireland Irlanda, l' *f (eer-LAHN-dah)*

iron (for clothes) ferro da
stiro, il/un *(FEHR-roh dah STEE-roh)*

is è *(eh)*

island isola, l' *f/*un' *(EE-zoh-lah)*
(le isole)

IT informatica, l' *f (een-fohr-MAH-tee-kah)*

it (subject) esso/a *(AYS-soh/-sah)*, (direct object) lo/la/l' *(loh/lah/l)*
  it's ___ è ___ *(eh ___)*
Italian Italiano/a *(ee-tah-LYAH-noh/-nah)*
Italy Italia, l' *f (ee-TAH-lyah)*
itch prurito, il/un *(proo-REE-toh)*
itinerary itinerario, l' *m/un (ee-tee-nay-RAH-ryoh)*
its (possessive) suo/a *(SOO-oh/-ah)*
IUD spirale, la/una *(spee-RAH-lay)*

J

J, j J, j *(ee-LOON-gah)*
jacket giacca, la/una *(JAHK-kah)*
  life jacket giubbotto di salvataggio, il/un *(joob-BOHT-toh dee sahl-vah-TAHD-joh)*
jail prigione, la/una *(pree-JOH-nay)*
jam marmellata, la/una *(mahr-mayl-LAH-tah)*
January gennaio *(jayn-NAH-yoh)*
Japan Giappone, il *(jahp-POH-nay)*
jar barattolo, il/un *(bah-RAHT-toh-loh)* (i barattoli)
jazz jazz, il *(jahz)*
jealous geloso/a *(jay-LOH-soh/-sah)*
jeans jeans, i *(jeenz)*
jet lag disturbi da fuso orario, i *(dees-TOOR-bee dah FOO-soh oh-RAHR-yoh)*
jewelry gioielli, i *(joh-YEL-lee)*
Jewish ebreo/a *(ay-BREH-oh/-ah)*
job lavoro, il/un *(lah-VOH-roh)* (i lavori)
jogging footing, il *(FOO-teeng)*

joke scherzo, lo/uno *(SKAYR-tsoh)* (gli scherzi)
journalist giornalista, il/la *(johr-nah-LEES-tah)*
juice succo, il *(SOOK-koh)*, (fresh) spremuta, la *(spray-MOO-tah)*
July luglio *(LOOL-lyoh)*
jump, to saltare *(sahl-TAH-ray)*
June giugno *(JOON-nyoh)*
just (=only) solo *(SOH-loh)*
  just a moment un momento *(oon moh-MAYN-toh)*

K

K, k K, k *(KAHP-pah)*
keep, to tenere *(tay-NAY-ray)*
  I keep tengo *(TAYN-goh)*
  we keep teniamo *(tay-NYAH-moh)*
  you keep tiene (form. sing.) *(TYEH-nay)*
ketchup ketchup, il *(KAY-choop)*
key chiave, la/una *(KYAH-vay)* (le chiavi)
  car key chiave della macchina, la *(KYAH-vay DAYL-lah MAHK-kee-nah)*
keyboard tastiera, la/una *(tahs-TYEH-rah)*
kick, to dare un calcio *(DAH-ray oon KAHL-choh)*
kill, to uccidere *(oot-CHEE-day-ray)*
kilogram chilo, il/un *(KEE-loh)* (i chili)

2 kilograms due chili *(DOO-ay KEE-lee)*

kilometer chilometro, il/un *(kee-LOH-may-troh)* (i chilometri)

kind (nice) gentile *(jayn-TEE-lay)*

king re, il/un *(ray)*

kiss bacio, il/un *(BAH-choh)* (i baci)

kiss, to baciare *(bah-CHAH-ray)*

kiss me baciami *(BAH-chah-mee)*

kitchen cucina, la/una *(koo-CHEE-nah)*

kitten gattino, il/un *(gaht-TEE-noh)* (i gattini)

kiwi (food) kiwi, il/un *(KEE-wee)*

knee ginocchio, il/un *(jee-NOHK-kyoh)* (le ginocchia)

knife coltello, il *(kohl-TEL-loh)* (i coltelli)

knock, to bussare *(boos-SAH-ray)*

know, to (knowledge) sapere *(sah-PAY-ray)*

he/she/it knows sa *(sah)*

I know so *(soh)*

I don't know Non lo so *(nohn loh soh)*

they know sanno *(SAHN-noh)*

we know sappiamo *(sahp-PYAH-moh)*

you know sa (form. sing.) *(sah)*

Who knows chissà *(kees-SAH)*

know, to (to be acquainted with) conoscere *(koh-NOHSH-shay-ray)*

kosher kasher *(kah-SHAYR)*

L

L, 1 L, l *(EL-lay)*

laborer manovale, il *(mah-noh-VAH-lay)*, lavoratore/lavoratrice, il/la *(lah-voh-rah-TOH-ray/-TREE-chay)*

lace merletto, il *(mayr-LAYT-toh)*

ladies' room signore *(seen-NYOH-ray)*

lady signora, la/una *(seen-NYOH-rah)* (le signore)

lager birra chiara, la/una *(BEER-rah KYAH-rah)*

lake lago, il/un *(LAH-goh)* (i laghi)

lamb agnello, l' *m*/un *(ahn-NYEL-loh)* (gli agnelli)

lamp lampada, la/una *(LAHM-pah-dah)*

land terra, la *(TEHR-rah)*

landlady padrona (di casa), la *(pah-DROH-nah [dee KAH-sah])*

land line (phone) rete fissa, la *(RAY-tay FEES-sah)*

landlord padrone (di casa), il *(pah-DROH-nay [dee KAH-sah])*

lane (alley) vicolo, il/un *(VEE-koh-loh)*

language lingua, la/una *(LEEN-gwah)* (le lingue)

laptop (computer) portatile, il/un *([kom-PYOO-ter] pohr-TAH-tee-lay)*

lard lardo, il *(LAHR-doh)*

large grande *(GRAHN-day)*, (clothing) forte *(FOHR-tay)*

lasagna lasagne, le *(lah-ZAHN-nyay)*

last ultimo/a *(OOL-tee-moh/-mah)*

  the last ___ l'ultimo/a ___ *(LOOL-tee-moh/-mah)*

late tardi *(TAHR-dee)*, in ritardo *(een ree-TAHR-doh)*

later più tardi *(pyoo TAHR-dee)*

  until later/see you later a più tardi *(ah pyoo TAHR-dee)*

laugh, to ridere *(REE-day-ray)*

laundry lavanderia, la/una *(lah-vahn-day-REE-ah)*, (coin-operated) lavanderia a gettone, la *(lah-vahn-day-REE-ah ah jayt-TOH-nay)*

  laundry service servizio lavanderia, il/un *(sayr-VEET-tsyoh lah-vahn-day-REE-ah)*

law legge, la *(LAYD-jay)*

lawyer avvocato/a, l'/l' *m/f (ahv-voh-KAH-toh/-tah)*

laxative lassativo, il/un *(lahs-sah-TEE-voh)*

lazy pigro/a *(PEE-groh/-grah)*

lead, to (=to conduct) condurre *(kohn-DOO-ray)*

leaded (gas) con piombo *(kohn PYOHM-boh)*

leader capo, il *(KAH-poh)*

leaf foglia, la/una *(FOHL-lyah)*

learn, to imparare *(eem-pah-RAH-ray)*, apprendere *(ahp-PREN-day-ray)*

lease, for affittasi *(ahf-feet-TAH-see)*

leather cuoio, il *(KWOH-yoh)*

  leather goods articoli di pelletteria, gli *(ahr-TEE-koh-lee dee payl-layt-tay-REE-ah)*

leave, to (=depart) partire *(pahr-TEE-ray)*

  he/she/it leaves parte *(PAHR-tay)*

  I leave parto *(PAHR-toh)*

  you leave/are you leaving? parte (form. sing.) *(PAHR-tay)*

leave (something), to lasciare *(lahsh-SHAH-ray)*

leek porro, il/un *(POHR-roh)* (i porri)

left sinistra *(see-NEES-trah)*

  to the left a sinistra *(ah see-NEES-trah)*

leg gamba, la/una *(GAHM-bah)* (le gambe)

legal legale *(lay-GAH-lay)*

lemon limone, il/un *(lee-MOH-nay)* (i limoni)

lemonade limonata, la/una *(lee-moh-NAH-tah)*

lend, to prestare *(prays-TAH-ray)*

lens obiettivo, l' *m*/un *(ohb-yayt-TEE-voh)*

Lent quaresima, la *(kwah-RAY-see-mah)*

lentil lenticchia, la *(layn-TEEK-kyah)* (le lenticchie)

lesbian lesbica, la/una *(LEZ-bee-kah)* (le lesbiche)

less meno *(MAY-noh)*

letter lettera, la/una *(LET-tay-rah)* (le lettere)

lettuce lattuga, la *(laht-TOO-gah)*

  red lettuce radicchio, il *(rah-DEEK-kyoh)*

liar bugiardo/a, il/la *(boo-JAHR-doh/-dah)*

library biblioteca, la/una *(bee-blyoh-TEH-kah)*

lice pidocchi, i *(pee-DOHK-kee)*

license plate targa, la *(TAHR-gah)*

license plate number numero di targa, il *(NOO-may-roh dee TAHR-gah)*

lie, to (e.g, in bed) giacere *(jah-CHAY-ray)*, (untruth) mentire *(mayn-TEE-ray)*

life vita, la *(VEE-tah)*

life jacket giubbotto di salvataggio, il/un *(joob-BOHT-toh dee sahl-vah-TAHD-joh)*

light luce, la *(LOO-chay)*

light bulb lampadina, la/una *(lahm- pah-DEE-nah)* (le lampadine)

light (e.g., weight) leggero/a *(layd-JEH-roh/-rah)*, (=bright) luminoso/a *(loo-mee-NOH-soh/-sah)*

light-colored chiaro/a *(KYAH-roh/-rah)*

lighter (cigarette) accendino, l' *m/*un *(aht-chayn-DEE-noh)*

like, to piacere *(pyah-CHAY-ray)*

I like (it) mi piace *(mee PYAH-chay)*

I like (them) mi piacciono *(mee PYAHT-choh-noh)*

I don't like (it) Non mi piace *(nohn mee PYAH-chay)*

I would like vorrei *(vohr-REH-ee)*, desidero *(day-ZEE-day-roh)*

we would like vorremmo *(vohr-REM-moh)*, desideriamo *(day-zee-dayr-YAH-moh)*

you would like desidera (form. sing.) *(day-ZEE-day-rah)*

like so così *(koh-SEE)*

lime limetta, la/una *(lee-MAYT-tah)* (le limette)

line (transportation, e.g. bus) linea, la *(LEE-nay-ah)* (le linee), coda, la *(KOH-dah)*, fila, la *(FEE-lah)*

lip labbro, il *(LAHB-broh)* (le labbra)

lip balm burro per le labbra, il *(BOOR-roh payr lay LAHB-brah)*

lipstick rossetto, il *(rohs-SAYT-toh)*

liquor store bottiglieria, la/una *(boht-teel-lyay-REE-ah)*, enoteca, l' *f/*un' *(ay-noh-TEH-kah)*

list lista, la *(LEES-tah)*

waiting list lista d'attesa, la/una *(LEES-tah daht-TAY-sah)*

wine list lista dei vini, la *(LEES-tah DAY-ee VEE-nee)*

listen, to ascoltare *(ahs-kohl-TAH-ray)*

liter litro, il/un *(LEE-troh)* (i litri)

little piccolo/a *(PEEK-koh-loh/-lah)*

little (of), a poco *(POH-koh)*, un po' (di) *(oon poh [dee])*

live, to vivere *(VEE-vay-ray)*

he/she/it lives vive *(VEE-vay)*

I live vivo *(VEE-voh)*

they live vivono *(VEE-voh-noh)*

we live vivamo *(vee-VYAH-moh)*

you live vive (form. sing.) *(VEE-vay)*

live, to (= reside) abitare *(ah-bee-TAH-ray)*

Do you live ___? Abita ___? *(AH-bee-tah ___)*

I live (with) ___. Abito (con) ___. *(AH-bee-toh [kohn] ___)*

liver fegato, il *(FAY-gah-toh)*

lizard lucertola, la/una *(loo-CHEHR-toh-lah)*

local locale *(loh-KAH-lay)*

lock (door) serratura, la/una *(sayr-rah-TOO-rah)*

locked chiuso/a *(KYOO-soh/-sah)*

locker armadietto, l' *m/*un *(ahr-mah-DYEHT-toh)*

locker room spogliatoio, lo/uno *(spohl-lyah-TOH-yoh)*

luggage locker deposito bagagli automatico, il/un *(day-POH-zee-toh bah-GAHL-lyee ow-toh-MAH-tee-koh)*, armadietto per il bagaglio, l' *m/*un *(ahr-mah-DYET-toh payr eel bah-GAHL-lyoh)*

lodging alloggio, l' *m (ahl-LOH-joh)*

log on, to accedere *(aht-CHEH-day-ray)*

Lombardy Lombardia, la *(lohm-bahr-DEE-ah)*

London Londra *(LOHN-drah)*

long lungo/a *(LOON-goh/-gah)*

look, to guardare *(gwahr-DAH-ray)*

I'm just looking Sto solo guardando *(stoh SOH-loh gwahr-DAHN-doh)*

I look guardo *(GWAHR-doh)*

we look guardiamo *(gwahr-DYAH-moh)*

you look guarda (form. sing.) *(GWAHR-dah)*

look after, to curare *(koo-RAH-ray)*

look for, to cercare *(chayr-KAH-ray)*

he/she/it looks for cerca *(CHAYR-kah)*

I look for cerco *(CHAYR-koh)*

we look for cerchiamo *(chayr-KYAH-moh)*

you look for cerca (form. sing.) *(CHAYR-kah)*

looking guardando *(gwahr-DAHN-doh)*

I'm just looking Sto solo guardando *(stoh SOH-loh gwahr-DAHN-doh)*

Look out! attenzione! *(aht-tayn-TSYOH-nay)*

lookout (view) veduta, la/una *(vay-DOO-tah)*

lose, to perdere *(PEHR-day-ray)*

I've lost ___. Ho perso ___. *(oh PEHR-soh ___)*

lost perso/a *(PEHR-soh/-sah)*

lost luggage bagagli smarriti, i *(bah-GAHL-lyee zmahr-REE-tee)*

lot, a molto *(MOHL-toh)*

loud/loudly forte *(FOHR-tay)*

louder/more loudly più forte *(pyoo FOHR-tay)*

love amore, l' *m (ah-MOH-ray)*

love, to amare *(ah-MAH-ray)*

I love you. Ti amo. (informal)

lover amante, l'/l' *m/f (ah-MAHN-tay)*

low basso/a *(BAHS-soh/-sah)*

lubricant lubrificante, il/un *(loo-bree-fee-KAHN-tay)*

luck fortuna, la *(fohr-TOO-nah)*

lucky fortunato/a *(fohr-too-NAH-toh/-tah)*

luggage bagaglio, il *(bah-GAHL-lyoh)*

lost luggage bagagli smarriti, i *(bah-GAHL-lyee zmahr-REE-tee)*

luggage cart carrello, il/un *(kahr-REL-loh)*

luggage checkroom deposito bagagli, il/un *(day-POH-zee-toh bah-GAHL-lyee)*

luggage locker deposito bagagli automatico, il/un *(day-POH-zee-toh bah-GAHL-lyee ow-toh-MAH-tee-koh)*, armadietto per i bagagli, l' *m/un (ahr-mah-DYET-toh payr ee bah-GAHL-lyee)*

luggage tag etichetta, l' *f/un' (ay-tee-KAYT-tah)*

my luggage il mio bagaglio *(eel MEE-oh bah-GAHL-lyoh)*

your luggage il suo bagaglio *(eel SOO-oh bah-GAHL-lyoh)*

lump nodulo, il/un *(NOH-doo-loh)*

lunch pranzo, il *(PRAHN-dzoh)*

lunch break pausa, la *(POW-zah)*

lunch hour ora di pranzo, l' *f (OH-rah dee PRAHN-dzoh)*

lung polmone, il *(pohl-MOH-nay)* (i polmoni)

luxurious di lusso *(dee LOOS-soh)*

M

M, m M, m *(EM-may)*

machine macchina, la/una *(MAHK-kee-nah)*

madam signora, la *(seen-NYOH-rah)*

made of fatto/a di *(FAHT-toh/-tah dee)*

magazine rivista, la/una *(ree-VEES-tah)* (le riviste)

mail posta, la *(POHS-tah)*

international express mail EMS

mailbox buca delle lettere, la/una *(BOO-kah DAYL-lay LET-tay-ray)*

registered mail posta raccomandata, la *(POHS-tah rahk-koh-mahn-DAH-tah)*

regular mail posta ordinaria, la *(POHS-tah ohr-dee-NAHR-yah)*

mail, to (a letter) imbucare *(eem-boo-KAH-ray)*

mailbox cassetta delle lettere, la/una *(kahs-SAYT-tah DAYL-lay LET-tay-ray)*, buca delle lettere, la/una *(BOO-kah DAYL-lay LET-tay-ray)*

main principale *(preen-chee-PAH-lay)*

main square piazza principale, la *(PYAHT-tsah preen-chee-PAH-lay)*

maintain, to mantenere *(mahn-tay-NAY-ray)*

make, to fare *(FAH-ray)*

make-up trucco, il *(TROOK-koh)*

M'am signora, la *(seen-NYOH-rah)*

mallet mazzuolo, il/un *(maht-TSWOH-loh)*

mammogram mammografia, la *(mahm-moh-grah-FEE-ah)*

man uomo, l' *m*/un *(WOH-moh)* (gli uomini)

manager direttore/trice, il/la *(dee-rayt-TOH-ray/TREE-chay)*, manager, il *(MAN-ee-juh)*

mandarin mandarino, il *(mahn-dah-REE-noh)*

mango mango, il/un *(MAHN-goh)* (i manghi)

manual manuale *(mah-noo-AH-lay)*

  manual worker manovale, il/la *(mah-noh-VAH-lay)*

many molti/e *m*/*f* *(MOHL-tee/-tay)*

map mappa, la/una *(MAHP-pah)*, carta, la/una *(KAHR-tah)*, cartina, la/una *(kahr-TEE-nah)*, pianta, la/una *(PYAHN-tah)*

marble marmo, il *(MAHR-moh)*

  marbled paper carta marmorizzata, la *(KAHR-tah mahr-moh-reed-DZAH-tah)*

March marzo *(MAHR-tsoh)*

margarine margarina, la *(mahr-gahr-EE-nah)*

marital status stato civile, lo *(STAH-toh chee-VEE-lay)*

market mercato, il/un *(mayr-KAH-toh)* (i mercati)

marmalade marmellata, la *(mahr-mayl-LAH-tah)*

marriage matrimonio, il/un *(mah-tree-MOHN-yoh)*

married sposato/a *(spoh-ZAH-toh/-tah)*

marry, to sposare *(spoh-ZAH-ray)*

martial arts arti marziali, le *(AHR-tee mahr-TSYAH-lee)*

mask maschera, la/una *(MAHS-kay-rah)* (le maschere)

  Carnevale mask maschera di Carnevale, la/una *(MAHS-kay-rah dee kahr-nay-VAH-lay)*

  masked in maschera *(een MAHS-kay-rah)*

mass (church) messa, la *(MAYS-sah)*

massage massaggio, il/un *(mahs-SAHD-joh)*

mat tappeto, il/un *(tahp-PAY-toh)*

match fiammifero, il/un *(fyahm-MEE-fay-roh)* (i fiammiferi)

mattress materasso, il/un *(mah-tay-RAHS-soh)*

may (=be able to) potere *(poh-TAY-ray)*

  may I?/I may posso (form. sing.) *(POHS-soh)*

  may you?/you may possa *(POHS-sah)*

may we?/we may possiamo *(pohs-SYAH-moh)*

May maggio *(MAHD-joh)*

maybe forse *(FOHR-say)*

mayonnaise maionese, la *(mah-yoh-NAY-say)*

mayor sindaco, il *(SEEN-dah-koh)*

meal pasto, il/un *(PAHS-toh)* (i pasti)

  a cheap meal un pasto economico *(oon PAHS-toh ay-koh-NOH-mee-koh)*

measles morbillo, il *(mohr-BEEL-loh)*

meat carne, la *(KAHR-nay)*

  meatball polpetta di carne, la/una *(pohl-PAYT-tah dee KAHR-nay)* (le polpette)

  meat dish piatto di carne, il/un *(PYAH-toh dee KAHR-nay)*

mechanic meccanico, il/la *(mayk-KAH-nee-koh)*

medication medicinale, il/un *(may-dee-chee-NAH-lay)* (i medicinali), medicina, la/una *(may-dee-CHEE-nah)*

medicine medicina, la/una *(may-dee-CHEE-nah)*

meditation meditazione, la *(may-dee-taht-TSYOH-nay)*

medium (cooked meat) a puntino *(ah poon-TEE-noh)*, (size) regolare *(ray-goh-LAH-ray)*

meet, to incontrare *(een-kohn-TRAH-ray)*

meeting riunione, la/una *(ree-oo-NYOH-nay)*

melon melone, il/un *(may-LOH-nay)* (i meloni)

melt, to fondere *(FOHN-day-ray)*

member socio, il/un *(SOH-choh)* (i soci)

memory card scheda di memoria, la/una *(SKEH-dah dee may-MOHR-yah)* (le schede di memoria)

memory stick chiavetta USB, la/una *(kyah-VAYT-tah OO-es-ay-bee)*

men's room uomo *(WOH-moh)*

menstrual pain dolori mestruali, i *(doh-LOH-ree mayn-stroo-AH-lee)*

menstrual period mestruazioni, le *(mays-troo-aht-TSYOH-nee)*

menstruation mestruazione, la *(mays-troo-aht-TSYOH-nay)*

menu menù, il/un *(may-NOO)*

  children's menu menù per bambini, il/un *(may-NOO payr bahm-BEE-nee)*

message messaggio, il/un *(mays-SAHD-joh)* (i messaggi)

  message board bacheca, la *(bah-KEH-kah)*

metal metallo, il *(may-TAHL-loh)*

meter (length) metro, il/un *(MET-roh)* (i metri)

metro (= urban) urbano/a *(oor-BAH-noh/-nah)*

metro (=subway) metrò, il *(may-TROH)*, metropolitana, la *(may-troh-poh-lee-TAH-nah)*

metro station stazione della metropolitana, la/una *(staht-TSYOH-nay DAYL-lah may-troh-poh-lee-TAH-nah)*

microphone microfono, il/un *(mee-KROH-foh-noh)* (i microfoni)

microwave oven microonde, il/un *(FOHR-noh ah mee-kroh-OHN-day)*

midday mezzogiorno, il *(mayd-dzoh-JOHR-noh)*

middle (of place) di mezzo *(dee MED-dzoh)*, centrale *(chayn-TRAH-lay)*; (in size/quality) medio/a *(MED-yoh/-yah)*

midnight mezzanotte, la *(mayd-dzah-NOHT-tay)*

might see *may*

I might be able to potrei *(poh-TREH-ee)*

you might be able to potrebbe (form. sing.) *(POH-tray-bay)*

migraine emicrania, l' *f*/un' *(ay-mee-KRAHN-yah)*

Milan Milano *(mee-LAH-noh)*

mild dolce *(DOHL-chay)*

mileage chilometraggio, il *(kee-loh-may-TRAHD-joh)*

military forze armate, le *(FOHRT-say ahr-MAH-tah)*

military service servizio militare, il *(sayr-VEET-tsyoh mee-lee-TAH-ray)*

milk latte, il *(LAHT-tay)*

millimeter millimetro, il/un *(meel-LEE-may-troh)* (i millimetri)

million milione, il *(mee-LYOH-nay)*

mine (possession) mio/a *(MEE-oh/-ah)*

mineral water acqua minerale, l' *f*/un' *(AHK-kwah mee-nay-RAH-lay)*

mini-bar frigobar, il/un *(free-goh-BAHR)*

minister pastore, il/un *(pahs-TOH-ray)*

mint (candy) caramella di menta, la/una *(kah-rah-MEL-lah dee MAYN-tah)* (le caramelle)

minus meno *(MAY-noh)*

minute minuto, il/un *(mee-NOO-toh)* (i minuti)

mirror specchio, lo/uno *(SPEK-kyoh)*

miss (young woman) signorina, la/una *(seen-nyoh-REE-nah)*

mistake errore, l' *m*//un *(ayr-ROH-ray)* (gli errori), sbaglio, lo/uno *(ZBAHL-lyoh)* (gli sbagli)

mister signore, il/un *(seen-NYOH-ray)*

mix, to mescolare *(may-skoh-LAH-ray)*

mixed misto/a *(MEES-toh/-tah)*

mobile number numero di cellulare, il *(NOO-may-roh dee chay-loo-LAH-ray)*

mobile phone (telefono) cellulare, il *([tay-LEH-foh-noh] chayl-loo-LAH-ray)*

modem modem, il/un *(MOH-daym)*

modern moderno/a *(moh-DEHR-noh/-nah)*

modify, to modificare *(moh-dee-fee-KAH-ray)*

moisturizer idratante, l' *m*/un *(ee-drah-TAHN-tay)*

moment, just a un momento *(oon moh-MAYN-toh)*

monastery monastero, il/un *(moh-nahs-TEH-roh)*

Monday lunedì *(loo-nay-DEE)*

money denaro, il *(day-NAH-roh)*, soldi, i *(SOHL-dee)*

month mese, il/un *(MAY-say)* (i mesi)

last month lo scorso mese *(loh SKOHR-soh MAY-say)*

next month il mese prossimo *(eel MAY-say PROH-see-moh)*

this month questo mese *(KWAYS-toh MAY-say)*

monument monumento, il/un *(moh-noo-MAYN-toh)*

moon luna, la *(LOO-nah)*

more più *(pyoo)*, ancora *(AHN-koh-rah)*

morning mattina, la/una *(maht-TEE-nah)*

in the morning di mattina *(dee maht-TEE-nah)*

this morning stamattina *(stah-maht-TEE-nah)*, stamani *(stah-MAH-nee)*

yesterday morning ieri mattina *(YEH-ree maht-TEE-nah)*

morning-after pill pillola del mattino dopo, la *(PEEL-loh-lah dayl maht-TEE-noh DOH-poh)*, pillola del giorno dopo, la *(PEEL-loh-lah dayl JOHR-noh DOH-poh)*

morning sickness nausea mattutina, la *(NOW-zay-ah maht-too-TEE-nah)*

mosque moschea, la/una *(mohs-KEH-ah)*

mosquito zanzara, la/una *(dzahn-DZAH-rah)* (le zanzare)

mother madre, la/una *(MAH-dray)*, mamma, la/una *(MAHM-mah)*

Mother's Day festa della mamma, la *(FES-tah DAYL-lah MAHM-mah)*

mother-in-law suocera, la *(SWOH-chay-rah)*

motorboat motoscafo, il/un *(moh-tohs-KAH-foh)*

motorcycle motocicletta, la/una *(moh-toh-chee-KLAYT-tah)*, moto, la/una *(MOH-toh)*

motor scooter motorino, il/un *(moh-toh-REE-noh)*

mountain montagna, la/una *(mohn-TAHN-nyah)* (le montagne)

mountain bike mountain bike, il/un *(MOWN-teen BAH-eek)*

mountain hut rifugio, il/un *(ree-FOO-joh)*

mountaineering alpinismo, l' *m* *(ahl-pee-NEEZ-moh)*

mouse (computer) mouse, il/un *(mows)*, (animal) topo, il/un *(TOH-poh)* (i topi)

mouth bocca, la *(BOHK-kah)*

movie film, il/un *(feelm)*

movie theater cinema, il/un *(CHEE-nay-mah)*

MP3 player lettore MP3, il/un *(layt-TOH-ray EM-may-pee-tray)*

Mrs. Signora *(seen-NYOH-rah)*

MSG glutammato monosodico *(gloo-tahm-MAH-toh moh-noh-SOH-dee-koh)*

much molto/a *(MOHL-toh/-tah)*

too much troppo *(TROHP-poh)*

mud fango, il *(FAHN-goh)*

muesli muesli, il *(MOOS-lee)*

muscle muscolo, il/un *(MOOS-koh-loh)* (i muscoli)

museum museo, il/un *(moo-ZEH-oh)* (i musei)

mushroom fungo, il/un *(FOON-goh)* (i funghi)

music musica, la *(MOO-zee-kah)*

musician musicista, il/la *(moo-zee-CHEES-tah)*

Muslim musulmano/a, il/la *(moo-sool-MAH-noh/-nah)*

mussel cozza, la/una *(KOHT-tsah)* (le cozze)

must dovere *(doh-VAY-ray)*

I must devo *(DAY-voh)*

we must dobbiamo *(dohb-BYAH-moh)*

you must (form. sing.) deve *(DAY-vay)*

mustard senape, la *(SEH-nah-pay)*, mostarda, la *(mohs-TAHR-dah)*

mute muto/a *(MOO-toh/-tah)*

my mio/a *(MEE-oh/-ah)*

N

N, n N, n *(EN-nay)*

nail clippers tagliaunghie, il/un *(tah-lyah-OON-gyay)*

name nome, il *(NOH-may)*

My name is ___. Mi chiamo ___. *(mee KYAH-moh ___.)*

What's your name? (form. sing.) Come si chiama? *(KOH-may see KYAH-mah?)*, (informal) Come ti chiami? *(KOH-may tee KYAH-mee?)*

napkin tovagliolo, il/un *(toh-vah-LYOH-loh)* (i tovaglioli)

Naples Napoli *(NAH-poh-lee)*

national nazionale *(naht-tsyoh-NAH-lay)*

national park parco nazionale, il/un *(PAHR-koh naht-tsyoh-NAH-lay)*

nationality nazionalità, la *(naht-tsyoh-nah-lee-TAH)*

nature natura, la *(nah-TOO-rah)*

naturopathy naturopatia, la *(nah-too-roh-pah-TEE-ah)*

nausea nausea, la *(NOW-zay-ah)*

near(by) (to) vicino (a) *(vee-CHEE-noh [ah])*

necessary necessario/a *(nay-chays-SAHR-yoh/-yah)*

neck collo, il *(KOHL-loh)*

  necklace catena, la/una *(kah-TAY-nah)* (le catene)

  necktie cravatta, la/una *(krah-VAHT-tah)* (le cravatte)

need bisogno, il/un *(bee-ZOH-nyoh)*

need, to avere bisogno *(ah-VAY-ray bee-ZOH-nyoh)*

  he/she/it needs ha bisogno di ___ *(ah bee-ZOH-nyoh dee ___)*

  I need ho bisogno di ___ *(oh bee-ZOH-nyoh dee ___)*

  you need ha bisogno di ___ (form. sing.) *(ah bee-ZOH-nyoh dee ___)*

  we need abbiamo bisogno di ___ *(ahb-BYAH-moh bee-ZOH-nyoh dee ___)*

needle ago, l' *m*/un *(AH-goh)*

negotiate, to negoziare *(nay-goht-TSYAH-ray)*

neither nessuno/a *(nays-SOO-noh/-nah)*

nephew nipote (di zii), il *(nee-POH-tay [dee TSEE-ee])*

net rete, la/una *(RAY-tay)*

Netherlands Paesi Bassi, i *(pah-AY-zay BAHS-see)*

never mai *(MAH-ee)*

new nuovo/a *(NWOH-voh/-vah)*

newspaper giornale, il *(johr-NAH-lay)* (i giornali)

newstand edicola, l' *f*/un' *(ay-DEE-koh-lah)*

next prossimo/a *(PROH-see-moh/-mah)*

  the next ___ il/la prossimo/a ___ *(PROH-see-moh/-mah)*

next to accanto (a) *(ahk-KAHN-toh [ah])*

nice bello/a *(BEL-loh/-lah)*; (person) simpatico/a *(seem-PAH-tee-koh/-kah)*, gentile *(jayn-TEE-lay)*

nickname soprannome, il/un *(soh-prahn-NOH-may)*

niece nipote (di zii), la *(nee-POH-tay [dee TSEE-ee])*

night notte, la/una *(NOHT-tay)*

  at night di notte *(dee NOHT-tay)*

  last night ieri notte *(YEH-ree NOHT-tay)*

nine nove *(NOH-vay)*

nine hundred novecento *(noh-vay-CHEN-toh)*

nineteen dicannove *(dee-chahn-NOH-vay)*

ninety novanta *(noh-VAHN-tah)*

  ninety-one novantuno *(noh-vahn-TOO-noh)*

  ninety-two novantadue *(noh-vahn-tah-DOO-ay)*

  ninety-three novantatré *(noh-vahn-tah-TRAY)*

  ninety-four novantaquattro *(noh-vahn-tah-KWAHT-troh)*

  ninety-five novantacinque *(noh-vahn-tah-CHEEN-kway)*

ninety-six novantasei *(noh-vahn-tah-SEH-ee)*

ninety-seven novantasette *(noh-vahn-tah-SET-tay)*

ninety-eight novantotto *(noh-vahn-TOHT-toh)*

ninety-nine novantanove *(noh-vahn-tah-NOH-vay)*

no no *(noh)*

noisy rumoroso/a *(roo-moh-ROH-soh/sah)*

non-carbonated naturale *(nah-too-RAH-lay)*

non-direct non-diretto/a *(nohn dee-RET-toh/-tah)*

none niente *(NYEHN-tay)*, nulla *(NOOL-lah)*

non-smoking non fumatore *(nohn foo-mah-TOH-ray)*

noodles pasta, la *(PAHS-tah)*

noon mezzogiorno, il *(mayd-dzoh-JOHR-noh)*

north nord *(nohrd)*

(to the) north (of) (a) nord (di) *([ah] nohrd [dee])*

nose naso, il *(NAH-soh)*

not non *(nohn)*

notebook quaderno, il/un *(kwah-DEHR-noh)*

nothing niente *(NYEN-tay)*

notify, to notificare *(noh-tee-fee-KAH-ray)*

novel romanzo, il/un *(roh-MAHN-dzoh)*

November novembre *(noh-VEM-bray)*

now adesso *(ah-DES-soh)*

nudist nudista, il/la un/una *(noo-DEES-tah)*

number numero, il *(NOO-may-roh)* (i numeri)

cell phone number numero di cellulare, il/un *(NOO-may-roh dee chayl-loo-LAH-ray)*

fax number numero di fax, il/un *(NOO-may-roh dee fahks)*

work number numero di lavoro, il/un *(NOO-may-roh dee lah-VOH-roh)*

nun suora, la/una *(SWOH-rah)*

nurse infermiere/a, l'/l' *m/f (een-fayr-MYEH-ray/-rah)*

nut noce, la/una *(NOH-chay)* (le noci), frutta secca, la *(FROOT-tah SAYK-kah)*

O

O, o O, o *(oh)*

oats avena, l' *f (ah-VAY-nah)*

obligatory obbligatorio/a *(ohb-blee-gah-TOHR-yoh/yah)*

obtain, to ottenere (see *to get*) *(oht-tay-NAY-ray)*

occupation (job) mestiere, il *(mays-TYEH-ray)*

occupied occupato/a *(ohk-koo-PAH-toh/-tah)*

occupy, to occupare *(ohk-koo-PAH-ray)*

ocean oceano, l' *m/un (oh-CHEH-ah-noh)*

October ottobre *(oht-TOH-bray)*

octopus polipo, il/un *(POH-lee-poh)* (i polipi)

of di *(dee)*

of course certo *(CHEHR-toh)*

off, to get scendere *(SHAYN-day-ray)*

 I get off here. Scendo qui. *(SHAYN-doh kwee)*

offend, to offendere *(ohf-FEN-day-ray)*

offer, to offrire *(ohf-FREE-ray)*

 I'll offer ___. Le offro ___. *(lay OHF-froh ___)*

office ufficio, l' *m/un (oof-FEE-choh)*

 office worker impiegato/a, l'/l' *m/f (eem-pyay-GAH-toh/-tah)*

often spesso *(SPAYS-soh)*

oil olio, l' *m (OHL-yoh)*

 olive oil olio d'oliva, l' *m (OHL-yoh doh-LEE-vah)*

OK bene *(BEH-nay)*

 Everything OK? tutto a posto? *(TOOT-toh ah POHS-toh?)*

 I'm OK. Sto bene. *(stoh BEH-nay)*

 That's OK va bene *(vah BEH-nay)*

old vecchio/a *(VAYK-kyoh/-kyah)*

 old city centro storico, il *(CHEN-troh STOH-ree-koh)*

 old part of town parte vecchia della città, la *(PAHR-tay VAYK-kyah DAYL-lah cheet-TAH)*

older people persone anziani *(payr-SOH-nay ahn-TSYAH-nee)*

olive oliva, l' *f/un' (oh-LEE-vah)* (le olive)

 olive oil olio d'oliva, l' *m (OHL-yoh doh-LEE-vah)*

omelette frittata, la/una *(freet-TAH-tah)*, omeletta, l' *f/un' (oh-*

muh-LET-tah)*, omelette, l' *f /un' (oh-muh-LET)*

on su *(soo)*, sopra *(SOH-prah)*

once una volta *(OO-nah VOHL-tah)*

one uno *(OO-noh)*

one-way (ticket) di sola andata *(dee SOH-lah ahn-DAH-tah)*, (traffic) a senso unico *(ah SEN-soh OO-nee-koh)*

onion cipolla, la/una *(chee-POHL-lah)* (le cipolle)

online online

only solo/a *(SOH-loh/-lah)*

open (to be) aperto/a *(ah-PEHR-toh/-tah)*

 When does it open? A che ora apre? *(ah kay OH-rah AH-pray?)*

open, to aprire *(ah-PREE-ray)*

opening apertura, l' *f (ah-payr-TOO-rah)*

 opening hours orario di apertura, l' *m (oh-RAHR-yoh dee ah-payr-TOO-rah)*

opera opera lirica, l' *f/un' (OH-pay-rah LEE-ree-kah)*

 opera house teatro dell'opera, il/un *(tay-AH-troh dayl-LOH-pay-roh)*

operation (surgery) intervento, l' *m (een-tayr-VEN-toh)*

operator operatore/operatrice, l'/l' *m/f (oh-pay-rah-TOH-ray/-TREE-chay)*

opinion opinione, l' *f/un' (oh-pee-NYOH-nay)*

opposite di fronte (a) *(dee FROHN-tay [ah])*

or o *(oh)*

orange (fruit) arancia, l' *f*/un' *(ah-RAHN-chah)* (le arance); (color) arancione *(ah-rahn-CHOH-nay)*

orange juice (bottled) succo d'arancia, il *(SOOK-koh dah-RAHN-chah)*; (fresh) spremuta d'arancia, lo *(spray-MOO-tah dah-RAHN-chah)*

orchestra orchestra, l' *f*/un' *(ohr-KES-trah)*

order ordine, l' *m*/un *(OHR-dee-nay)*

order, to place an ordinare *(ohr-dee-NAH-ray)*

order, to put in ordinare *(ohr-dee-NAH-ray)*

organic organico/a *(ohr-GAH-nee-koh/-kah)*

organize, to organizzare *(ohr-gah-need-DZAH-ray)*

origin origine, l' *f (oh-REE-jee-nay)*

original originale *(oh-ree-jee-NAH-lay)*

ostrich struzzo, lo/uno *(STROOT-tsoh)* (gli struzzi)

other altro/a *(AHL-troh/-trah)*

others altri/e *(AHL-tree/-tray)*

our nostro/a *(NOHS-troh/-trah)*

outside fuori *(FWOH-ree)*

oven forno, il/un *(FOHR-noh)*

over (above) sopra *(SOH-prah)*

overcoat cappotto, il/un *(kahp-POHT-toh)*

overdose dose eccessiva, la/una *(DOH-zay ayt-chays-SEE-vah)*

own, on one's da solo/a *(dah SOH-loh)*

owner proprietario/a *(proh-pryay-TAHR-yoh/-yah)*

oxygen ossigeno, l' *m (ohs-SEE-jay-noh)*

oyster ostrica, l' *f*/un' *(OHS-tree-kah)* (le ostriche)

P

P, p P, p *(pee)*

pacemaker pacemaker, il/un *(PAYS-may-kuh)*

pacifier ciucciotto, il/un *(choot-CHOHT-toh)* (i ciucciotti)

package pacco, il/un *(PAHK-koh)* (i pacchi), pacchetto, il/un *(pahk-KAYT-toh)*

packet sacchetto, il/un *(sahk-KAYT-toh)*, pacchetto, il/un *(pahk-KAYT-toh)*

packing material imballaggio, l' *m (eem-bahl-LAHD-joh)*

padlock lucchetto, il/un *(look-KAYT-toh)* (i lucchetti)

Padua Padova *(PAH-doh-vah)*

page pagina, la/una *(PAH-jee-nah)* (le pagine)

paid parking lot parcheggio a pagamento, il/un *(pahr-KAYD-joh ah pah-gah-MAYN-toh)*

paid parking zone zona disco, la/una *(DZOH-nah DEES-koh)*

pain dolore, il/un *(doh-LOH-ray)*

painful doloroso/a *(doh-loh-ROH-soh/-sah)*

painkiller analgesico, l' *m*/un *(ah-nahl-JEH-zee-koh)*

paint, to dipingere *(dee-PEEN-jay-ray)*

painter pittore/pittrice, il/la *(peet-TOH-ray/-TREE-chay)*

painting pittura, la/una *(peet-TOO-rah)*

pair (couple) paio, un *(PAH-yoh)*

palace palazzo, il/un *(pah-LAHT-tsoh)* (i palazzi)

pan pentola, la/una *(PAYN-toh-lah)*

pants pantaloni, i *(pahn-tah-LOH-nee)*

pantyhose collant, il *(koh-LAH)*

panty liners salva slip, i *(SAHL-vah sleep)*

paper carta, la *(KAHR-tah)*

  marbled paper carta marmorizzata, la *(KAHR-tah mahr-moh-reed-DZAH-tah)*

  toilet paper carta igienica, la *(KAHR-tah ee-JEH-nee-kah)*

papers (documents) documenti, i *(doh-koo-MAYN-tee)*

paperwork moduli, i *(MOH-doo-lee)*

parcel pacchetto, il/un *(pahk-KAYT-toh)* (i pacchetti)

pardon me! mi scusi! *(mee SKOO-zee)*

parents genitori, i *(jay-nee-TOH-ree)*

Paris Parigi *(pah-REE-jee)*

park parco, il/un *(PAHR-koh)* (i parchi)

parking sostare *(sohs-TAH-ray)*

  no parking divieto sostare/divieto di sostare *(dee-VYEH-toh dee sohs-TAH-ray)*

  paid parking lot parcheggio a pagamento, il/un *(pahr-KAYD-joh ah pah-gah-MAYN-toh)*

  paid parking zone zona disco, la/una *(DZOH-nah DEES-koh)*

  parking disk disco orario, il/un *(DEES-koh oh-RAHR-yoh)*

  parking lot parcheggio, il/un *(pahr-KAYD-joh)*

  parking meter parchimetro, il/un *(pahr-KEE-may-troh)*

part parte, la *(PAHR-tay)*, pezzo, il *(PET-tsoh)* (=piece) (i pezzi)

  to order a replacement part ordinare il pezzo di ricambio *(ohr-dee-NAH-ray eel PET-tsoh dee ree-KAHM-byoh)*

partly in parte *(een PAHR-tay)*

partner compagno/a, il/la *(kohm-PAHN-nyoh/-nyah)*

  my partner il mio compagno *(eel MEE-oh kohm-PAHN-nyoh)*, la mia compagna *(lah MEE-ah kohm-PAHN-nyah)*

part-time part time *(PAHT tym)*

party festa, la/una *(FES-tah)*, (political) partito, il/un *(pahr-TEE-toh)*

pass (mountain) passo, il *(PAHS-soh)*

passenger passeggero/a, il/la *(pahs-sayd-JEH-roh/-rah)*

passport passaporto, il *(pahs-sah-POHR-toh)* (i passaporti)

my passport il mio passaporto *(eel MEE-oh pahs-sah-POHR-toh)*

passport control controllo passaporti, il *(kohn-TROHL-loh pahs-sah-POHR-tee)*

passport photo foto tessera, la *(FOH-toh TES-say-rah)*

Your passport, please. Il Suo passaporto, per favore. *(eel SOO-oh pahs-sah-POHR-toh, payr fah-VOH-ray)*

past passato, il *(pahs-SAH-toh)*

pasta pasta, la *(PAH-stah)*

pastry pasta, la *(PAH-stah)*

pastry shop pasticceria, la/una *(pahs-teet-chay-REE-ah)*

path sentiero, il/un *(sayn-TYEH-roh)*

pause pausa, la/una *(POW-zah)*

pay, to pagare *(pah-GAH-ray)*

pay attention! attenzione! *(aht-tayn-TSYOH-nay)*

payment pagamento, il *(pah-gah-MAYN-toh)* (i pagamenti)

pea pisello, il *(pee-SEL-loh)* (also slang for *penis*) (i piselli)

peace pace, la *(PAH-chay)*

peach pesca, la/una *(PES-kah)* (le pesche)

peak cima, la/una *(CHEE-mah)* (le cime)

peanut arachide, l' *f* /un' *(ah-RAH-kee-day)* (le arachidi)

pear pera, la/una *(PAY-rah)* (le pere)

peas piselli, i *(pee-SEL-lee)*

pedal pedale, il *(pay-DAH-lay)*

pedestrian pedone, il/la *(pay-DOH-nay)*

pedestrian crossing passaggio zebrato, il/un *(pahs-SAHD-joh dzay-BRAH-toh)*

pedestrian zone isola pedonale, l' *f* /un' *(EE-zoh-lah pay-doh-NAH-lay)*

pen, ballpoint penna, la/una *(PAYN-nah)*

pencil matita, la/una *(mah-TEE-tah)* (le matite)

penicillin penicillina, la *(pay-nee-cheel-LEE-nah)*

penis pene, il *(PEH-nay)*

people persone, le *(payr-SOH-nay)*, gente, la *(JEN-tay)*

pepper pepe, il *(PAY-pay)*

per per *(payr)*, a *(ah)*

percent per cento *(payr CHEN-toh)*

perfect perfetto/a *(payr-FAYT-toh/-tah)*

performance spettacolo, lo *(spayt-TAH-koh-loh)*

perfume profumo, il *(proh-FOO-moh)*

perfumery profumeria, la *(proh-foo-may-REE-ah)*

period (time) periodo, il *(pay-RYOH-doh)*; (menstrual) mestruazioni, le *(mays-troo-aht-TSYOH-nee)*

period pain dolori mestruali, i *(doh-LOH-ree may-stroo-AH-lee)*

permanent permanente *(payr-mah-NEN-tay)*

permission (also, =to get past) permesso, il *(payr-MAYS-soh)*

permit permesso, il *(payr-MAYS-soh)*

permit, to permettere *(payr-MAYT-tay-ray)*

person persona, la/una *(payr-SOH-nah)*

personal personale *(payr-soh-NAH-lay)*

personality personalità, la/una *(payr-sohn-ah-lee-TAH)*

pet animale domestico, l' *m*/un *(ah-nee-MAH-lay doh-MES-tee-koh)*

pharmacy farmacia, la/una *(fahr-mah-CHEE-ah)*

phone telefono, il/un *(tay-LEH-foh-noh)*

  cell phone cellulare, il/un *(chayl-loo-LAH-ray)*

  public phone telefono pubblico, il/un *(tay-LEH-foh-noh POOB-blee-koh)*

  phone book elenco telefonico, l' *m*/un *(ay-LEN-koh tay-lay-FOH-nee-koh)*

  phone booth cabina telefonica, la/una *(kah-BEE-nah tay-lay-FOH-nee-kah)*

  phone call chiamata, la/una *(kyah-MAH-tah)*

  phone card scheda telefonica, la/una *(SKEH-dah tay-lay-FOH-nee-kah)*; (international) scheda internazionale, la/una *(SKEH-dah een-tayr-naht-tsyoh-NAH-lay)*, carta telefonica internazionale, la/una *(KAHR-tah tay-lay-FOH-nee-kah een-tayr-naht-tsyoh-NAH-lay)*

  phone charger caricabatterie, il/un *(kah-ree-kah-baht-tay-REE-ah)*

  phone number numero di telefono, il/un *(NOO-may-roh dee tay-LEH-foh-noh)*

photo foto, la/una *(FOH-toh)*

  digital photo foto digitale, la/una *(FOH-toh dee-jee-TAH-lay)*

  photo shop/store negozio di fotocine, il/un *(nay-GOHT-tsyoh dee foh-toh-CHEE-nay)*

  print photos, to stampare foto *(stahm-PAH-ray FOH-toh)*

photocopy fotocopia, la/una *(foh-toh-KOHP-yah)*

photographer fotografo/a, il/la *(foh-TOH-grah-foh/-fah)*

photography fotografia, la *(foh-toh-grah-FEE-ah)*

photo shop/store negozio di fotocine, il/un *(nay-GOHT-tsyoh dee foh-toh-CHEE-nay)*

phrasebook vocabularietto, il/un *(voh-kah-boh-lah-RYET-toh)*

pickle sottaceto, il/un *(soh-tah-CHAY-toh)* (i sottaceti)

picnic picnic, il/un *(PEEK-neek)*

pick up, to (e.g., ticket) ritirare *(ree-tee-RAH-ray)*, raccogliere *(rahk-KOHL-lyay-ray)*

picture (painting) pittura, la/una *(peet-TOO-rah)* (le pitture)

pictures, to take fotografare *(foh-toh-grah-FAH-ray)*

pie torta, la/una *(TOHR-tah)*

piece pezzo, il/un *(PET-tsoh)*

  two pieces due pezzi *(DOO-ay PET-tsee)*

Piedmont Piemonte, il *(pyay-MOHN-tay)*

pig maiale, il/un *(mah-YAH-lay)*

Pill, the pillola, la *(PEEL-loh-lah)* (le pillole)

  morning-after pill pillola del mattino dopo, la *(PEEL-loh-lah dayl maht-TEE-noh DOH-poh)*

pillow guanciale, il/un *(gwahn-CHAH-lay)* (i guanciali), cuscino, il/un *(koosh-SHEE-noh)*

pillowcase federa, la/una *(FEH-day-rah)*

PIN PIN, il *(peen)*

  my PIN il mio PIN *(eel MEE-oh peen)*

  your PIN il suo PIN *(eel SOO-oh peen)*

pineapple ananas, l' *m*/un *(AH-nah-nahs)*

pink rosa *(ROH-sah)*

pint pinta, la/una *(PEEN-tah)*

pistachio pistacchio, il/un *(pees-STAHK-kyoh)* (i pistacchi)

pizzeria pizzeria, la/una *(peet-tsay-REE-ah)*

place (seat) posto, il/un *(POHS-toh)*, (location) luogo, il/un *(LWOH-goh)*

place of birth luogo di nascita, il *(LWOH-goh dee NAHSH-shee-tah)*

plane, (air-) aereo, l' *m*/un *(ah-EH-ray-oh)*, aereoplano, l' *m*/un *(ah-ay-roh-PLAH-noh)*

plant pianta, la/una *(PYAHN-tah)* (le piante)

plastic plastica, la *(PLAHS-tee-kah)*

plate piatto, il/un *(PYAHT-toh)* (i piatti)

plateau altopiano, l' *m*/un *(ahl-toh-PYAH-noh)*

platform (train station) binario, il *(bee-NAHR-yoh)* (i binari)

play (theater) teatro, il/un *(tay-AH-troh)*, commedia, la/una *(kohm-MEH-dyah)*

play, to (e.g., a game/sport) giocare *(joh-KAH-ray)*, (e.g., an instrument) suonare *(swoh-NAH-ray)*

playground parco giochi, il/un *(PAHR-koh JOH-kee)*

please per favore *(payr fah-VOH-ray)*, per piacere *(payr pyah-CHAY-ray)*

pleased to meet you (molto) piacere *([MOHL-toh] pyah-CHAY-ray)*

plug (sink) tappo, il/un *(TAHP-poh)*, (electrical) spina, la/una *(SPEE-nah)*

plum prugna, la/una *(PROON-nyah)* (le prugne)

plumber idraulico, l' *m (ee-DRAW-lee-koh)*

p.m. (afternoon) del pomeriggio *(dayl poh-may-REED-joh)*, (evening) di sera *(dee SAY-rah)*

PMS tensione premestruale, la *(tayns-SYOH-nay pray-may-stroo-AH-lay)*

P.O. Box casella postale, la/una *(kah-SEL-lah pohs-TAH-lay)*

pocket tasca, la/una *(TAHS-kah)* (le tasche)

poetry poesia, la *(poh-ay-ZEE-ah)*

point punto, il/un *(POON-toh)* (i punti)

point, to indicare *(een-dee-KAH-ray)*

poisonous velenoso/a *(vay-lay-NOH-soh/-sah)*

police polizia, la *(poh-leet-TSEE-ah)*

   miltary police carabinieri, i *(kah-rah-bee-NYEH-ree)*

   police station posto di polizia, il *(POHS-toh dee poh-leet-TSEE-ah)*

politician politico/a, il/la *(poh-LEE-tee-koh/-kah)*

politics politica, la *(poh-LEE-tee-kah)*

pollen polline, il *(POHL-lee-nay)*

pollute, to inquinare *(een-kwee-NAH-ray)*

pollution inquinamento, l' *m (een-kwee-nah-MAYN-toh)*

pony cavallino, il *(kah-vahl-LEE-noh)*

pool (swimming) piscina, la *(peesh-SHEE-nah)*

pop bibita frizzante, la *(bee-BEE-tah freed-ZAHN-tay)*

popular popolare *(poh-poh-LAH-ray)*

pork maiale, il *(mah-YAH-lay)*

port porto, il/un *(POHR-toh)*

porter (for luggage) portobagagli, i *(pohr-toh-bah-GAHL-lyee)*, facchino, il *(fahk-KEE-noh)*

portion porzione, la/una *(pohr-TSYOH-nay)* (le porzioni)

   children's portions porzioni per (i) bambini, le *(pohr-TSYOH-nee payr [ee] bahm-BEE-nee)*

possible possibile *(pohs-SEE-bee-lay)*

postage stamp francobollo, il/un *(frahn-koh-BOHL-loh)* (i francobolli)

postal address indirizzo postale, l' *m (een-dee-REET-tsoh pohs-TAH-lay)*

postcard cartolina, la *(kahr-toh-LEE-nah)* (le cartoline)

poste restante fermo posta, il *(FAYR-moh POHS-tah)*

post office ufficio postale, l' *m (oof-FEE-choh pohs-TAH-lay)*

pot (cooking) pentola, la/una *(PAYN-toh-lah)*, (ceramic) pignatta, la/una *(peen-NYAHT-tah)*, (marijuana) erba, l' *f (EHR-bah)*

potato patata, la/una *(pah-TAH-tah)* (le patate)

pottery ceramiche, le *(chay-RAH-mee-kay)*

potty (chair) vasino, il/un *(vah-SEE-noh)*

poultry pollame, il *(pohl-LAH-may)*

Prague Praga *(PRAH-gah)*

prawn gambero, il/un *(GAHM-bay-roh)* (i gamberi)

pray, to pregare *(pray-GAH-ray)*

prayer preghiera, la/una *(pray-GYEH-rah)*

prefer, to preferire *(pray-fay-REE-ray)*

  I prefer x to y preferisco __ al __ *(pray-fayr-EES-koh __ ahl __)*

prefix prefisso, il *(pray-FEES-soh)*

pregnancy test kit test di gravidanza, il/un *(test dee grah-vee-DAHN-tsah)*

pregnant incinta *(een-CHEEN-tah)*

prepare, to preparare *(pray-pah-RAH-ray)*

prescription ricetta, la/una *(ree-CHET-tah)* (le ricette)

present (gift) regalo, il/un *(ray-GAH-loh)* (i regali)

president presidente/tessa, il/la *(pray-see-DEN-tay/dayn-TAYS-sah)*

press, to spingere *(SPEEN-jay-ray)*, premere *(PREM-ay-ray)*

pressure pressione, la *(prays-SYOH-nay)*

  tire pressure pressione delle gomme, la *(prays-SYOH-nay DAYL-lay GOHM-may)*

pretty bello/a *(BEL-loh/-lah)*, carino/a *(kah-REE-noh/-nah)*

previous precedente *(pray-chay-DEN-tay)*

price prezzo, il *(PRET-tsoh)* (i prezzi)

priest prete, il/un *(PREH-tay)*

prime minister primo ministro, il/la *(PREE-moh mee-NEES-troh)*

print (reproduction) riproduzione, la/una *(ree-proh-doot-TSYOH-nay)*

print, to stampare *(stahm-PAH-ray)*

printer (computer) stampante, la/una *(stahm-PAHN-tay)*

  use a printer usare una stampante *(oo-ZAH-ray OO-nah stahm-PAHN-tay)*

priority mail posta prioritaria, la *(POHS-tah pree-oh-ree-TAHR-yah)*

prison prigione, la/una *(pree-JOH-nay)*

private privato/a *(pree-VAH-toh/-tah)*

problem problema, il/un *(proh-BLEH-mah)* (i problemi)

  no problem Non c'è problema. *(nohn cheh proh-BLEH-mah)*

produce, to produrre *(proh-DOOR-ray)*

professor professore/essa, il/la *(proh-fays-SOH-ray/-soh-RAYS-sah)*

profit profitto, il/un *(proh-FEET-toh)* (i profitti)

program programma, il/un *(proh-GRAHM-mah)*

prohibit, to vietare *(vyay-TAH-ray)*

prohibited vietato/a *(vyay-TAH-toh/-tah)*, proibito/a *(proh-ee-BEE-toh/-tah)*

prohibition (against) divieto (di), il/un *(dee-VYEH-toh [dee])*

projector proiettore, il/un *(proh-yayt-TOH-ray)*

  overhead projector lavagna luminosa, la/una *(lah-VAHN-nyah loo-mee-NOH-sah)*

promise promessa, la/una *(proh-MAYS-sah)*

promise, to promettere *(proh-MAYT-tay-ray)*

  I promise prometto *(proh-MAYT-toh)*

  Do you promise? promette? *(proh-MAYT-tay?)*

pronounce, to pronunciare *(proh-noon-CHAH-ray)*

protect, to proteggere *(proh-TED-jay-ray)*

protected protetto/a *(proh-TET-toh/-tah)*

protest manifestazione, la/una *(mah-nee-fays-taht-TSYOH-nay)*

protest, to protestare *(proh-tays-TAH-ray)*

provisions provviste, le *(prohv-VEES-tay)*

prune prugna secca, la/una *(PROON-nyah SAYK-kah)* (le prugne secche)

pub pub, il/un *(poob)*

public pubblica *(POOB-blee-kah)*

  public relations relazioni pubbliche, le *(ray-laht-TSYOH-nee POOB-blee-kay)*

public telephone telefono pubblico, il/un *(tay-LEH-foh-noh POOB-blee-koh)*

public toilet gabinetto pubblico, il/un *(gah-bee-NAYT-toh POOB-blee-koh)*

public transportation mezzi pubblici, i *(MED-dzee POOB-blee-chee)*

pudding budino, il *(boo-DEE-noh)*

pull, to tirare *(tee-RAH-ray)*

pullover (sweater) maglione, il/un *(mahl-LYOH-nay)*

pump pompa, la/una *(POHM-pah)*

pumpkin zucca, la/una *(TSOOK-kah)* (le zucche)

puncture bucatura, la/una *(boo-kah-TOO-rah)*

punish, to punire *(poo-NEE-ray)*

puppy cucciolo, il/un *(KOOT-choh-loh)*

purchase, to acquistare *(ahk-kwees-TAH-ray)*

pure puro/a *(POO-roh/rah)*

purple viola *(vee-OH-lah)*

purse borsa, la/una *(BOHR-sah)*, borsetta, la/una *(bohr-SAYT-tah)*

push, to spingere *(SPEEN-jay-ray)*

put, to mettere *(MAYT-tay-ray)*

Q

Q, q Q, q *(koo)*

quality qualità, la *(kwah-lee-TAH)*

quantity quantità, la *(kwahn-tee-TAH)*

quarrel bisticcio, il/un *(bees-TEET-choh)*

quarter quarto, un *(KWAHR-toh)* (le quarti)

  one-quarter un quarto *(oon KWAHR-toh)*

  three-quarters tre quarti *(tray KWAHR-tee)*

queen regina, la/una *(ray-JEE-nah)*

question domanda, la/una *(doh-MAHN-dah)* (le domande)

queue coda, la/una *(KOH-dah)*

quick rapido/a *(RAH-pee-doh/-dah)*

quiet tranquillo/a *(trahn-KWEEL-loh/-lah)*

R

R, r R, r *(EHR-ray)*

rabbit coniglio, il/un *(koh-NEEL-lyoh)* (i conigli)

racetrack pista, la/una *(PEES-tah)*

racquet racchetta, la/una *(rahk-KAYT-tah)*

radiator radiatore, il *(rahd-yah-TOH-ray)*

railing corrimano, il *(kohr-ree-MAH-noh)* (i corrimani)

rail station stazione ferroviaria, la *(staht-TSYOH-nay fayr-roh-VYAH-ryah)*

rain pioggia, la *(PYOHD-jah)*

rain, to piovere *(PYOH-vay-ray)*

  it's raining piove *(PYOH-vay)*

raincoat impermeabile, l' *m*/un *(eem-payr-may-AH-bee-lay)*

ramp rampa, la/una *(RAHM-pah)*

raisins uva passa, l' *f* *(OO-vah PAHS-sah)*

rape stupro, lo *(STOO-proh)*

rape, to stuprare *(stoo-PRAH-ray)*, violentare *(vee-oh-layn-TAH-ray)*

rare (cooked meat) al sangue *(ahl SAHN-gway)*, (unusual) raro/a *(RAH-roh/-rah)*

  very rare (cooked meat) quasi crudo/a *(KWAH-zee KROO-doh/-dah)*

rash (medical) sfogo, lo/uno *(SFOH-goh)*

raspberry lampone, il/un *(lahm-POHN-nay)* (i lamponi)

rat topo, il/un *(TOH-poh)* (i topi)

rate tariffa, la/una *(tah-REEF-fah)* (le tariffe)

raw crudo/a *(KROO-doh/-dah)*

razor rasoio, il/un *(rah-SOH-yoh)* (i rasoi)

  disposable razor rasoio radi e getta, il/un *(rah-SOH-yoh RAH-dee ay JET-tah)*

  electric razor rasoio elettrico, il/un *(rah-SOH-yoh ay-LET-tree-koh)*

  razor blades lamette da barba, le *(lah-MAYT-tay dah BAHR-bah)*

read, to leggere *(LED-jay-ray)*

ready pronto/a *(PROHN-toh/-tah)*

realistic realistico/a *(ray-ah-LEES-tee-koh/-kah)*

reason ragione, la *(rah-JOH-nay)* (le ragioni)

receipt ricevuta, la/una *(ree-chay-VOO-tah)*, (when prepaying) scontrino, lo/uno *(skohn-TREE-noh)*

receive, to ricevere *(ree-CHAY-vay-ray)*

recently di recente *(dee ray-CHEN-tay)*

recharge, to ricaricare *(ree-kah-ree-KAH-ray)*

to recharge the battery ricaricare la batteria *(ree-kah-ree-KAH-ray lah baht-tay-REE-ah)*

recommend, to consigliare *(kohn-seel-LYAH-ray)*, raccomandare *(rah-koh-mahn-DAH-ray)*

recyclable riciclabile *(ree-chee-KLAH-bee-lay)*

recycle, to riciclare *(ree-chee-KLAH-ray)*

recycling riciclaggio *(ree-chee-KLAHD-joh)*

red rosso/a *(ROHS-soh/-sah)*

red wine vino rosso, il/un *(VEE-noh ROHS-soh)*

referee arbitro, l' *m (AHR-bee-troh)*

refrigerator frigo, il/un *(FREE-goh)*

refund rimborso, il/un *(reem-BOHR-soh)*

refuse, to rifiutare *(ree-fyoo-TAH-ray)*

region regione, la *(ray-JOH-nay)*

registered mail posta raccomandata, la *(POHS-tah rahk-koh-mahn-DAH-tah)*

regular normale *(nohr-MAH-lay)*

regulate, to (= to adjust) regolare *(ray-goh-LAH-ray)*

re-heated riscaldato/a *(rees-kahl-DAH-toh/-tah)*

reimbursement rimborso, il/un *(reem-BOHR-soh)*

relationship rapporto, il/un *(rahp-POHR-toh)*

relatives parenti, i *(pah-REN-tee)*

relax, to rilassarsi *(ree-lahs-SAH-ray)*

relic reliquia, la/una *(ray-LEE-kwyah)*

religion religione, la/una *(ray-lee-JOH-nay)*

religious religioso/a *(ray-lee-JOH-soh/-sah)*

remote control telecomando, il/un *(tay-lay-koh-MAHN-doh)*

Renaissance Rinascimento, il *(ree-nahsh-shee-MAYN-toh)*

rent affitto, l' *m (ahf-FEET-toh)*

for rent affittasi *(ahf-feet-TAH-see)*

rent, to noleggiare *(noh-layd-JAH-ray)*, prendere in affitto *(PREN-day-ray een ahf-FEET-toh)*

repair, to riparare *(ree-pah-RAH-ray)*, aggiustare *(ahd-joos-TAH-ray)*

repeat, to ripetere *(ree-PEH-tay-ray)*

replacement part pezzo di ricambio, il/un *(PET-tsoh dee ree-KAHM-byoh)*

to order a replacement part ordinare un pezzo di ricambio *(ohr-dee-NAH-ray oon PET-tsoh dee ree-KAHM-byoh)*

represent, to rappresentare *(rahp-pray-zayn-TAH-ray)*

reproduction riproduzione, la/una *(ree-proh-doot-TSYOH-nay)*

required obbligatorio/a *(ohb-blee-gah-TOHR-yoh/yah)*

reservation prenotazione, la/una *(pray-noh-tah-TSYOH-nay)* (le prenotazioni)

reserve, to prenotare *(pray-noh-TAH-ray)*

residency permit permesso di soggiorno, il/un *(payr-MAYS-soh dee sohd-JOHR-noh)*

rest, to riposare *(ree-poh-SAH-ray)*

restaurant ristorante, il/un *(rees-toh-RAHN-tay)*

résumé curriculum vitae, il/un *(koor-REE-koo-loom VEE-tay)*

retired in pensione *(een payn-SYOH-nay)*

retired person pensionato/a *(payn-syoh-NAH-toh/-tah)*

return, to ritornare *(ree-tohr-NAH-ray)*

return (something), to restituire *(rays-tee-too-EE-ray)*

I would like to return this. Vorrei restituire questo/a. *(vohr-REH-ee rays-tee-too-EE-ray KWAYS-toh/-tah)*

return ticket biglietto di andata e ritorno, il/un *(beel-LYAYT-toh dee (ahn-DAH-tah ay ree-TOHR-noh)*

rice riso, il *(REE-soh)*

brown rice riso integrale, il *(REE-soh een-tay-GRAH-lay)*

rich (money) ricco/a *(REEK-koh/-kah)*

right (direction) destra *(DES-trah)*, (correct) giusto/a *(JOOS-toh/-tah)*

to the right a destra *(ah DES-trah)*

right away (=quickly) subito *(SOO-bee-toh)*

ring (jewelry) anello, l' *m*/un *(ah-NEL-loh)* (gli anelli)

rip-off fregatura, la/una *(fray-gah-TOO-rah)*

risk rischio, il/un *(REES-kyoh)* (i rischi)

river fiume, il/un *(FYOO-may)*

road strada, la/una *(STRAH-dah)*

roasted arrosto/a *(ahr-ROHS-toh/-tah)*

rob, to derubare *(day-roo-BAH-ray)*

rock roccia, la/una *(ROHT-chah)* (le rocce)

rock climbing andare su roccia, il *(ahn-DAH-ray soo ROHT-chah)*

rock group (music) gruppo rock, il/un *(GROO-poh rock)*

roll (bread) panino, il/un *(pah-NEE-noh)* (i panini)

Romanesque romanico/a *(roh-MAH-nee-koh/-kah)*

romantic romantico/a *(roh-MAHN-tee-koh/-kah)*

Rome Roma *(ROH-mah)*

room camera, la/una *(KAH-may-rah)* (le camere)

double room camera doppia, la/una *(KAH-may-rah DOHP-pyah)*

room number numero di camera, il *(NOO-may-roh dee KAH-may-rah)*

single room camera singola, la/una *(KAH-may-rah SEEN-goh-lah)*

triple room camera tripla, la/una *(KAH-may-rah TREEP-lah)*

rooster gallo, il/un *(GAHL-loh)*

rope corda, la/una *(KOHR-dah)*

round rotondo/a *(roh-TOHN-doh/-dah)*

roundabout rotatoria, la *(roh-tah-TOHR-yah)*

round trip andata e ritorno *(ahn-DAH-tah ay ree-TOHR-noh)*

route corsa, la/una *(KOHR-sah)*, itinerario, l' *m*/un *(ee-tee-nay-RAH-ryoh)*

rug tappeto, il/un *(tah-PAY-toh)*

rugby rugby, il *(ROOG-bee)*

ruin rovina, la/una *(roh-VEE-nah)* (le rovine)

rule regola, la/una *(REH-goh-lah)* (le regole)

run, to correre *(KOHR-ray-ray)*

running (sport) footing, il *(FOO-teeng)*

S

S, s S, s (ES-say)

Sabbath sabato, il *(SAH-bah-toh)*

sad triste *(TREE-stay)*

safe (=secure) sicuro/a *(see-KOO-roh/-rah)*

safe (box) cassaforte, la/una *(kahs-sah-FOHR-tay)*

safety sicurezza, la *(see-koo-RAYT-tsah)*

sage (spice) salvia, la *(SAHL-vyah)*

sail, to navigare *(nah-vee-GAH-ray)*

saint santo/a, il/la un/una *(SAHN-toh/-tah)* (i santi/le sante)

salad insalata, l' *f*/un' *(een-sah-LAH-tah)*

mixed salad insalata mista, l' *f*/un' *(een-sah-LAH-tah MEES-tah)*

salami salame, il *(sah-LAH-may)*

salary stipendio, lo *(stee-PEN-dyoh)*

sale saldo, il/un *(SAHL-doh)* (i saldi), vendita, la/una *(VAYN-dee-tah)*

on sale in vendita *(een VAYN-dee-tah)*

sales saldi, i *(SAHL-dee)*

salesperson commesso/a, il/la *(kohm-MAYS-soh/-sah)*

sales representative rappresentante di commercio, il/la *(rahp-pray-zayn-TAHN-tay dee kohm-MEHRT-choh)*

sales tax IVA, L' *f (LEE-vah)*

salmon salmone, il *(sahl-MOH-nay)*

salt sale, il *(SAH-lay)*

  salt-free senza sale *(SEN-tsah SAH-lay)*

same stesso/a *(STAYS-soh/-sah)*

sand sabbia, la *(SAHB-byah)*

sandal sandalo, il/un *(SAHN-dah-loh)* (i sandali)

sandwich tramezzino, il/un *(trah-mayd-DZEE-noh)* (i tramezzini)

sanitary napkin assorbente igienico, l' *m/*un *(ahs-sohr-BEN-tay ee-JEH-nee-koh)* (gli assorbenti igienici)

sardine sardina, la/una *(sahr-DEE-nah)* (le sardine)

Sardinia Sardegna, la *(sahr-DAYN-nyah)*

Saturday sabato *(SAH-bah-toh)*

sauce salsa, la/una *(SAHL-sah)*, sugo, il *(SOO-goh)*

saucepan pentola, la/una *(PAYN-toh-lah)*

sauna sauna, la/una *(SOW-nah)*

sausage salsiccia, la/una *(sahl-SEET-chah)*

say, to dire *(DEE-ray)*

scan, to (=use a scanner) scandire *(skahn-DEE-ray)*

scanner scanner, lo/uno *(SKAHN-ner)*

scarf sciarpa, la/una *(SHAHR-pah)* (le sciarpe)

schedule orario, l' *m/*un *(oh-RAHR-yoh)*

school scuola, la/una *(SKWOH-lah)*

science scienza, la *(SHEN-tsah)*

scientist scienziato/a, lo/la *(shayn-TSYAH-toh/-tah)*

scissors forbici, le *(FOHR-bee-chee)*

score punteggio, il *(poon-TAYD-joh)*

score, to segnare *(sayn-NYAH-ray)*

scoreboard tabellone segnapunti, il *(tah-bayl-LOH-nay sayn-nyah-POON-tee)*

Scotland Scozia, la *(SKOHT-tsyah)*

screen schermo, lo/uno *(SKAYR-moh)*

sculptor scultore, lo *(skool-TOH-ray)*, scultrice, la *(skool-TREE-chay)*

sculpture scultura, la/una *(skool-TOO-rah)*

sea mare, il *(MAH-ray)*

  seafood frutti di mare, i *(FROOT-tee dee MAH-ray)*

  seafood chowder cacciucco, il *(kaht-CHOOK-koh)*

  seasickness mal di mare, il *(mahl dee MAH-ray)*

  I'm seasick. Ho il mal di mare. *(oh eel mahl dee MAH-ray)*

seaside al mare *(ahl MAH-ray)*

season stagione, la *(stah-JOH-nay)* (le stagioni)

seat (chair) sedia, la/una *(SED-yah)* (le sedie), (e.g., bus) posto, il/un *(POHS-toh)*

aisle seat posto sul corridoio, il/un *(POHS-toh sool kohr-ree-DOH-yoh)*

child seat seggiolino (per bambini), il/un *(sayd-joh-LEE-noh [payr bahm-BEE-nee])*

Is this seat free? È libero questo posto? *(eh LEE-bay-roh KWAYS-toh POHS-toh?)*

window seat posto vicino al finestrino, il/un *(POHS-toh vee-CHEE-noh ahl fee-nays-TREE-noh)*

seatbelt cintura di sicurezza, la/una *(cheen-TOO-rah dee see-koo-RAYT-tsah)*

second (time) secondo, il/un *(say-KOHN-doh)* (i secondi)

second (placement) secondo/a *(say-KOHN-doh/-dah)*

second-class (di) seconda classe, la *([dee] say-KOHN-dah KLAHS-say)*

secretary segretario/a, il/la *(say-gray-TAHR-yoh/-yah)*

security sicurezza, la *(see-koo-RAYT-tsah)*

security deposit cauzione, la/una *(kowt-TSYOH-nay)*

see, to vedere *(vay-DAY-ray)*

self-employed, I'm Lavoro in proprio *(lah-VOH-roh een PROH-pyoh)*

self-service self-service *(self-SEHR-vees)*

self-service station distributore automatico, il *(dees-tree-boo-TOH-ray ow-toh-MAH-tee-koh)*

sell, to vendere *(VEN-day-ray)*

send, to (e-mail, fax) mandare *(mahn-DAH-ray)*

Can you send it overseas? Può spedirlo all'estero? *(pwoh spay-DEER-loh ahl-LES-tay-roh?)*

senior person (age) persona anziana, la/una *(payr-SOH-nah ahn-TSYAH-nah)*

separate/separated separato/a *(say-pah-RAH-toh/-tah)*

separately separatamente *(say-pah-rah-tah-MAYN-tay)*

September settembre *(sayt-TEM-bray)*

series (TV) serie televisiva, la/una *(SEHR-yay tay-lay-vee-ZEE-vah)*

serious serio/a *(SEHR-yoh/-yah)*

serve, to servire *(sayr-VEE-ray)*

service servizio, il *(sayr-VEET-tsyoh)*

service center (on highway) area servizio, l' *f* /un' *(AH-ray-ah sayr-VEET-tsyoh)*

service charge servizio, il *(sayr-VEET-tsyoh)*

service station stazione di servizio, la/una *(staht-TSYOH-nay dee sayr-VEET-tsyoh)*

set-priced meal menù a prezzo fisso, il/un *(may-NOO ah PRET-tsoh FEES-soh)*

set-up, to sistemare *(sees-tay-MAH-ray)*

seven sette *(SET-tay)*

seven hundred settecento *(sayt-tay-CHEN-toh)*

seventeen diciassette *(dee-chahs-SET-tay)*

seventy settanta *(sayt-TAHN-tah)*

  seventy-one settantuno *(sayt-tahn-TOO-noh)*

  seventy-two settantadue *(sayt-tahn-tah-DOO-ay)*

  seventy-three settantatré *(sayt-tahn-tah-TRAY)*

  seventy-four settantaquattro *(sayt-tahn-tah-KWAHT-troh)*

  seventy-five settantacinque *(sayt-tahn-tah-CHEEN-kway)*

  seventy-six settantasei *(sayt-tahn-tah-SEH-ee)*

  seventy-seven settantasette *(sayt-tahn-tah-SET-tay)*

  seventy-eight settantotto *(sayt-tahn-TOHT-toh)*

  seventy-nine sessantanove *(sayt-tahn-tah-NOH-vay)*

several diversi/e *(dee-VEHR-see/-say)*

sew, to cucire *(koo-CHEE-ray)*

sex sesso, il *(SES-soh)*

sexy erotico/a *(ay-ROH-tee-koh/-kah)*

shade/shadow ombra, l' *f (OHM-brah)*

shampoo shampoo, lo/uno *(SHAHM-poo)*

shape forma, la/una *(FOHR-mah)*

sharp (flavor) piccante *(peek-KAHN-tay)*, (point) affilato/a *(ahf-fee-LAH-toh/-tah)*

shave rasatura, la *(rah-sah-TOO-rah)*

shave, to fare la barba *(FAH-ray lah BAHR-bah)*

shaving cream crema da barba, la *(KREH-mah dah BAHR-bah)*

she lei *(LEH-ee)*

sheep pecora, la/una *(PEH-kohr-rah)* (le pecore)

sheet (bed) lenzuolo, il/un *(layn-TSWOH-loh)* (le lenzuola)

  bottom sheet lenzuolo sotto, il/un *(layn-TSWOH-loh SOHT-toh)*

  top sheet lenzuolo sopra, il/un *(layn-TSWOH-loh SOHP-rah)*

shellfish crostacei, i *(krohs-TAH-chay-ee)*

ship nave, la/una *(NAH-vay)*

ship, to spedire *(spay-DEE-ray)*

shipping, surface pacco ordinario, il/un *(pahk-koh ohr-dee-NAH-ryoh)*

shirt camicia, la/una *(kah-MEE-chah)* (le camicie)

shivers brividi, i *(BREE-vee-dee)*

shoe scarpa, la/una *(SKAHR-pah)* (le scarpe)

  shoe store negozio di scarpe, il/un *(nay-GOH-tsyoh dee SKAHR-pay)*

shop negozio, il/un *(nay-GOH-tsyoh)*, bottega, la/una *(boht-TAY-gah)*

shopping center centro commerciale, il/un *(CHEN-troh kohm-mayr-CHAH-lay)*

short (length) corto/a *(KOHR-toh/tah)*, (height) basso/a *(BAHS-soh/-sah)*

short stays periodi brevi, i *(pay-RYOH-dee BREV-ee)*

shorts shorts, gli *(shorts)*, pantaloncini, i *(pahn-tah-lohn-CHEE-nee)*

shot of, a (alcohol) un sorso di *(oon SOHR-soh dee)*

shoulder spalla, la *(SPAHL-lah)* (le spalle)

show (event) spettacolo, lo/uno *(spayt-TAH-koh-loh)*

show, to mostrare *(mohs-TRAH-ray)*

Can you show me ___? Può mostrarmi ___? *(pwoh mohs-TRAHR-mee ___?)*

shower doccia, la/una *(DOHT-chah)* (le docce)

shower facilities servizio doccia, il *(sayr-VEET-tsyoh DOHT-chah)*

shrine santuario, il/un *(sahn-too-AHR-yoh)*

shut chiuso/a *(KYOO-soh/-sah)*

shut, to chiudere *(KYOO-day-ray)*

shy timido/a *(TEE-mee-doh/-dah)*

Sicily Sicilia, la *(see-CHEE-lyah)*

sick malato/a *(mah-LAH-toh/-tah)*

I'm sick Mi sento male *(mee SAYN-toh MAH-lay)*

side lato, il *(LAH-toh)*

on the side a parte *(ah PAHR-tay)*

side dishes contorni, i *(kohn-TOHR-nee)*

sign cartello, il/un *(kahr-TEL-loh)*, segno, il/un *(SAYN-nyoh)*

sign, to firmare *(feer-MAH-ray)*

signal segnale, il/un *(sayn-NYAH-lay)*

signature firma, la/una *(FEER-mah)*

silk seta, la *(SAY-tah)*

silver (metal) argento, l' *m (ahr-JEN-toh)*, (color) argenteo/a *(ahr-JEN-tay-oh/-ah)*

SIM card carta sim, la/una *(KAHR-tah seem)*, SIM card, il/un *(seem kahrd)*

similar simile *(SEE-mee-lay)*

simple semplice *(SAYM-plee-chay)*

since (time) da *(dah)*

sing, to cantare *(kahn-TAH-ray)*

singer cantante, il/la *(kahn-TAHN-tay)*

single singolo/a *(SEEN-goh-loh/-lah)*, (man) celibe *(CHEH-lee-bay)*, (woman) nubile *(NOO-bee-lay)*

single room camera singola, la/una *(KAH-may-rah SEEN-goh-lah)*

sir signore, il/un *(seen-NYOH-ray)*

sister sorella, la/una *(soh-REL-lah)*

sister-in-law cognata, la *(kohn-NYAH-tah)*

sit, to sedere *(say-DAY-ray)*

sit down, to sedersi *(say-DAYR-see)*

site sito, il/un *(SEE-toh)*

six sei *(SEH-ee)*

six hundred seicento *(say-ee-CHEN-toh)*

sixteen sedici *(SAY-dee-chee)*

sixty sessanta *(says-SAHN-tah)*

sixty-one sessantuno *(says-sahn-TOO-noh)*

sixty-two sessantadue *(says-sahn-tah-DOO-ay)*

sixty-three sessantatré *(says-sahn-tah-TRAY)*

sixty-four sessantaquattro *(says-sahn-tah-KWAHT-troh)*

sixty-five sessantacinque *(says-sahn-tah-CHEEN-kway)*

sixty-six sessantasei *(says-sahn-tah-SEH-ee)*

sixty-seven sessantasette *(says-sahn-tah-SET-tay)*

sixty-eight sessantotto *(says-sahn-TOHT-toh)*

sixty-nine sessantanove *(says-sahn-tah-NOH-vay)*

size misura, la *(mee-ZOO-rah)*, dimensioni, le *(dee-mayn-SYOH-nee)*, (clothes) taglia, la *(TAHL-lyah)*

ski sci, lo/uno *(shee)* (gli sci)

  ski lift sciovia, la/una *(shoh-VEE-ah)*

  ski resort stazione sciistica, la/una *(staht-TSYOH-nay shee-EES-tee-kah)*

ski, to sciare *(shee-AH-ray)*

skiing sci, lo *(shee)*

  Alpine skiing sci alpino, lo *(lo shee ahl-PEE-noh)*

  cross-country skiing sci di fondo, lo *(lo shee dee FOHN-doh)*

skillet tegame, il/un *(tay-GAH-may)*

skim milk latte scremato, il *(LAHT-tay skray-MAH-toh)*

skin pelle, la *(PEL-lay)*

skirt gonna, la/una *(GOHN-nah)* (le gonne)

sky cielo, il *(CHEH-loh)*

Skype, to usare Skype *(oo-ZAH-ray skipe)*

slacks pantaloni, i *(pahn-tah-LOH-nee)*

sleep, to dormire *(dohr-MEE-ray)*

  sleeping bag sacco a pelo, il/un *(SAHK-koh ah PAY-loh)*

  sleeping berth cuccetta, la/una *(koot-CHAYT-tah)*

  sleeping car vagone letto, il/un *(vah-GOH-nay LET-toh)*

  sleeping pill sonnifero, il/un *(sohn-NEE-fay-roh)* (i sonniferi)

sleepy, to be avere sonno *(ah-VAY-ray SOHN-noh)*

  I'm sleepy Ho sonno *(oh SOHN-noh)*

slice fetta, la/una *(FAYT-tah)* (le fette)

  by the slice all'taglio *(ahl TAHL-lyoh)*

slope (ski) pista, la *(PEES-tah)*

Slovenia Slovenia, la *(zloh-VEN-yah)*

slow lento/a *(LEN-toh/-tah)*

Slow down, please Rallenti, per favore. *(rahl-LAYN-tee, payr fah-VOH-ray)*

slowly lentamente *(layn-tah-MAYN-tay)*, piano *(pyah-noh)*

small piccolo/a *(PEEK-koh-loh/-lah)*

smell odore, l' *m/un *(oh-DOH-ray)*

smile sorriso, il/un *(sohr-REE-soh)*

smile, to sorridere *(sohr-REE-day-ray)*

smoke, to fumare *(foo-MAH-ray)*

smoked (food) fumicato/a *(foo-mee-KAH-toh/-tah)*

smoking fumare, il *(foo-MAH-ray)*, fumo, il *(FOO-moh)*

snack spuntino, lo/uno *(spoon-TEE-noh)*

  afternoon snack merenda, la *(may-REN-dah)*

  snack bar snack-bar, lo/uno *(SNEK-bahr)*, tavola calda/fredda, la/una *(TAH-voh-lah KAHL-dah/FRAYD-dah)*

snail lumaca, la/una *(loo-MAH-kah)* (le lumache)

snake serpente, il/un *(sayr-PEN-tay)* (i serpenti)

snorkel boccaglio, il/un *(bohk-KAHL-lyoh)*

snorkelling snorkelling *(snohr-kayl-LEENG)*

snow neve, la *(NAY-vay)*

  It's snowing nevica *(NAY-vee-kah)*

snowboarding surf da neve, il *(soorf dah NAY-vay)*

snow chains catene da neve, le *(kah-TAY-nay dah NAY-vay)*

soap sapone, il *(sah-POH-nay)*

  bar of soap saponetta, la/una *(sah-poh-NAYT-tah)*

soap opera telenovela, la/una *(tay-lay-noh-VEH-lah)*

soccer calcio, il *(KAHL-choh)*

sock calzino, il/un *(kahl-TSEE-noh)* (i calzini)

soda pop bibita frizzante, la/una *(BEE-bee-tah freed-ZAHN-tay)*

soft molle *(MOHL-lay)*, morbido/a *(MOHR-bee-doh/-dah)*

soft drink bibita frizzante, la/una *(BEE-bee-tah freed-ZAHN-tay)*

softly piano/a *(PYAH-noh/-nah)*

software software, il *(SOHFT-weh-uh)*

soldier soldato, il/un *(sohl-DAH-toh)* (i soldati)

some alcuni/e (plural) *(ahl-KOO-nee/-nay)*

someone qualcuno/a *(kwahl-KOO-noh/-nah)*

something qualcosa *(kwahl-KOH-sah)*

sometimes a volte *(ah VOHL-tay)*

son figlio, il/un *(FEEL-lyoh)* (i figli)

  my son mio figlio *(MEE-oh FEEL-lyoh)*

  son-in-law genero, il *(JEH-nay-roh)*

song canzone, la/una *(kahn-TSOH-nay)* (i canzoni)

soon presto *(PRES-toh)*, fra poco *(frah POH-koh)*

sore doloroso/a *(doh-loh-ROH-soh/-sah)*

sorry, I'm mi dispiace *(mee dees-PYAH-chay)*

soup zuppa, la/una *(TSOO-pah)* (le zuppe), minestra, la/una *(mee-NES-trah)* (le minestre)

  soup of the day zuppa del giorno, la *(TSOO-pah dayl JOHR-noh)*

sour acido/a *(AH-chee-doh/-dah)*

  sour cream panna acida, la *(PAHN-nah AH-cee-dah)*

south sud *(sood)*

  (to the) south (of) (a) sud (di) *([ah] sood [dee])*

souvenir ricordino, il/un *(ree-kohr-DEE-noh)* (i ricordini)

  souvenir shop negozio di souvenir, il/un *(nay-GOH-tsyoh dee soo-vah-NEER)*

soy soia, le *(SOH-yah)*

  soy milk latte di soia, il *(LAHT-tay day SOH-yah)*

  soy sauce salsa di soia, la *(SAHL-sah dee SOH-yah)*

spa (thermal baths) terme, le *(TEHR-may)*

space spazio, lo *(SPAHT-tsyoh)*

spade vanga, la/una *(VAHN-gah)*

spaghetti spaghetti, gli *(spah-GAYT-tee)*

Spain Spagna, la *(SPAHN-nyah)*

speak, to parlare *(pahr-LAHR-ay)*

  Do you speak? parla? *(PAHR-lah)*

  I speak parlo *(PAHR-loh)*

special speciale *(spay-CHAH-lay)*

  special offer offerta speciale, l' *f* /un' *(ohf-FEHR-tah spay-CHAH-lay)*, in offerta *(een ohf-FEHR-tah)*

specialist specialista, il/la *(spay-chah-LEES-tah)*

speed velocità, la *(vay-loh-chee-TAH)*

  speed limit limite di velocità, il *(LEE-mee-tay dee vay-loh-chee-TAH)*

speeding eccesso di velocità *(ayt-CHES-soh dee vay-loh-chee-TAH)*

speedometer tachimetro, il *(tah-KEE-may-troh)*

spend, to spendere *(SPEN-day-ray)*

spicy piccante *(peek-KAHN-tay)*

spider ragno, il/un *(RAHN-nyoh)* (i ragni)

spinach spinaci, gli *(spee-NAH-chee)*

splendid splendido/a *(SPLEN-dee-doh/-dah)*

spoon cucchiaio, il/un *(kook-KYAH-yoh)* (i cucchiai)

sport sport, lo *(spohrt)*

  sports store negozio di articoli, il/un *(nay-GOH-tsyoh dee ahr-TEE-koh-lee)*

sprain storta, la/una *(STOHR-tah)*

spring (season) primavera, la *(pree-mah-VEH-rah)*

square (town) piazza, la/una *(PYAHT-tsah)*

stadium stadio, lo/uno *(STAH-dyoh)*

stain, to macchiare *(mahk-KYAH-ray)*

I stained ___. Ho macchiato ___. *(oh mahk-KYAH-toh ___.)*

stairs scale, le *(SKAH-lay)*

stamp francobollo, il/un *(frahn-koh-BOH-loh)* (i francobolli)

stamp, to timbrare *(teem-BRAH-ray)*

stand-by list lista d'attesa, la/una *(LEES-tah daht-TAY-sah)*

start, to cominciare *(koh-meen-CHAH-ray)*

station stazione, la/una *(staht-TSYOH-nay)*

  Which station is next? Che stazione è prossima? *(kay staht-TSYOH-nay eh PROHS-see-mah?)*

  Which station is this? Che stazione è questa? *(kay staht-TSYOH-nay eh KWAYS-tah?)*

statue statua, la/una *(STAH-too-ah)*

stay, to (=lodge) alloggiare *(ahl-lohd-JAH-ray)*, fermarsi *(fayr-MAHR-see)*

steak bistecca, la *(bee-STAYK-kah)*

steal, to rubare *(roo-BAH-ray)*

steamed cotto/a a vapore *(KOHT-toh/-tah ah vah-POH-ray)*

steep ripido/a *(REE-pee-doh/-dah)*

step gradino, il *(grah-DEE-noh)* (i gradini)

stew stufato, lo/uno *(stoo-FAH-toh)*

stingy avaro/a *(ah-VAH-roh/-rah)*

Stockholm Stoccolma *(stohk-KOHL-mah)*

stocking calza, la/una *(KAHL-tsah)* (le calze)

stolen rubato/a *(roo-BAH-toh/-tah)*

stomach stomaco, lo *(STOH-mah-koh)*

  stomachache mal di stomaco, il/un *(mahl dee STOH-mah-koh)*

stop (e.g., bus) fermata, la/una *(fayr-MAH-tah)*

  the next stop la prossima fermata *(lah PROHS-see-mah fayr-MAH-tah)*

stop, to fermare *(fayr-MAH-ray)*, fermarsi *(fayr-MAHR-see)*

  stop! fermi! *(FAYR-mee!)*, fermo! *(FAYR-moh!)*

  Stop here, please. Si fermi qui. *(see FAYR-mee kwee)*

store/shop negozio, il/un *(nay-GOHT-tsyoh)* (i negozi)

storm temporale, il/un *(taym-poh-RAH-lay)*

stove stufa, la/una *(STOO-fah)*

straight diritto/a *(dee-REET-toh/-tah)*, (alcohol) liscio/a *(LEE-shoh/-shah)*

straight ahead dritto *(DREET-toh)*

strange strano/a *(STRAH-noh/-nah)*

stranger sconosciuto/a *(skoh-nohsh-SHOO-toh/-tah)*

strawberry fragola, la/una *(FRAH-goh-lah)* (i fragole)

stream ruscello, il/un *(roosh-SHEL-loh)*

street via, la *(VEE-ah)*, viale, il *(vee-AH-lay)*, strada, la *(STRAH-dah)*

streetcar tram, il/un *(trahm)*

strike sciopero, lo/uno *(SHOH-pay-roh)*

on strike in sciopero *(een SHOH-pay-roh)*

string spago, lo/uno *(SPAH-goh)*

stroller (baby) passeggino, il *(pahs-sayd-JEE-noh)*

strong forte *(FOHR-tay)*

student studente/essa, lo/la *(stoo-DEN-tay/stoo-dayn-TAYS-sah)*

students studenti, i *(stoo-DEN-tee)*

student's ticket biglietto per studenti, il/un *(beel-LYAYT-toh payr stoo-DEN-tee)*

studio studio, lo/uno *(STOO-dyoh)*

study, to studiare *(stoo-DYAH-ray)*

I'm studying ___. Sto studiando ___. *(stoh stoo-DYAHN-doh)*

What are you studying? Cosa studia? *(KOH-sah STOO-dyah?)*, (informal) Cosa studi? *(KOH-sah STOO-dee?)*

stupendous stupendo/a *(stoo-PEN-doh/-dah)*

stupid stupido/a *(STOO-pee-doh/-dah)*

style stile, lo *(STEE-lay)*

subtitles sottotitoli, i *(soht-toh-TEE-toh-lee)*

subtract, to sottrarre *(soht-TRAHR-ray)*

suburb quartiere, il/un *(kwahr-TYEH-ray)*

subway metropolitana, la *(may-troh-poh-lee-TAH-nah)*, metro, il *(MEH-troh)*

sugar zucchero, lo *(TSOO-kay-roh)*

suitcase valigia, la/una *(vah-LEEJ-jah)* (le valigie)

sulfur zolfo, lo *(TSOHL-foh)*

summer estate, l' *f (ays-TAH-tay)*

sun sole, il *(SOH-lay)*

sun umbrella ombrellone, l' *m/un (ohm-brayl-LOH-nay)*

sunblock crema solare, la/una *(KREH-mah soh-LAH-ray)*

sunburn scottatura, la/una *(skoht-tah-TOO-rah)*

Sunday domenica, la *(doh-MAY-nee-kah)*

sunglasses occhiali da sole, gli *(oh-KYAH-lee dah SOH-lay)*

sunny, it's c'è il sole *(cheh eel SOH-lay)*

sunrise alba, l' *f (AHL-bah)*

sunscreen crema solare protettiva, la/una *(KREH-mah soh-LAH-ray proh-tayt-TEE-vah)*

sunset tramonto, il *(trah-MOHN-toh)*

suntan cream crema solare, la/una *(KREH-mah soh-LAH-ray)*

suntan oil olio solare, l' *m (OHL-yoh soh-LAH-ray)*

sun umbrella ombrellone, l' *m/un (ohm-brayl-LOH-nay)*

supermarket supermercato, il/un *(soo-payr-mayr-KAH-toh)*

supper cena, la *(CHAY-nah)*

supplement (e.g., train ticket) supplemento, il/un *(soop-play-MAYN-toh)*

supplementary supplemento/a *(soo-play-MAYN-toh/-tah)*

supplies provviste, le *(prohv-VEES-tay)*

sure certo *(CHEHR-toh)*

surface mail posta ordinaria, la *(POHS-tah ohr-dee-NAHR-yah)*

surface shipping pacco ordinario, il/un *(pahk-koh ohr-dee-NAH-ryoh)*

surname cognome, il *(kohn-NYOH-may)*

surprise sorpresa, la/una *(soh-PRAY-sah)*

suspended sospeso/a *(sohs-PAY-soh/-sah)*

sweater maglione, il/un *(mahl-LYOH-nay)*

sweatshirt felpa, la/una *(FAYL-pah)* (le felpe)

Sweden Svezia, la *(ZVET-syah)*

sweet dolce *(DOHL-chay)*

swelling gonfiore, il *(gohn-FYOH-ray)*

swim, to nuotare *(nwoh-TAH-ray)*

swimming nuotare *(nwoh-TAH-ray)*
  no swimming vietato nuotare *(vyay-TAH-toh nwoh-TAH-ray)*
  swimming pool piscina, la/una *(peesh-SHEE-nah)*

swimsuit costume da bagno, il/un *(kohs-TOO-may dah BAHN-nyoh)*

Switzerland Svizzera, la *(ZVEET-tsay-rah)*

synagogue sinagoga, la/una *(see-nah-GOH-gah)*

synthetic sintetico/a *(seen-TEH-tee-koh/-kah)*

syringe siringa, la/una *(see-REEN-gah)* (le siringhe)

T

T, t T, t *(tee)*

table tavola, la/una *(TAH-voh-lah)* (le tavole)

tablecloth tovaglia, la/una *(toh-VAHL-lyah)*

table tennis ping-pong, il *(peeng-PONG)*

tailor sarto, il *(SAHR-toh)*

take, to prendere *(PREN-day-ray)*
  I'll take it lo/la prendo *(loh/lah PREN-doh)*
  you take prenda *(PREN-dah)*

take, to (transport) portare *(pohr-TAH-ray)*
  take me to ___ mi porti a ___ *(mee POHR-tee ah ___)*

take-away/take-out (e.g., food) da asporto *(dah ahs-POHR-toh)*

talk, to parlare *(pahr-LAH-ray)*

tall alto/a *(AHL-toh/-tah)*

tampon tampone, il/un *(tahm-POH-nay)* (i tamponi), assorbente interno, l' *m*/un *(ahs-sohr-BEN-tay een-TEHR-noh)*

tan, to abbronzare *(ahb-brohn-DZAH-ray)*

tap, on alla spina *(AHL-lah SPEE-nah)*
  tap water acqua del rubinetto, l' *f* *(AHK-kwah dayl roo-bee-NAYT-toh)*

tapestry tappezzeria, la/una *(tahp-payt-tsay-REE-ah)*

taste sapore, il *(sah-POH-ray)*

It tastes good/bad ha un buon/cattivo sapore *(ah oon bwohn/kaht-TEE-voh sah-POH-ray)*

taste, to (= try something) assaggiare *(ahs-ahd-JAH-ray)*

tasty gustoso/a *(goos-TOH-soh/-sah)*

tax tassa, la *(TAHS-sah)*

taxi taxi, il/un *(TAHK-see)*, tassì, il/un *(tahs-SEE)*

by taxi con il taxi/tassì *(kohn eel TAHK-see/tahs-SEE)*

taxi meter tassametro, il *(tahs-SAH-may-troh)*

taxi stand posteggio dei tassi, il *(pohs-TAYD-joh DAY-ee tahs-SEE)*

tea tè, il *(tay)*

teach, to istruire *(ees-troo-EE-ray)*

teacher insegnante, l'/l' *m/f* *(een-sayn-NYAHN-tay)*

team squadra, la/una *(SKWAH-drah)*

teaspoon cucchiaino, il/un *(kook-kyah-EE-noh)* (i cucchiaini)

technique tecnica, la/una *(TEK-nee-kah)*

teeth denti, i *(DEN-tee)*

telegram telegramma, il/un *(tay-lay-GRAHM-mah)*

telephone telefono, il/un *(tay-LEH-foh-noh)*

telephone, to telefonare *(tay-lay-fohn-NAH-ray)*

television televisione, la *(tay-lay-vee-SYOH-nay)*, (set) televisore, il *(tay-lay-vee-ZOH-ray)*,

tell me mi dica (also=May I help you?) *(mee DEE-kah)*

temperature temperatura, la *(taym-pay-rah-TOO-rah)*

temple tempio, il/un *(TEM-pyoh)*

ten dieci *(DYEH-chee)*

tennis tennis, il *(TEN-nees)*

tennis court campo da tennis, il/un *(KAHM-poh dah TEN-nees)*

tent tenda, la/una *(TEN-dah)* (le tende)

terrible terribile *(tayr-REE-bee-lay)*

terrific fantastico/a *(fahn-TAHS-tee-koh/-kah)*

test esame, l' *m*/un *(ay-ZAH-may)*

tetanus tetano, il *(TEH-tah-noh)*

thank, to ringraziare *(reen-graht-TSYAH-ray)*

thank you (very much) (mille) grazie *([MEEL-lay] GRAHT-tsyay or GRAHT-tsee)*

that (thing) quello/a *(KWAYL-loh/-lah)*

that's all è tutto *(eh TOOT-toh)*

that's it a posto *(ah POHS-toh)*

theater teatro, il/un *(tay-AH-troh)*

movie theater cinema, il/un *(CHEE-nay-mah)*

theft furto, il/un *(FOOR-toh)*

then poi *(poy)*

there là *(lah)*

there are ecco! *(EK-koh) [= here (they) are!]*; ci sono *(chee SOH-noh) [= there are, there exist]*

there is ecco! *(EK-koh) [= here (it) is!]*; c'è *(cheh) [= there is, there exists]*

they loro *(LOH-roh)*

thick spesso/a *(SPAYS-soh/-sah)*

thief ladro, il/un *(LAH-droh/-drah)*

thin magro/a *(MAH-groh/-grah)*

thing cosa, la/una *(KOH-sah)*

think, to pensare *(payn-SAH-ray)*

  I think penso *(PAYN-soh)*

  I think so penso di si *(PAYN-soh dee see)*

  I don't think so penso di no *(PAYN-soh dee noh)*

third terzo/a *(TEHR-tsoh/-tsah)*

  one-/a third un terzo *(oon TEHR-tsoh)*

  two-thirds due terzi *(DOO-ay TEHR-tsee)*

thirst sete, la *(SAY-tay)*

  to "have" thirst (=to be thirsty) avere sete *(ah-VAY-ray SAY-tay)*

  I'm thirsty. Ho sete. *(oh SAY-tay)*

thirteen tredici *(TRAY-dee-chee)*

thirty trenta *(TRAYN-tah)*

  thirty-one trentuno *(trayn-TOO-noh)*

  thirty-two trentadue *(trayn-tah-DOO-ay)*

  thirty-three trentatré *(trayn-tah-TRAY)*

  thirty-four trentaquattro *(trayn-tah-KWAHT-troh)*

  thirty-five trentacinque *(trayn-tah-CHEEN-kway)*

  thirty-six trentasei *(trayn-tah-SEH-ee)*

  thirty-seven trentasette *(trayn-tah-SET-tay)*

  thirty-eight trentotto *(trayn-TOHT-toh)*

  thirty-nine trentanove *(trayn-tah-NOH-vay)*

this questo/a *(KWAYS-toh/-tah)*

thousand mille *(MEEL-lay)*

thread (fabric) filo, il *(FEE-loh)*

three tre *(tray)*

three hundred trecento *(tray-CHEN-toh)*

throat gola, la *(GOH-lah)*

throw, to gettare *(jayt-TAH-ray)*

Thursday giovedì *(joh-vay-DEE)*

Tiber Tevere, il *(TAY-vay-ray)*

ticket biglietto, il/un *(beel-LYAYT-toh) (i biglietti)*

  child's ticket biglietto per bambini, il *(beel-LYAYT-toh payr bahm-BEE-nee)*

  for one ride biglietto ordinario, il/un *(beel-LYAYT-toh ohr-dee-NAH-ryoh)*

  one-way ticket biglietto di sola andata, il/un *(beel-LYAYT-toh dee SOH-lah ahn-DAH-tah)*

  return (two-way) ticket biglietto di andata e ritorno, il/un *(beel-LYAYT-toh dee ahn-DAH-tah ay ree-TOHR-noh)*

  student's ticket biglietto per studenti, il/un *(beel-LYAYT-toh payr stoo-DEN-tee)*

ticket collector controllore, il *(kohn-trohl-LOH-ray)*

ticket machine distributore automatico di biglietti, il/un *(dees-tree-boo-TOH-ray ow-toh-MAH-tee-koh dee beel-LYAYT-tee)*

ticket office biglietteria, la *(beel-lyayt-tay-REE-ah)*

ticket vendor biglietteria, la *(beel-lyayt-tay-REE-ah)*

tide marea, la *(mah-REH-ah)*

tie cravatta, la/una *(krah-VAHT-tah)* (le cravatte)

tight stretto/a *(STRAYT-toh/-tah)*

till a *(ah)*

till tomorrow a domani *(ah doh-MAH-nee)*

time tempo, il *(TEM-poh)*

at what time? a che ora? *(ah kay OH-rah?)*

time difference differenza di fuso orario, la *(deef-fay-REN-tsah dee FOO-soh oh-RAH-ryoh)*

timetable orario, l' *m*/un *(oh-RAH-ryoh)*

tiny minuscolo/a *(mee-NOOS-koh-loh/-lah)*

tip (money) mancia, la *(MAHN-chah)*

tire (car) gomma, la/una *(GOHM-mah)* (le gomme), pneumatico, lo/uno *(pnay-oo-MAH-tee-koh)*

flat tire gomma bucata, la/una *(GOHM-mah boo-KAH-tah)*

tire pressure pressione delle gomme, la *(prays-SYOH-nay DAYL-lay GOHM-may)*

tired stanco/a *(STAHN-koh/-kah)*

tissue fazzoletto, il/un *(faht-tsoh-LAYT-toh)*

facial tissues fazzoletti di carta, i *(faht-tsoh-LAYT-tee dee KAHR-tah)*

to a *(ah)*, (flight/airmail/train) per *(payr)*

to Milan/the United States per Milano/gli Stati Uniti

toast pane tostato, il *(PAH-nay tohs-TAH-toh)*

toaster tostapane, il/un *(tohs-tah-PAH-nay)*

tobacco tabacco, il *(tah-BAHK-koh)*

tobacconist's shop tabaccheria, la/una *(tah-bahk-kay-REE-ah)*, tabaccaio, il/un *(tah-bah-KAH-yoh)*

today oggi *(OH-jee)*

toe dito del piede, il/un *(DEE-toh dayl PYEH-day)* (le dita)

together (as in the bill) unico/a *(OO-nee-koh/-kah)*, insieme *(een-SYEH-may)*

to-go (food) da asporto *(dah ahs-POHR-toh)*

toilet toilette, la *(twah-LET)*, toeletta, la *(toh-ay-LET-tah)*, gabinetto, il *(gah-bee-NAYT-toh)*

public toilets servizi igienici, i *(sayr-VEET-tsee ee-JEH-nee-chee)*

Where are the toilets? Dove sono i gabinetti? *(DOH-vay SOH-noh ee gah-bee-NAYT-tee?)*

toilet paper carta igienica, la *(KAHR-tah ee-JEH-nee-kah)*

token gettone, il/un *(jayt-TOH-nay)* (i gettoni)

  some tokens dei gettoni *(DAY-ee jayt-TOH-nee)*

toll (on road) pedaggio, il *(pay-DAHD-joh)*

  toll-free number numero verde, il/un *(NOO-may-roh VAYR-day)*

tomato pomodoro, il/un *(poh-moh-DOH-roh)*

  tomato juice succo di pomodoro, il *(SOOK-koh dee poh-moh-DOH-roh)*

  tomato sauce salsa di pomodoro, la *(SAHL-sah dee poh-moh-DOH-roh)*

tomorrow domani *(doh-MAH-nee)*

  day after tomorrow dopodomani *(doh-poh-doh-MAH-nee)*

  tomorrow afternoon domani pomeriggio *(doh-MAH-nee poh-may-REED-joh)*

  tomorrow evening domani sera *(doh-MAH-nee SAY-rah)*

  tomorrow morning domani mattina *(doh-MAH-nee maht-TEE-nah)*

tonight questa notte *(KWAYS-tah NOHT-tay)*, stasera *(stah-SAY-rah)*

tonsil tonsilla, la *(tohn-SEEL-lay)* (le tonsille)

too (=also) anche *(AHN-kay)*

  too many troppi/e *(TROHP-pee/-pay)*

too much troppo *(TROHP-poh)*

tooth dente, il *(DEN-tay)* (i denti)

toothache mal di denti, il/un *(mahl dee DEN-tee)*

toothbrush spazzolino da denti, lo/uno *(spaht-tsoh-LEE-noh dah DEN-tee)*

toothpaste dentifricio, il/un *(dayn-tee-FREE-choh)*

toothpick stuzzicadenti, lo/uno *(stoot-tsee-kah-DEN-tee)*

touch, to toccare *(tohk-KAH-ray)*

  don't touch! non toccare! *(nohn tohk-KAH-ray)*

tour gita turistica, la *(JEE-tah too-REES-tee-kah)*

tourist turista, il/la *(too-REES-tah)*

  tourist information office ufficio turistico, l' *m*/un *(oof-FEE-choh too-REES-tee-koh)*

towel asciugamano, l' *m*/un *(ahsh-shoo-gah-MAH-noh)* (gli asciugamani)

tower torre, la/una *(TOHR-ray)*

town hall municipio, il *(moo-nee-CHEE-pyoh)*

town square piazza principale, la *(PYAHT-tsah preen-chee-PAH-lay)*

toystore negozio di giocattoli, il/un *(nay-GOHT-syoh dee joh-KAHT-toh-lee)*

track (train) binario, il *(bee-NAH-ryoh)*, (path) sentiero, il *(sayn-TYEH-roh)*

trade commercio, il *(kohm-MEHR-choh)*

trade fair fiera commerciale, la/una *(FYEH-rah kohm-mayr-CHAH-lay)*

traditional tradizionale *(trah-dee-tsyoh-NAH-lay)*

traffic traffico, il *(TRAHF-fee-koh)*

traffic jam ingorgo (del traffico), l' *m*/un *(een-GOHR-goh [dayl TRAHF-fee-koh])*

traffic light semaforo, il/un *(say-MAH-foh-roh)*

  at the traffic light al semaforo *(ahl say-MAH-foh-roh)*

trail pista, il *(PEE-stah)*

train treno, il/un *(TREH-noh)*

  by train con il treno *(kohn eel TREH-noh)*

  Do I have to change trains? Devo cambiare treno? *(DAY-voh kahm-BYAH-ray TREH-noh?)*

  train car vagone di treno, il *(vah-GOH-nay dee TREH-noh)*

  train information informazioni treni *(een-fohr-maht-TSYOH-nay TREH-nee)*

  train platform binario, il *(bee-NAHR-yoh)*

  train station stazione ferroviaria, la *(staht-TSYOH-nay fayr-roh-VYAH-ryah)*

  train ticket biglietto, il/un *(beel-LYAYT-toh)* (i biglietti)

  train track binario, il *(bee-NAHR-yoh)* (i binari)

tram tram, il/un *(trahm)*

transfer, to (e.g., electronically) trasferire *(trahs-fay-REE-ray)*

  to transfer money trasferire soldi *(trahs-fay-REE-ray SOHL-dee)*

transit, in in transito *(een TRAHN-see-toh)*

translate, to tradurre *(trah-DOOR-ray)*

transportation trasporto, il *(trahs-POHR-toh)*

travel viaggio, il *(vee-AHD-joh)*

travel, to viaggiare *(vee-ahd-JAH-ray)*

travel agency agenzia di viaggi, l' *f*/un' *(ah-jayn-TSEE-ah dee vee-AHD-jee)*

traveler viaggiatore/trice, il/la *(vee-ahd-jah-TOH-ray/-TREE-chay)*

traveler's check assegno turistico, l' *m*/un *(ahs-SAYN-nyoh too-REES-tee-koh)* (gli assegni), assegno di viaggio, il/un *m* *(ahs-SAYN-nyoh dee vee-AHD-joh)*

traveling viaggare, il *(vee-ahd-JAH-ray)*

tree albero, l' *m*/un *(AHL-bay-roh)* (gli alberi)

trip viaggio, il/un *(vee-AHD-joh)*, gita, la/una *(JEE-tah)*

triple room camera tripla, la/una *(KAH-may-rah TREEP-lah)*

trout trota, la *(TROH-tah)*

truck camion, il/un *(KAH-myohn)*

true vero/a *(VAY-roh/-rah)*

try, to (attempt) provare *(proh-VAH-ray)*

try on, to provare *(proh-VAH-ray)*
  Can I try it on? Posso provarmelo/a? *(POHS-soh proh-vahr-may-loh/lah?)*

T-shirt T-shirt, la/una *(TEE-shirt)*, maglietta, la/una *(mahl-LYAYT-tah)*

Tuesday martedì *(mahr-tay-DEE)*

tuna tonno, il *(TOHN-noh)*

tune melodia, la *(may-loh-DEE-ah)*

tunnel galleria, la *(gahl-lay-REE-ah)*

Turin Torino *(toh-REE-noh)*

turkey tacchino, il/un *(tahk-KEE-noh)*

turn, to girare *(jee-RAH-ray)*
  Turn ___. Giri ___. *(JEE-ree __)*

turquoise azzurro/a *(ahd-DZOOR-roh/-rah)*

Tuscany Toscana, la *(tohs-KAH-nah)*

TV TV, la *(tee-VOO)*, (set) televisore, il *(tay-lay-vee-ZOH-ray)*

tweezers pinzette, le *(peen-TSAYT-tay)*

twelve dodici *(DOH-dee-chee)*

twenty venti *(VAYN-tee)*
  twenty-one ventuno *(vayn-TOO-noh)*
  twenty-two ventidue *(vayn-tee-DOO-ay)*
  twenty-three ventitré *(vayn-tee-TRAY)*
  twenty-four ventiquattro *(vayn-tee-KWAHT-troh)*
  twenty-five venticinque *(vayn-tee-CHEEN-kway)*
  twenty-six ventisei *(vayn-tee-SEH-ee)*
  twenty-seven ventisette *(vayn-tee-SET-tay)*
  twenty-eight ventotto *(vayn-TOHT-toh)*
  twenty-nine ventinove *(vayn-tee-NOH-vay)*

twice due volte *(DOO-ay VOHL-tay)*

twin beds due letti *(DOO-ay LET-tee)*, letti separati *(LET-tee say-pah-RAH-tee)*

twins gemelli/e, i/le *(jay-MEL-lee/-lay)*

two due *(DOO-ay)*

two hundred duecento *(doo-ay-CHEN-toh)*

type tipo/a, il/la *(TEE-poh/-pah)*

typical tipico/a *(TEE-pee-koh/-kah)*

Tyrrhenian Sea mar Tirreno, il *(mahr teer-REH-noh)*

U

U, u U, u *(oo)*

ugly brutto/a *(BROOT-toh/-tah)*

umbrella ombrello, l' *m*/un *(ohm-BREL-loh)*

uncle zio, lo *(TSEE-oh)*

uncomfortable scomodo/a *(SKOH-moh-doh/-dah)*

under sotto *(SOHT-toh)*

underpants mutande, le *(moo-TAHN-day)*

underpass sottopassaggio, il/un *(soht-toh-pahs-SAHD-joh)*

undershirt maglietta, la/una *(mahl-LYAYT-tah)*

understand, to capire *(kah-PEE-ray)*

  I understand capisco *(kah-PEES-koh)*

  I don't understand non capisco *(nohn kah-PEES-koh)*

  Do you understand? Capisce? *(kah-PEESH-shay?)*

  We understand capiamo *(kah-PYAH-moh)*

underwear mutande, le *(moo-TAHN-day)*

undo, to disfare *(dees-FAH-ray)*

unemployed disoccupato/a *(deez-ohk-koo-PAH-toh/-tah)*

unfurnished non ammobiliato/a *(nohn ahm-moh-bee-LYAH-toh/-tah)*

United States, the Stati Uniti, gli *(STAH-tee oo-NEE-tee)*

  to the United States per gli Stati Uniti *(payr lyee STAH-tee oo-NEE-tee)*

university università, la/una *(oo-nee-vayr-see-TAH)*

unleaded (gas) senza piombo *(SEHN-tsah PYOHM-boh)*, benzina verde, la *(bayn-DZEE-nah VAYR-day)*

unsafe pericoloso/a *(pay-ree-koh-LOH-soh/-sah)*

until a *(ah)*

up su *(soo)*

upfront (=in advance) in anticipo *(een ahn-TEE-chee-poh)*

uphill in salita *(een sah-LEE-tah)*

urban urbana *(oor-BAH-nah)*

urgent urgente *(oor-JEN-tay)*

USA U.S.A. *(OO-zah)*, Stati Uniti, gli *(STAH-tee oo-NEE-tee)*

use, to usare *(oo-ZAH-ray)*

  Can I use ___? Posso usare ___? *(POHS-soh oo-ZAH-ray)*

use up, to esaurire *(ay-zow-REE-ray)*

  I have used up ___. Ho esaurito ___. *(oh ay-zow-REE-toh ___)*

  We have used up ___. Abbiamo esaurito ___. *(ahb-BYAH-moh ay-zow-REE-toh ___)*

  You have used up ___. Ha esaurito ___. *(ah ay-zow-REE-toh ___)*

used to, to get abituarsi *(ah-bee-too-AHR-see)*

useful utile *(OO-tee-lay)*

V

V, v V, v *(voo)*

vacancy, no completo/a *(kohm-PLEH-toh/-tah)*

vacant libero/a *(LEE-bay-roh/-rah)*

vacation vacanza, la/una *(vah-KAHN-tsah)*

  on vacation in vacanza *(een vah-KAHN-tsah)*

vaccination vaccinazione, la/una *(vaht-chee-naht-TSYOH-nay)*

vagina vagina, la *(vah-JEE-nah)*

validate, to convalidare *(kohn-vah-lee-DAH-ray)*

valley valle, la/una *(VAHL-lay)*

valuable prezioso/a *(prayt-TSYOH-soh/-sah)*

valuables oggetti di valore, gli *(ohd-JET-tee dee vah-LOH-ray)*

value valore, il *(vah-LOH-ray)*

van furgone, il/un *(foor-GOH-nay)*

vanilla vaniglia *(vah-NEEL-lyah)*, (ice cream) crema *(KREH-mah)*

vanish, to svanire *(zvah-NEE-ray)*

Vatican, the Vaticano, il *(vah-tee-KAH-noh)*

veal vitello, il *(vee-TEL-loh)*

vegan vegetaliano/a *(vay-jay-tah-LYAH-noh/-nah)*

vegetable verdura, la *(vayr-DOO-rah)* (le verdure)

mixed vegetables verdura mista , la *(vayr-DOO-rah MEES-tah)*

vegetable accompaniment contorni, i *(kohn-TOHR-nee)*

vegetable soup minestrone, il *(mee-nays-TROH-nay)*

vegetarian vegetariano/a *(vay-jay-tah-RYAH-noh/nah)*

vegetarian restaurant ristorante vegetariano, il/un *(ree-stoh-RAHN-tay vay-jay-tah-RYAH-noh)*

vehicle macchina, la/una *(MAHK-kee-nah)*, veicolo, il/un *(vay-EE-koh-loh)*

Venice Venezia *(vay-NAYT-tsyah)*

venue locale, il/un *(loh-KAH-lay)*

very molto/a *(MOHL-toh/-tah)*

video video, il/un *(VEE-day-oh)*

video camera videocamera, la/una *(vee-day-oh-KAH-may-rah)*

video cassette videocassetta, la/una *(vee-day-oh-kahs-SAYT-tah)*

video tape videonastro, il/un *(vee-day-oh-NAHS-troh)*

view vista, la/una *(VEES-tah)*

villa villa, la/una *(VEEL-lah)* (le ville)

village villaggio, il/un *(veel-LAHD-joh)*

vinegar aceto, l' *m (ah-CHAY-toh)*

vineyard vigneto, il/un *(veen-NYAY-toh)*

virus virus, il/un *(VEE-roos)*

visa visto, il/un *(VEES-toh)*

visit visita, la/una *(VEE-zee-tah)*

visit, to visitare *(vee-zee-TAH-ray)*

vitamins vitamine, le *(vee-tah-MEE-nay)*

voice voce, la *(VOH-chay)*

voice mail segreteria telefonica, la *(say-gray-tay-REE-ah tay-lay-FOH-nee-kah)*

volleyball pallavolo, la *(pahl-lah –VOH-loh)*

vomit, to vomitare *(voh-mee-TAH-ray)*

vomiting vomito, il *(VOH-mee-toh)*

vote, to votare *(voh-TAH-ray)*

voyage viaggio, il/un *(vee-AHD-joh)*

W

W, w w, w *(DOHP-pyoh voo)*

wait, to attendere *(aht-TEN-day-ray)*

  I wait attendo *(aht-TEN-doh)*

  you wait attende *(aht-TEN-day)*

wait for, to aspettare *(ahs-payt-TAH/-ray)*

  he/she/it waits for aspetta *(ahs-PAYT-tah)*

  I wait for aspetto *(ahs-PAYT-toh)*

  you wait for aspetta *(ahs-PAYT-tah)*

  Wait a moment un attimo solo *(oon AHT-tee-moh SOH-loh)*

  Wait here, please. Mi aspetti qui. *(mee ahs-PET-tee kwee)*

waiter/waitress cameriere/a, il/la *(kah-may-RYEH-ray/-rah)*

  waiter! cameriere! *(kah-may-RYEH-ray)*, signore! *(seen-NYOH-ray)*

  waitress! cameriera! *(kah-may-RYEH-rah)*, signora! *(seen-NYOH-rah)*

waiting room sala d'attesa, la *(SAH-lah daht-TAY-sah)*

wake up, to svegliare *(zvah-LYAH-ray)*

  Wake me at ___. Mi svegli alle ___. *(mee ZYAYL-lyee AHL-lay ___.)*

Wales Galles, il *(GAHL-lays)*

walk passeggiata, la/una *(pahs-sayd-JAH-tah)*

  to take a walk fare una passeggiata *(FAH-ray OO-nah pahs-sayd-JAH-tah)*

walk, to camminare *(kahm-mee-NAH-ray)*

walker (frame) deambulatore, il/un *(day-ahm-boo-lah-TOH-ray)*

walking stick bastone da passeggio, il/un *(bahs-TOH-nay dah pahs-SAYD-joh)*

wall (outside) muro, il *(MOO-roh)*, (inside) parete, la *(pah-RAY-tay)*

wallet portafoglio, il/un *(pohr-tah-FOHL-lyoh)*

want, to volere *(voh-LAY-ray)*

want, to desiderare *(day-zee-day-RAH-ray)*

  I want desidero *(day-ZEE-day-roh)*

  we want desideriamo *(day-zee-day-RYAH-moh)*

  you want desidera *(day-ZEE-day-rah)*,

war guerra, la *(GWEHR-rah)*

wardrobe (closet) armadio, l' *m*/un *(ahr-MAH-dyoh)*

warm caldo/a *(KAHL-doh/-dah)*, tiepido/a *(TYEH-pee-doh/-dah)*

warm up, to riscaldare *(rees-kahl-DAH-ray)*

warn, to avvertire *(ahv-vayr-TEE-ray)*

was (it) era *(EH-rah)*, (I) ero *(EH-roh)*

wash, to lavare *(lah-VAH-ray)*

wash detergent detersivo, il *(day-tayr-SEE-voh)*

washing machine lavatrice, la/una *(lah-vah-TREE-chay)*

wastebasket cestino per la cartaccia, il/un *(chays-TEE-noh payr lah kahr-TAHT-chah)*

watch orologio, l' *m*/un *(oh-roh-LOH-joh)*

watch, to guardare *(gwahr-DAH-ray)*

Watch out! attenzione! *(ah-tayn-TSYOH-nay)*

water acqua, l' *f (AHK-kwah)*

  mineral water acqua minerale, l' *f (AHK-kwah mee-nay-RAH-lay)*

  still water acqua non gassata, l' *f (AHK-kwah nohn gahs-SAH-tah)*

  tap water acqua del rubinetto, l' *f (AHK-kwah dayl roo-bee-NAYT-toh)*

water bottle borraccia, la/una *(bohr-RAHT-chah)*

waterbus vaporetto, il/un *(vah-poh-RAYT-toh)*

waterfall cascata, la/una *(kahs-KAH-tah)*

watermelon anguria, l' *f*/un' *(ahn-GOOR-yah)*, cocomero, il/un *(koh-KOH-may-roh)*

waterproof impermeabile *(eem-payr-may-AH-bee-lay)*

wave onda, l' *f*/un' *(OHN-dah)*

way via, la *(VEE-ah)*

we noi *(noy)*

weak debole *(DAY-boh-lay)*

wealthy ricco/a *(REEK-koh/-kah)*

wear, to portare *(pohr-TAH-ray)*

weather tempo, il *(TEM-poh)*

Web Web, il *(web)*, Internet, l' *m (EEN-tehr-net)*

  Web page pagina Web, la/una *(PAH-jee-nah web)*

wedding matrimonio, il *(mah-tree-MOHN-yoh)*

Wednesday mercoledì *(mayr-koh-lay-DEE)*

week settimana, la/una *(sayt-tee-MAH-nah)* (le settimane)

  last week settimana scorsa, la *(sayt-tee-MAH-nah SKOHR-sah)*

  next week settimana prossima, la *(sayt-tee-MAH-nah PROHS-see-mah)*

  this week questa settimana *(KWAYS-tah sayt-tee-MAH-nah)*

week day giorno feriale, il/un *(JOHR-noh fay-RYAH-lay)*, giorno lavorativo, il/un *(JOHR-noh lah-voh-rah-TEE-voh)*

weekend fine settimana, il/un *(FEE-nay sayt-tee-MAH-nah)*

weekly alla settimana *(AHL-lah sayt-tee-MAH-nah)*

weight peso, il *(PAY-soh)*

welcome, you're prego *(PREH-goh)*

well bene *(BEH-nay)*

well done/well cooked (cooked meat) ben cotto/a *(ben KOHT-toh/-tah)*

west ovest *(OH-vayst)*

  (to the) west (of) (a) ovest (di) *([ah] OH-vayst [dee])*

wet bagnato/a *(bahn-NYAH-toh/-tah)*

  wetsuit muta, la/una *(MOO-tah)*

wet wipe salviettina detergente, la/una *(sahl-vyayt-TEE-nah day-tayr-JEN-tay)* (salviettine detergenti)

what che cosa *(kay KOH-sah)*, che *(kay)*, quale *(KWAH-lay)*

what is___? Cos'è___? *(KOH-say___?)*

what is that? che cos'è quello? *(kay KOH-say KWAYL-loh?)*

wheel ruota, la/una *(RWOH-tah)* (le ruote)

wheelchair sedia a rotelle, la/una *(SED-yah ah roh-TEL-lay)*

when quando *(KWAHN-doh)*

at what time? a che ora? *(ah kay OH-rah?)*

where dove *(DOH-vay)*

where from da dove *(dah DOH-vay)*

where is ___? dov'è___? *(doh-VEH___?)*

which quale *(KWAH-lay)*

whipped cream panna montata, la *(PAHN-nah mohn-TAH-tah)*

white bianco/a *(BYAHN-koh/-kah)*

white wine vino bianco, il *(VEE-noh BYAHN-koh)*

whiteboard lavagna bianca, la/una *(lah-VAHN-nyah BYAHN-kah)*

who chi *(kee)*

Who knows? Chissà? *(kees-SAH)*

why perché *(payr-KAY)*

wide largo/a *(LAHR-goh/-gah)*

widow vedova, la/una *(VAY-doh-vah)*

widowed vedovo/a *(VAY-doh-voh/-vah)*

widower vedovo, il/un *(VAY-doh-voh)*

wife moglie, la/una *(MOHL-lyay)*

my wife mia moglie *(MEE-ah MOHL-lyay)*

Wi-Fi Wi-Fi *(wy-fy)*

win, to vincere *(VEEN-chay-ray)*

wind vento, il/un *(VEN-toh)*

window finestra, la/una *(fee-NEHS-trah)*, (small) finestrino, il/un *(fee-nays-TREE-noh)*

windshield parabrezza, il *(pah-rah-BRAYD-dzah)*

windy ventoso/a *(vayn-TOH-soh/-sah)*

It's windy. Tira vento *(TEE-rah VEN-toh)*

wine vino, il/un *(VEE-noh)*

house wine vino della casa, il *(VEE-noh DAYL-lah KAH-sah)*

red wine vino rosso, il/un *(VEE-noh ROHS-soh)*

white wine vino bianco, il/un *(VEE-noh BYAHN-koh)*

wine cellar cantina, la/una *(kahn-TEE-nah)*

wine list lista dei vini, la/una *(LEES-tah DAY-ee VEE-nee)*

wine tasting degustazione dei vini, la/una *(day-goos-taht-TSYOH-nay DAY-ee VEE-nee)*

winter inverno, l' *m (een-VEHR-noh)*

wipe (cleaning cloth) salviettina, la/una *(sahl-vayt-TEE-nah)* (le salviettine)

baby wipes salviettine detergenti per bambini, le *(sahl-vyayt-TEE-nay day-tayr-JEN-tee payr bahm-BEE-nee)*

wet wipes salviettine detergenti, le *(sahl-vyayt-TEE-nay day-tayr-JEN-tee)*

wish, to desiderare *(day-see-day-RAH-ray)*

with con *(kohn)*

within entro *(AYN-troh)*

without senza *(SEN-tsah)*

woman donna, la/una *(DOHN-nah)* (le donne)

wood legno, il *(LAYN-nyoh)*

woodcarvings legno intagliato, il *(LAYN-nyoh een-tahl-LYAH-toh)*

wool lana, la *(LAH-nah)*

word parola, la/una *(pah-ROH-lah)* (le parole)

work (job) lavoro, il *(lah-VOH-roh)*

work, to (=occupation) lavorare *(lah-voh-RAH-ray)*

work, to (=to function) funzionare *(foon-tsyoh-NAH-ray)*

It doesn't work non funziona *(nohn foon-TSYOH-nah)*, guasto/a *(GWAHS-toh/-tah)* (e.g., Internet)

work day giorno lavorativo, il/un *(JOHR-noh lah-voh-rah-TEE-voh)*, giorno feriale, il/un *(JOHR-noh fay-RYAH-lay)*

worker lavoratore/ lavoratrice, il/la *(lah-voh-rah-TOH-ray/TREE-chay)*

work number numero di lavoro, il/un *(NOO-may-roh dee lah-VOH-roh)*

work permit permesso di lavoro, il/un *(payr-MAYS-soh dee lah-VOH-roh)*

workshop bottega, la/una *(boht-TAY-gah)*, laboratorio, il/un *(lah-boh-rah-TOH-ryoh)*

world mondo, il *(MOHN-doh)*

World Cup Coppa del Mondo, la *(KOHP-pah dayl MOHN-doh)*

worm verme, il *(VEHR-may)* (i vermi)

worried preoccupato/a *(pray-ohk-koo-PAH-toh/-tah)*

would like

he/she/it would like vorrebbe *(VOHR-rayb-bay)*

I would like vorrei *(vohr-REH-ee)*, desidero *(day-ZEE-day-roh)*

they would like vorrebbero *(vohr-RAYB-bay-roh)*

we would like vorremmo *(vohr-REM-moh)*, desideriamo *(day-zee-dayr-YAH-moh)*

you would like vorrebbe (form. sing.) *(VOHR-rayb-bay)*

wrist polso, il *(POHL-soh)*

wristwatch orologio da polso, l' *m*/un *(oh-roh-LOH-joh dah POHL-soh)*

write, to scrivere *(SKREE-vay-ray)*

write it, please lo scriva, per favore *(loh SKREE-vah, payr fah-VOH-ray)*

writer scrittore/scrittrice *(skree-TOH-ray/-TREE-chay)*

writing paper carta da lettere, la *(KAHR-tah dah LET-tay-ray)*

wrong sbagliato/a *(zbahl-LYAH-toh/-tah)*

X

X, x X, x *(eeks)*

Y

Y, y Y, y *(EEP-see-lohn)*

year anno, l' *m*/un *(AHN-noh)* (gli anni)

  last year anno scorso, l' *m* *(LAHN-noh SKOHR-soh)*

  next year anno prossimo, l' *m* *(LAHN-noh PROH-see-moh)*

  this year quest'anno *(kwayst AHN-noh)*

yellow giallo/a *(JAHL-loh/-lah)*

yes sì *(see)*

yesterday ieri *(YEH-ree)*

  day before yesterday l'altro ieri *(LAHL-troh YEH-ree)*

  yesterday afternoon ieri pomeriggio *(YEH-ree poh-may-REED-joh)*

  yesterday evening ieri sera *(YEH-ree SAY-rah)*

  yesterday morning ieri mattina *(YEH-ree maht-TEE-nah)*

yet ancora *(ahn-KOH-rah)*

  not yet non ancora *(nohn ahn-KOH-rah)*

yoga yoga, la *(YOH-gah)*

yogurt yogurt, il *(YOH-goort)*

you (form. sing.) lei *(LEH-ee)*, (inf. sing.) tu *(too)*

young giovane *(JOH-vah-nay)*

your Suo/a (form. sing.) *(SOO-oh/-ah)*, (inf.) tuo/a (inf. sing.) *(TOO-oh/-ah)*

you're welcome prego *(PREH-goh)*

youth hostel ostello della gioventù, l' *m*/un *(ohs-TEL-loh DAYL-lah joh-vayn-TOO)*

Z

Z, z Z, z *(DZEH-tah)*

zero zero *(DZEH-roh)*

zip code codice postale, il *(KOH-dee-chay pohs-TAH-lay)*

zoo giardino zoologico, il/un *(jahr-DEE-noh dzoh-oh-LOH-jee-koh)*

zoom lens zoom, lo/uno *(zoom)*

zucchini zucchina, la/una *(tsook-KEE-nah)* (le zcchuine)

Italian-English Dictionary

How to use this dictionary

The purpose of this dictionary is to help you understand written and spoken Italian. Because you will be exposed to more Italian than you will need to produce, this dictionary contains more entries than the English-Italian dictionary that precedes it. It is by no means comprehensive, however.

Italian words are listed in bold. Verbs are listed in the infinitive form, as well as separate listings for some common inflected forms. Nouns are usually listed in singular form, followed by the definite article and, if necessary, *m* or *f* to show whether the noun is masculine or feminine. Plural forms of many nouns are noted in parentheses. Adjectives are listed in their masculine forms with alternate feminine endings (unless they end in –e, which works for both genders).

A

A, a *(ah)* A, a

a *(ah)* until, to, till, per, in, at

abbacchio, l' *m (ahb-BAHK-kyoh)* roast young lamb

abbacchio alla scottadita, l' *m (ahb-BAHK-kyoh AHL-lah skoht-tah-DEE-tah)* grilled lamb cutlets

abbandonare *(ahb-bahn-doh-NAH-ray)* to abandon

abbastanza *(ahb-bahs-TAHN-tsah)* enough

abbiamo *(ahb-BYAH-moh)* we have

abbigliamento, l' *m (ahb-beel-lyah-MAYN-toh)* clothing, clothing store

abboccato/a *(ahb-bohk-KAH-toh/tah)* medium sweet, semi-dry

abbonamento, l' *m (ahb-boh-nah-MAYN-toh)* subscription, season pass

abbondante *(ahb-bohn-DAHN-tay)* abundant

abbracciare *(ahb-braht-CHAH-ray)* to hug

abbronzante, l' *m (ahb-brohn-DZAHN-tay)* suntan lotion or oil

abbronzare *(ahb-brohn-DZAH-ray)* to tan

abbuono, l' *m (ahb-BWOH-noh)* (gli abbuoni) discount

abile *(AH-bee-lay)* skillful, able

abitare *(ah-bee-TAH-ray)* to reside

abita *(AH-bee-tah)* You (form.)/he/she/it lives/resides

abitano *(AH-bee-tah-noh)* they live/reside

abiti *(AH-bee-tee)* you (inf.) live/reside

abitiamo *(ah-bee-TYAH-moh)* we live/reside

abito *(AH-bee-toh)* I live/reside

abito, l' *m (AH-bee-toh)* (gli abiti) dress, suit

abituale *(ah-bee-too-AH-lay)* usual, regular

abituarsi *(ah-bee-too-AHR-see)* to get used to

abnorme *(ahb-NOHR-may)* abnormal, extraordinary

abruzzese, all' *(ahl ah-broot-TSAY-say)* with red peppers and possibly ham

abusare *(ah-boo-ZAH-ray)* to abuse, to take advantage of

accanto (a) *(ahk-KAHN-toh [ah])* nearby (to)

accappatoio, l' *m (ahk-kahp-pah-TOH-yoh)* (gli accappatoi) bathrobe, beachrobe

accattone/a, l'/l' *m/f (ahk-kaht-TOH-nay/-nah)* beggar

accendino, l' *m (aht-chayn-DEE-noh)* (gli accendini) cigarette lighter

accesso, l' *m (aht-CHES-soh)* access

accesso permanente, l' *m (aht-CHES-soh payr-mah-NEN-tay)* 24-hour access

vietato l'accesso *(vyay-TAH-toh aht-CHES-soh)* no entry

accetazione, l' *f (aht-chayt-taht-TSYOH-nay)* acceptance, reception

accettazione bagagli, l' *f (aht-chayt-taht-TSYOH-nay bah-GAHL-lyee)* (airport) check-in desk

accettabile *(aht-chayt-TAH-bee-lay)* acceptable

accidentale *(aht-chee-dayn-TAH-lay)* accidental

accidente, l' *m (aht-chee-DEN-tay)* (gli accidenti) accident

acciottolato, l' *m (aht-choht-toh-LAH-toh)* cobblestones

acciuga, l' *f (aht-CHOO-gah)* (le acciughe) anchovy

accompagnare *(ahk-kohm-pahn-NYAH-ray)* to accompany

accordo, d' *(dahk-KOHR-doh)* I agree

accurato/a *(ahk-koo-RAH-toh/-tah)* accurate, careful

aceto, l' *m (ah-CHAY-toh)* vinegar

sotto aceto *(SOHT-toh ah-CHAY-toh)* pickled

acetosella, l' *f (ah-chay-toh-SEL-lah)* (wood)sorrel

acido/a *(AH-chee-doh/dah)* sour, tart

acqua, l' *f (AHK-kwah)* (le acque) water

acqua calda, l' *f (AHK-kwah KAHL-dah)* hot water

acqua del rubinetto, l' *f (AHK-kwah dayl roo-bee-NAYT-toh)* tap water

acqua di mare, l' *f (AHK-kwah dee MAH-ray)* sea water

acqua di seltz, l' *f (AHK-kwah dee selts)* seltzer water

acqua distillata, l' *f (AHK-kwah dees-teel-LAH-tah)* distilled water

acqua dolce, l' *f (AHK-kwah DOHL-chay)* fresh water

acqua minerale, l' *f (AHK-kwah mee-nay-RAH-lay)* mineral water

acqua non gassata, l' *f (AHK-kwah nohn gahs-SAH-tah)* still water (no bubbles)

acqua pazza, l' *f (AHK-kwah PAHT-tsah)* fish soup, poached white fish

acqua potabile, l' *f (AHK-kwah poh-TAH-bee-lay)* drinking water

acqua salata, l' *f (AHK-kwah sah-LAH-tah)* salt water

acqua tonica, l' *f (AHK-kwah TOH-nee-kah)* tonic water

acquacotta, l' *f (ahk-kwah-KOHT-tah)* soup of

bread/vegetables, possibly
egg/cheese also

acqua pazza, l' *f (AHK-kwah PAHT-tsah)* fish soup, poached white
fish

acquistare *(ahk-kwees-TAH-ray)* to
acquire, to buy, to purchase

adesso *(ah-DES-soh)* now

adorare *(ah-doh-RAH-ray)* to adore

adulto/a, l'/l' *m/f (ah-DOOL-toh/-tah)* (gli adulti/le adulte) adult

aerea, via *(VEE-ah ah-EH-ray-ah)* via
air mail

aereo, l' *m (ah-EH-ray-oh)* (gli aerei)
plane

aerobica, l' *f (ah-ay-ROH-bee-kah)*
aerobics

aeroplano, l' *m (ah-ay-roh-PLAH-noh)*
(gli aeroplani) airplane

aeroporto, l' *m (ah-ay-roh-POHR-toh)*
(gli aeroporti) airport

affari, gli *(ahf-FAH-ree)* business

affettato, l' *m (ahf-fayt-TAH-toh)*
sliced salami or ham

affilato/a *(ahf-fee-LAH-toh/-tah)*
sharp

affittasi *(ahf-feet-TAH-see)* for rent,
for lease

affitto, l' *m (ahf-FEET-toh)* rent

affogato *(ahf-foh-GAH-toh)* poached
(egg)

affollato/a *(ahf-fohl-LAH-toh/-tah)*
crowded

affresco, l' *m (ahf-FRAYS-koh)*
fresco

affumicato/a *(ahf-foo-mee-KAH-toh/-tah)* smoked

agenda, l' *f (ah-JEN-dah)* diary

agenzia di viaggi, l' *f (ahd-jayn-TSEE-ah dee vee-AHD-jee)* travel
agency

aggiustare *(ahd-joos-TAH-ray)* to
repair

aggressivo/a *(ahg-grays-SEE-voh/-vah)* aggressive

agile *(AH-jee-lay)* agile, nimble

agio, l' *m (AH-joh)* ease,
comfort

aglio, l' *m (AHL-yoh)* garlic

aglio e olio *(AHL-yoh ay OHL-yoh)* garlic and oil sauce

agnellino, l' *m (ah-nyayl-LEE-noh)*
baby lamb

agnello, l' *m (ahn-NYEL-loh)* (gli
agnelli) lamb

agnello abbacchio *(ahn-NYEL-loh ahb-BAHK-kyoh)* very
young lamb

agnello ai funghi *(ahn-NYEL-loh AH-ee FOON-gee)* lamb with
mushrooms

agnello al forno *(ahn-NYEL-loh ahl FOHR-noh)* lamb with
garlic

agnolini, gli *(ahn-yoh-LEE-nee)*
type of stuffed pasta, often

filled with beef/egg/cheese
mixture

agnolotti ripieni, gli *(ahn-yoh-LOHT-tee ree-PYEH-nee)* pasta
filled with meat/egg/cheese
mixture

ago, l' *m (AH-goh)* (gli aghi) needle

agopuntura, l' *f (ah-goh-poon-TOO-rah)* acupuncture

agosto, l' *m (ah-GOHS-toh)* August

agricoltore/agricoltrice, l'/l'
m/f (ah-gree-kohl-TOH-ray/-TREE-chay) farmer

agricoltura, l' *f (ah-gree-kohl-TOO-rah)* agriculture

agriturismo, l' *m (ah-gree-too-REEZ-moh)* farm vacations

agro, all' *(ahl AH-groh)* lemon
juice/oil dressing

agrodolce, l' *m (ah-groh-DOHL-chay)*
sweet and sour sauce

aguzzo/a *(ah-GOOT-tsoh/-tsah)*
sharp

aiutare *(ah-yoo-TAH-ray)* to help
  aiuta *(ah-YOO-tah)* You
  (form.)/he/she/it helps
  aiutano *(ah-yoo-TAH-noh)* they
  help
  aiuti *(ah-YOO-tee)* you (inf.) help
  aiutiamo *(ah-yoo-TYAH-moh)* we
  help
  aiuto *(ah-YOO-toh)* I help
  aiuto! *(ah-YOO-toh)* Help!

al *(ahl)* with, in the style of

al dente *(ahl DEN-tay)* state of
cooked pasta still firm

al mare *(ahl MAH-ray)* seaside

al sangue *(ahl SAHN-gway)*
rare (meat)

ala, l' *f (AH-lah)* (le ali) wing

alba, l' *f (AHL-bah)* sunrise

Albania, l' *f (ahl-bah-NEE-ah)*
Albania

albergo, l' *m (ahl-BEHR-goh)* (gli
alberghi) hotel

albero, l' *m (AHL-bay-roh)* (gli
alberi) tree

albicocca, l' *f (ahl-bee-KOHK-kah)*
(le albicocche) apricot

alcolico, l' *m (ahl-KOH-lee-koh)*
alcohol

alcuni/e *(ahl-KOO-nee/-nay)*
some (pl.), a few

alfabeto, l' *m (ahl-fah-BEH-toh)*
alphabet

alfredo *(ahl-FRAY-doh)* cream/
butter/parmesan sauce

ali, le *(AH-lee)* wings

alice, l' *f (ah-LEE-chay)* (le alici)
anchovy

alici, le *(ah-LEE-chee)* anchovies
  alici a crudo *(ah-LEE-chee ah
  KROO-doh)* raw, marinated
  anchovies

alieno/a, l'/l' *m/f (ah-LYEH-noh/-nah)* alien

alimentari, l' *m* **negozio di**
(nay-GOHT-syoh dee ah-lee-mayn-

TAH-ree) grocery store, convenience store

alimento, l' *m* *(ah-lee-MAYN-toh)* food

aliscafo, l' *m* *(ah-lees-KAH-foh)* hydrofoil

all'/alla *(ahl/AH-lah)* with, in the style of

allarme, l' *m* *(ahl-LAHR-may)* alarm

allegro/a *(ahl-LAY-groh/-grah)* cheerful, bright, lively

allergia, l' *f* *(ahl-layr-JEE-ah)* (le allergie) allergy

allergico/a (a) *(ahl-LEHR-jee-koh/-kah [ahl])* allergic (to)

all'estero *(ahl-LES-tay-roh)* abroad

allodola, l' *f* *(ahl-LOH-doh-lah)* (le allodole) (sky)lark

alloggio, l' *m* *(ahl-LOH-joh)* accommodation

allora *(ahl-LOH-rah)* now

alloro, l' *m* *(ahl-LOH-roh)* bay leaf, laurel

all'taglio *(ahl-TAHL-lyoh)* by the slice (pizza)

alluce, l' *m* *(AHL-loo-chay)* big toe

allucinazione, l' *f* *(ahl-loo-chee-naht-TSYOH-nay)* hallucination

alluvione, l' *f* *(ahl-loo-VYOH-nay)* flood

al mare *(ahl MAH-ray)* seaside

alpe, l' *f* *(AHL-pay)* (le alpi) alp

Alpi, le *(AHL-pee)* the Alps

alpinismo, l' *m* *(ahl-pee-NEEZ-moh)* mountain climbing

al sangue *(ahl SAHN-gway)* rare (meat)

alt! *(ahlt)* stop!

altare, l' *m* *(ahl-TAH-ray)* altar

altezza, l' *f* *(ahl-TAYT-tsah)* height, altitude

altitudine, l' *f* *(ahl-tee-TOO-dee-nay)* altitude

alto/a *(AHL-toh/-tah)* high, tall

altopiano, l' *m* *(ahl-toh-PYAH-noh)* plateau

altro/a *(AHL-troh/-trah)* other, different

  altro ieri *(AHL-troh YEH-ree)* day before yesterday

  un altro *(oon AHL-troh)* another

alveare, l' *m* *(ahl-vay-AH-ray)* (bee)hive

amabile *(ah-MAH-bee-lay)* slightly sweet (wine), pleasant

amaca, l' *f* *(ah-MAH-kah)* (le amache) hammock

amante, l'/l' *m/f* *(ah-MAHN-tay)* lover

amare *(ah-MAH-ray)* to love

amarena, l' *f* *(ah-mah-REH-nah)* (le amarene) black cherry

amaretti, gli *(ah-mah-RAY-tee)* almond cookies

amaretto, l' *m (ah-mah-RAYT-toh)*
almond-flavored liqueur

amaro/a *(ah-MAH-roh/-rah)* bitter

amaro, l' *m (ah-MAH-roh)* (gli
amari) after-dinner drink,
bitters

amatriciana, l' *f (ah-mah-tree-CHAH-nah)* spicy sauce of bacon or
salami, tomatoes, hot pepper,
cheese

ambasciata, l' *f (ahm-bahsh-SHAH-tah)* embassy

ambasciatore/ambasciatrice,
l'/l' *m/f (ahm-bahsh-shah-TOH-ray/-TREE-chay)* ambassador

ambiente, l' *m (ahm-BYEN-tay)*
environment

ambrosia, l' *f (ahm-BROHZ-yah)*
ambrosia

ambulanza, l' *f (ahm-boo-LAHN-tsah)*
(le ambulanze) ambulance

America, l' *f (ah-MEH-ree-kah)*
America

americano, l' *m (ah-may-ree-KAH-noh)* (aperitif) vermouth,
bitters, brandy, lemon peel

amico/a, l'/l' *m/f (ah-MEE-koh/-kah)*
(gli amici/le amiche) friend

amministrazione, l' *f (ahm-mee-nees-traht-TSYOH-nay)*
administration

ammirare *(ahm-mee-RAH-ray)* to
admire

amuleto, l' *m (ah-moo-LEH-toh)*
lucky charm

analcolico/a *(ah-nahl-KOH-lee-koh/-kah)* non-alcoholic

analgesico, l' *m (ah-nahl-JEH-zee-koh)* painkiller

ananas, l' *m (AH-nah-nahs)*
pineapple

anatra, l' *f (AH-nah-trah)* (le
anatre) duck

anche *(AHN-kay)* also, too

ancora *(ahn-KOH-rah)* still, yet,
again, more

ancora, l' *f (AHN-koh-rah)*
anchor

andare *(ahn-DAH-ray)* to go
andiamo *(ahn-DYAH-moh)* we
go
va *(vah)* You (form.) go,
he/she/it goes
vado *(VAH-doh)* I go
vai *(VAH-ee)* you (inf.) go
vanno *(VAHN-noh)* they go

andata, l' *f (ahn-DAH-tah)* (le
andate) outward journey
andata e ritorno *(ahn-DAH-tah
ay ree-TOHR-noh)* round trip
(di) solo andata *([dee] SOH-loh ahn-DAH-tah)* one-way
(ticket)

andiamo *(ahn-DYAH-moh)* we
go

anello, l' *m (ah-NEL-loh)* (gli
anelli) small pasta ring; ring
(jewelry)

angiulottus *(ahn-joo-LOHT-toos)* stuffed pasta squares with sauce

angolo, l' *m (AHN-goh-loh)* corner

anguilla, l' *f (ahn-GWEEL-lah)* (le anguille) eel

anguria, l' *f (ah-GOOR-yah)* (le angurie) watermelon (north)

anice, l' *m (AH-nee-chay)* anise, aniseed, anisette

animale, l' *m (ah-nee-MAH-lay)* (gli animali) animal

animale domestico, l' *m (ah-nee-MAH-lay doh-MES-tee-koh)* pet

anisetta, l' *f (ah-nee-ZAYT-tah)* anisette

anitra, l' *f (AH-nee-trah)* (le anitre) duck

annata, l' *f (ahn-NAH-tah)* vintage year

anno, l' *m (AHN-noh)* (gli anni) year

anno accademico, l' *m (AHN-noh ahk-kah-DEH-mee-koh)* academic year

anno finanziario, l' *m (AHN-noh fee-nahn-TSYAH-ryoh)* financial year

anno sabbatico, l' *m (AHN-noh sahb-BAH-tee-koh)* sabbatical year

annoglia, l' *f (ahn-NOH-lyah)* pork sausage

annoiare *(ahn-noh-YAH-ray)* to annoy, to bore

annoiato/a *(ahn-noh-YAH-toh/-tah)* bored

annuale *(ah-noo-AH-lay)* annual

annulla *(ahn-NOOL-lah)* annul, clear (ATM), cancel

annullamento, l' *m (ahn-nool-lah-MAYN-toh)* cancellation, annulment

annuncio, l' *m (ahn-NOON-choh)* announcement, advertisement

anolini, gli *(ah-noh-LEE-nee)* round pasta stuffed with beef/egg/cheese mixture

anormale *(ah-nohr-MAH-lay)* abnormal

antiacido, l' *m (ahn-tee-AH-chee-doh)* (gli antiacidi) antacid

antiallergico/a *(ahn-tee-ahl-LEHR-jee-koh/-kah)* hypoallergenic

antibiotici, gli *(ahn-tee-bee-OH-tee-chee)* antibiotics

antico/a *(ahn-TEE-koh/-kah)* ancient

anticoncezionale, l' *m (ahn-tee-kohn-chay-tsyoh-NAH-lay)* contraceptive

antidoto, l' *m (ahn-TEE-doh-toh)* antidote

antipasti, gli *(ahn-tee-PAHS-tee)* appetizers

antipasti a scelta, gli *(ahn-tee-PAHS-tee ah SHAYL-tah)* appetizers of one's choice

antipasti assortiti, gli *(ahn-tee-PAHS-tee ahs-sohr-TEE-tee)* assorted appetizers

antipasti di mare, gli *(ahn-tee-PAHS-tee dee MAH-ray)* seafood appetizers

antipasto, l' *m (ahn-tee-PAHS-toh)* (gli antipasti) appetizer

antisettico, l' *m (ahn-tee-SET-tee-koh)* antiseptic

antistaminico, l' *m (ahn-tees-tah-MEE-nee-koh)* (gli antistaminici) antihistamine

antro, l' *m (AHN-troh)* (gli antri) cave, cavern

ape, l' *f (AH-pay)* (le api) bee

aperitivo, l' *m (ah-pay-ree-TEE-voh)* (gli aperitivi) aperitif

Aperol *(AH-pay-rohl)* (aperitif) bitters, non-alcoholic

aperto/a *(ah-PEHR-toh/-tah)* open

apparecchio acustico, l' *m (ahp-pah-RAYK-kyoh ah-KOOS-tee-koh)* hearing aid

appartamento, l' *m (ahp-pahr-tah-MAYN-toh)* apartment

appendice, l' *f (ahp-payn-DEE-chay)* appendix

appetito, l' *m (ahp-pay-TEE-toh)* appetite

apprendere *(ahp-PREN-day-ray)* to learn

approdo, l' *m (ahp-PROH-doh)* approach, landing

appuntamento, l' *m (ahp-poon-tah-MAYN-toh)* appointment, date

apribottiglie, l' *m (ah-pree-boht-TEEL-lyay)* bottle opener

aprile, l' *m (ah-PREE-lay)* April

aprire *(ah-PREE-ray)* to open

apriscatole, l' *m (ah-prees-KAH-toh-lay)* can opener

arachide, l' *f (ah-RAH-kee-day)* (le arachidi) peanut

arachidi, le *(ah-RAH-kee-dee)* peanuts

aragosta, l' *f (ah-rah-GOHS-tah)* (le aragoste) lobster

arancia, l' *f (ah-RAHN-chah)* (le arance) orange

aranciata, l' *f (ah-rahn-CHAH-tah)* orangeade

arancini, gli *(ah-rahn-CHEE-nee)* meat-filled rice balls

arancione *(ah-rahn-CHOH-nay)* orange (color)

aranzada, l' *f (ah-rahn-TSAH-dah)* sweet made of oranges, almonds and honey

arazzo, l' *m (ah-RAHT-tsoh)* tapestry (gli arazzi)

arbitro, l' *m (AHR-bee-troh)* (gli arbitri) referee, umpire

arborio *(ahr-BOHR-yoh)* type of short-grained rice

arcata, l' *f (ahr-KAH-tah)* arcade

archeologico/a *(ahr-kay-oh-LOH-jee-koh/-kah)* archeological

architetto, l' *m (ahr-kee-TAYT-toh)* architect

architettura, l' *f (ahr-kee-tayt-TOO-rah)* architecture

archivio, l' *m* (gli archivi) *(ahr-KEEV-yoh)* archives, filing cabinet

arcivescovo, l' *m* *(ahr-chee-VAYS-koh-voh)* archbishop

arco, l' *m* *(AHR-koh)* (gli archi) arch

arcobaleno, l' *m* *(ahr-koh-bah-LAY-noh)* rainbow

ardere *(AHR-day-ray)* to burn

arduo/a *(AHR-doo-oh/-ah)* arduous, difficult

area servizio, l' *f* *(AH-ray-ah sayr-VEET-tsyoh)* highway service center

arenaria, l' *f* *(ah-ray-NAHR-yah)* sandstone

argenteo/a *(ahr-JEN-tay-oh/-ah)* silver (color)

argento, l' *m* *(ahr-JEN-toh)* silver (metal)

argilla, l' *f* *(ahr-JEEL-lah)* clay

aria, l' *f* *(AHR-yah)* air, look, manner

  aria condizionata, l' *f* *(AHR-yah kohn-deet-tsyoh-NAH-tah)* air conditioning

aringa, l' *f* *(ah-REEN-gah)* (le aringhe) herring

arista, l' *f* *(AH-rees-tah)* (le ariste) pork loin

  arista alla fiorentina *(AH-rees-tah AHL-lah fyoh-rayn-TEE-nah)* pork

roast with garlic, rosemary, cloves

arma, l' *f* *(AHR-mah)* (le armi) weapon

armadietto per il bagaglio, l' *m* *(ahr-mah-DYET-toh payr eel bah-GAHL-lyoh)* luggage locker

  armadietti per i bagagli, gli *(ahr-mah-DYET-tee payr ee bah-GAHL-lyee)* luggage lockers

armadio, l' *m* *(ahr-MAH-dyoh)* (gli armadi) wardrobe (closet)

aromi, gli *(ah-ROH-mee)* herbs

arpa, l' *f* *(AHR-pah)* harp

arrabbiato/a *(ahr-rahb-BYAH-toh/-tah)* angry, rabid

  all' arrabbiata *(ahl ahr-rahb-BYAH-tah)* with a spicy sauce

arredatore/-trice, l'/l' *m/f* *(ahr-ray-dah-TOH-ray/-TREE-chay)* interior designer

arrivare *(ahr-reev-VAH-ray)* to arrive

  arriva *(ahr-REE-vah)* (it) arrives, (it is) loading (e.g., Web page)

arrivederci *(ahr-ree-vay-DAYR-chee)* goodbye

arrivi, gli *(ahr-REE-vee)* arrivals

arrivo, l' *m* *(ahr-REE-voh)* (gli arrivi) arrival

arrosticini, gli *(ahr-roh-stee-CHEE-nee)* sheep-meat kebabs

arrosto/a *(ahr-ROHS-toh)* roasted, grilled

   arrosto alla griglia *(ahr-ROHS-toh AHL-lah GREEL-lyah)* barbecued

arte, l' *f (AHR-tay)* art

artefatto/a *(ahr-tay-FAHT-toh/-tah)* artificial

artificiale *(ahr-tee-fee-CHAH-lay)* artificial, unnatural

artigianale *(ahr-tee-jah-NAH-lay)* home-made

artista, l'/l' *m/f (ahr-TEES-tah)* (gli artisti/le artiste) artist

artrite, l' *f (ahr-TREE-tay)* arthritis

ascensore, l' *m (ahsh-shayn-SOH-ray)* elevator

asciugacapelli, l' *m (ahsh-shoo-gah-kah-PAYL-lee)* hair dryer

asciugamano, l' *m (ahsh-shoo-gah-MAH-noh)* (gli asciugamani) towel

asciugare *(ahsh-shoo-GAH-ray)* to dry

ascoltare *(ahs-kohl-TAH-ray)* to listen

ascolto, l' *m (ahs-KOHL-toh)* reception (radio)

asiago *(ah-see-AH-goh)* cow's milk cheese, flavor similar to parmesan

asilo, l' *m (ah-ZEE-loh)* daycare, nursery

asino, l' *m (AH-see-noh)* donkey, ass

asma, l' *f (AHZ-mah)* asthma

asparago, l' *m (ahs-PAH-rah-goh)* (gli asparagi) asparagus

   asparagi alla fiorentina *(ahs-PAH-rah-jee AHL-lah fyoh-rayn-TEE-nah)* asparagus with fried eggs/cheese

aspettare *(ahs-spayt-TAH-ray)* to wait for

aspirina, l' *f (ahs-pee-REE-nah)* (le aspirine) aspirin

asporto, d' *(dahs-POHR-toh)* "to go" (food), takeaway

aspro/a *(AHS-proh/-prah)* sour

assaggiare *(ahs-sahd-JAH-ray)* to taste

assegno, l' *m (ahs-SAYN-nyoh)* (gli assegni) check

   assegno turistico, l' *m (ahs-SAYN-nyoh too-REES-tee-koh)* (gli assegni turistici) traveler's check

   assegno di viaggo, l' *m (ahs-SAYN-nyoh dee VYAH-joh)* traveler's check

assenso, l' *m (ahs-SEN-soh)* assent, approval

assenza, l' *f (ahs-SEN-tsah)* absence

assicuratore/-trice, l'/l' *m/f (ahs-see-koo-rah-TOH-ray/-TREE-chay)* insurance agent

assicurazione, l' *f (ahs-see-koo-raht-TSYOH-nay)* insurance

assistenza, l' *f* *(ahs-sees-TEN-tsah)* assistance

assistere *(ahs-SEES-tay-ray)* to assist

assolato/a *(ahs-soh-LAH-toh/-tah)* sunny

assorbente igienice, l' *f* *(ahs-sohr-BEN-tay ee-JEH-nee-chay)* (le assorbenti igienici) sanitary napkin

assortito/a *(ahs-sohr-TEE-toh/-tah)* assorted

astice, l' *m* *(AHS-tee-chay)* (gli astici) lobster

astronomia, l' *f* *(ahs-troh-noh-MEE-ah)* astronomy

ateismo, l' *m* *(ah-tay-EEZ-moh)* atheism

atelier, l' *m* *(ah-tuh-LYAY)* fashion house, studio

atipico/a *(ah-TEE-pee-koh/-kah)* atypical

atrio, l' *m* *(AHT-ryoh)* foyer, lobby

atroce *(ah-TROH-chay)* atrocious, terrible

attendere *(aht-TEN-day-ray)* to wait for

attendere a *(aht-TEN-day-ray ah)* to attend to

attento! *(aht-TEN-toh)* careful!

attenzione! *(aht-tayn-TSYOH-nay)* attention!, careful!, caution!

attesa, l' *f* *(aht-TAY-sah)* wait

attesa: 20 minuti waiting time: 20 minutes

attraversare *(ah-trah-vayr-SAH-ray)* to cross, to traverse

attrezzatura, l' *f* *(aht-trayt-tsah-TOO-rah)* equipment

attuale *(aht-too-AH-lay)* current, present

audio, l' *m* *(OWD-yoh)* sound

Australia, l' *f* *(ows-TRAHL-yah)* Australia

Austria, l' *f* *(OWS-tree-ah)* Austria

auto, l' *f* *(OW-toh)* (le auto) car

autobus, l' *m* *(OW-toh-boos)* (gli autobus) city bus

autogrill, l' *m* *(ow-toh-GREEL)* (gli autogrill) roadside restaurant

automatico/a *(ow-toh-MAH-tee-koh/-kah)* automatic

automobilismo, l' *m* *(ow-toh-moh-bee-LEEZ-moh)* auto racing

autonoleggio, l' *m* *(ow-toh-noh-LAYD-joh)* (gli autonoleggi) car rental

autore/-trice, l'/l' *m/f* *(ow-TOH-ray/ow-toh-TREE-chay)* author

autostop, l' *m* *(ow-tohs-TOP)* hitchhiking

fare l'autostop *(FAH-ray low-tohs-TOP)* to hitchhike

autostrada, l' *f (ow-tohs-TRAH-dah)*
(le autostrade)
freeway/express highway that
requires a toll, indicated by
green sign, numbered by A
plus a number

autunno, l' *m (ow-TOON-noh)* (gli
autunni) fall, autumn

avanti *(ah-VAHN-tee)* ahead,
forward, before

avaro/a *(ah-VAH-roh/-rah)* stingy

avena, l' *f (ah-VAY-nah)* oats

avere *(ah-VAY-ray)* to have
  abbiamo *(ahb-BYAH-moh)* we
  have
  ha *(ah)* You (form.) have,
  he/she/it has
  hai *(AH-ee)* you (inf.) have
  hanno *(AHN-noh)* they have
  ho *(oh)* I have
  avere bisogno di *(ah-VAY-ray
  bee-ZOHN-nyoh dee)* to need
  avere fame *(ah-VAY-ray FAH-may)*
  to be hungry
  avere sete *(ah-VAY-ray SAY-tay)* to
  be thirsty

avocado, l' *m (ah-voh-KAH-doh)*
avocado

a volte *(ah VOHL-tay)* sometimes,
at times

avventura, l' *f (ahv-vayn-TOO-rah)*
adventure

avvertire *(ahv-vayr-TEE-ray)* to
warn, to inform

avvocato/a, l'/l' *m/f (ahv-voh-
KAH-toh/-tah)* lawyer

azzurro/a *(ahd-DZOOR-roh/-rah)*
azure, turquoise, light blue

B

B, b *(bee)* B, b

babà, il *(bah-BAH)* a dry cake,
usually with raisins, often
served with rum or
whipped cream

baby, il/la *(BAY-bee)* infant

babysitter, il/la *(BAY-bee-see-ter)*
babysitter

baccalà, il (i baccalà) *(bahk-kah-
LAH)* dried salted cod
  baccalà alla pizzaiola *(bahk-
  kah-LAH AHL-lah peet-tsah-YOH-
  lah)* dried salt cod with a
  tomato sauce
  baccalà alla romana *(bahk-
  kah-LAH AHL-lah roh-MAH-nah)*
  dried salt cod with tomato
  sauce, garlic, parsley
  baccalà alla vicentina
  *(bahk-kah-LAH AHL-lah vee-chayn-
  TEE-nah)* dried salt cod
  cooked in milk
  baccalà mantecato *(bahk-
  kah-LAH AHL-lah mahn-tay-KAH-
  toh)* puree of dried salt cod

baci, i *(BAH-chee)* "kisses,"
dark chocolate candies filled
with milk chocolate and

hazelnuts; chocolate/hazelnut cookies

baciare *(bah-CHAH-ray)* to kiss

bacio, il *(BAH-choh)* (i baci) kiss; Rocky Road ice cream

badia, la *(bah-DEE-ah)* abbey

badile, il *(bah-DEE-lay)* shovel

baffo, il *(BAHF-foh)* moustache, whiskers

bagaglio, il *(bah-GAHL-lyoh)* (i bagagli) luggage

 bagaglio a mano, il *(bah-GAHL-lyoh ah MAH-noh)* carry-on luggage

 bagaglio consentito, il *(bah-GAHL-lyoh kohn-sayn-TEE-toh)* baggage allowance

 bagaglio in eccedenza, il *(bah-GAHL-lyoh een ayt-chay-DEN-tsah)* excess baggage

 bagagli smarriti, i *(bah-GAHL-lyee zmahr-REE-tee)* lost luggage

bagnetto verde, il *(bahn-NYAYT-toh VAYR-day)* garlic, anchovy, and parsley sauce

bagno, il *(BAHN-nyoh)* (i bagni) bath, bathroom

balcone, il *(bahl-KOH-nay)* balcony

baldacchino, il *(bahl-dahk-KEE-noh)* canopy

baldo/a *(BAHL-doh/-dah)* bold

ballare *(bahl-LAH-ray)* to dance

balletto, il *(bahl-LAYT-toh)* ballet

ballo, il *(BAHL-loh)* ball (dance)

balsamo per capelli, il *(BAHL-sah-moh payr kah-PAYL-lee)* hair conditioner

bambino/a, il/la *(bahm-BEE-noh/-nah)* (i bambini/le bambine) baby, child, boy/girl

bambola, la *(BAHM-boh-lah)* (le bambole) doll

banana, la *(bah-NAH-nah)* (le banane) banana

banca, la *(BAHN-kah)* (le banche) bank (money)

banco, il *(BAHN-koh)* (i banchi) seat, bench; bank

Bancomat, il *(BAHN-koh-maht)* automated banking, ATM, cash machine

bancone, il *(BAHN-koh-nay)* bar counter

banconota, la *(bahn-koh-NOH-tah)* bank note, bill

bar, il *(bahr)* (i bar) cafè

baratro, il *(BAHR-ah-troh)* abyss

barattolo, il *(bah-RAHT-toh-loh)* (i barattoli) jar, can

barba, la *(BAHR-bah)* (le barbe) beard

barbabietola, la *(bahr-bah-BYEH-toh-lah)* (le barbabietole) beet

barbiere, il *(bahr-BYEH-ray)* barber

barca, la *(BAHR-kah)* (le barche) boat

baseball, il *(BAYS-bol)* baseball

basilica, la *(bah-ZEE-lee-kah)* basilica

basilico, il *(bah-ZEE-lee-koh)* (sweet) basil

basso/a *(BAHS-soh/-sah)* short, low

basta *(BAHS-tah)* all, enough

bastante *(bahs-TAHN-tay)* sufficient

batsoà, il *(baht-soh-AH)* breaded and fried meat from pig's feet (or veal)

battello, il *(baht-TEL-loh)* boat

batteria, la *(baht-tay-REE-ah)* (le batterie) battery

battesimo, il *(baht-TAY-zee-moh)* baptism

battistero, il *(baht-tees-TEH-roh)* baptistry

battuto, il *(baht-TOO-toh)* finely chopped onion, garlic and herbs cooked in lard or other oil, used for seasoning; mirepoix

batuffoli di cotone, i *(bah-TOOF-foh-lee dee koh-TOH-nay)* cotton balls

bavaglino, il *(bah-vahl-LYEE-noh)* (i bavaglini) bib

bavette, le *(bah-VAYT-tay)* narrow ribbon noodles

bebé, il/la *(bay-BEH)* baby

beige *(behzh)* beige

Belgio, il *(BEL-joh)* Belgium

bella, la *(BEL-lah)* beauty

bellissimo/a *(bayl-LEES-see-moh/-mah)* most beautiful

bello/a *(BEL-loh/-lah)* nice, beautiful, pretty, handsome

bel paese, il *(bel pah-AY-zay)* semi-soft, mild cow's-milk cheese

ben cotto/a *(ben KOHT-toh/-tah)* well done (meat)

benda, la *(BEN-dah)* (le bende) bandage

bene *(BEH-nay)* good, well

benvenuto/a *(bayn-vayn-NOO-toh/-tah)* (benvenuti/-te) welcome

benzina, la *(bayn-DZEE-nah)* gasoline

benzina senza piombo, la *(bayn-DZEE-nah SEN-tsah PYOHM-boh)* unleaded gas

benzina verde, la *(bayn-DZEE-nah VAYR-day)* unleaded gas

fare la benzina *(FAH-ray lah bayn-DZEE-nah)* to get gasoline

benzinaio, il *(bayn-dzee-NAH-yoh)* gas station

bere *(BAY-ray)* to drink

Berlino *(bayr-LEE-noh)* Berlin

Berna *(BEHR-nah)* Bern

besciamella, la *(baysh-shah-MEL-lah)* white sauce, béchamel sauce

bevanda, la *(bay-VAHN-dah)* (le bevande) drink, beverage

bevande, le *(bay-VAHN-day)* drinks

biancheria, la *(byahn-kay-REE-ah)* lingerie, lingerie shop

bincheria intima, la *(byahn-kay-REE-ah EEN-tee-mah)* underwear

bianco/a *(BYAHN-koh/kah)* white

bianco d'uovo *(BYAHN-koh DWOH-voh)* egg white

bibbia, la *(BEEB-byah)* bible

biberon, il *(bee-buh-ROHN)* baby bottle

bibita (frizzante), la *(BEE-bee-tah [freed-DZAHN-tay])* drink, soda pop, soft drink

bibite, le *(BEE-bee-tay)* beverages, soft drinks

biblioteca, la *(bee-blyoh-TEH-kah)* library

bibliotecario/-ria, il/la *(bee-blyoh-tay-KAH-ryoh/-ryah)* librarian

bicchiere, il *(beek-KYEH-ray)* (i bicchieri) glass (for drinking)

bici, la *(BEE-chee)* bike

bicicletta, la *(bee-chee-KLAYT-tah)* (le biciclette) bicycle

bidè/bidet, il *(bee-DEH)* bidet

biglietteria, la *(beel-lyayt-tay-REE-ah)* ticket vendor

biglietto, il *(beel-LYAYT-toh)* (i biglietti) ticket

biglietto giornaliero, il *(beel-LYAYT-toh johr-nahl-LYEH-roh)* one-day ticket

biglietto ordinario, il *(beel-LYAYT-toh ohr-dee-NAH-ryoh)* one-ride ticket

bigné, il *(been-NYAY)* cream puff

bigoli, i *(BEE-goh-lee)* long, thick tubular pasta made of buckwheat or whole wheat

bikini, il *(bee-KEE-nee)* bikini

bilancio, il *(bee-LAHN-choh)* balance, balance sheet

biliardo, il *(bee-LYAHR-doh)* pool (game)

bilingue *(bee-LEEN-gway)* bilingual

bimbo/a, il/la *(BEEM-boh/-bah)* baby, child

binario, il *(bee-NAH-ryoh)* (i binari) train platform

binocolo, il *(bee-NOH-koh-loh)* binoculars

biondo/a *(BYOHN-doh/-dah)* fair, blond, light (beer)

birra, la *(BEER-rah)* (le birre) beer

birra alla spina, la *(BEER-rah AHL-lah SPEE-nah)* draft beer

birra chiara, la *(BEER-rah KYAH-rah)* lager

birra rossa, la *(BEER-rah ROHS-sah)* dark beer

birra scura, la *(BEER-rah SKOO-rah)* stout

bisaccia, la *(bee-ZAHT-chah)* (le bisacce) backpack

biscotto, il *(bees-KOHT-toh)* (i biscotti) cookie

bisi, i *(BEE-see)* peas

bisogno, il *(bee-ZOHN-nyoh)* (i bisogni) need

bistecca, la *(bees-TAYK-kah)* (le bistecche) steak

bistecca alla fiorentina, la *(bees-TAYK-kah AHL-lah fyoh-rayn-TEE-nah)* thick, grilled, bone-in steak with pepper, lemon juice, parsley

bistecca di cinghiale, la *(bees-TAYK-kah dee cheen-GYAH-lay)* wild boar in sweet/sour sauce

bistecca di filetto, la *(bees-TAYK-kah dee fee-LAYT-toh)* rib steak

bitto, il *(BEET-toh)* aged cow's-milk cheese

bivio, il *(BEEV-yoh)* fork, split, crossroads

blanc manger, il *(blahnk MAHN-zhay)* sweet dessert of thickend cream or milk with sugar and usually almonds

blando/a *(BLAHN-doh/-dah)* mild, gentle, weak

bloccato/a *(blohk-KAH-toh/-tah)* blocked

blocchetto, il *(blohk-KAYT-toh)* notebook

blu *(bloo)* dark blue

bocca, la *(BOHK-kah)* (le bocche) mouth

boccaglio, il *(bohk-KAHL-lyoh)* snorkel

boccale, il *(bohk-KAH-lay)* jug, mug

bocciare *(boht-CHAH-ray)* to fail, to reject

bocconcini, i *(bohk-kohn-CHEE-nee)* small, spongy, mild unripened cheese

bolletta, la *(bohl-LAYT-tah)* (le bollette) bill

bollino, il *(bohl-LEE-noh)* (i bollini) coupon

bollire *(bohl-LEE-ray)* to boil

bollito/a *(bohl-LEE-toh/-tah)* boiled

bollito, il *(bohl-LEE-toh)* boiled beef

bollito misto, il *(bohl-LEE-toh MEES-toh)* sausages and other boiled meats

bollo, il *(BOHL-loh)* stamp

bollo di circolazione, il *(BOHL-loh dee cheer-koh-lah-TSYOH-nay)* car registration

bologna, la *(boh-LOHN-nyah)* mild, smooth sausage

bolognese *(boh-lohn-NYAY-say)* sauce of tomatoes, meat, onions, herbs

bomba di riso, la *(BOHM-bah dee REE-soh)* molded, baked rice dish, traditionally with pigeon meat

bonèt, il *(boh-NET)* dessert pudding made with almond cookies, cocoa and rum

bordo, il *(BOHR-doh)* (i bordi) border, edge

a bordo *(ah BOHR-doh)* on board

borgo, il *(BOHR-goh)* (i borghi) district, village, suburb

borotalco, il *(boh-roh-TAHL-koh)* talcum powder

borraccia, la *(bohr-RAHT-chah)* water bottle

borsa, la *(BOHR-sah)* (le borse) purse

borsaiolo/a, il/la *(bohr-sah-YOH-loh/-lah)* pickpocket

borsetta, la *(bohr-SAYT-tah)* (le borsette) handbag, purse

bosco, il *(BOHS-koh)* (i boschi) wood

bostrengo, il *(bohs-TREN-goh)* cake, often made with rice, dried fruit and nuts

bottega, la *(boht-TAY-gah)* shop, workshop

bottiglia, la *(boht-TEEL-lyah)* (le bottiglie) bottle

bottiglieria, la *(boht-teel-lyay-REE-ah)* wine shop

bottone, il *(boht-TOH-nay)* (i bottoni) button

boudin, il *(boo-DEEN)* blood sausage

bra, il *(brah)* cheese from Bra, can be hard or soft, milk flavor

bracciale, il *(braht-CHAH-lay)* (i bracciali) bracelet

braccio, il *(BRAHT-choh)* (le braccia) arm

braciola, la *(brah-CHOH-lah)* (le braciole) chop, steak, cutlet

braciolone napoletano *(brah-choh-LOH-nay nah-poh-lay-TAH-noh)* stuffed meat rolls with tomato and wine sauce

brandina, la *(brahn-DEE-nah)* (le brandine) cot

branzi, i *(BRAHN-tsee)* semi-firm Alpine cow's milk cheese with mild nutty flavor

branzino, il *(brahn-TSEE-noh)* (i branzini) bass (fish)

brasare *(brah-ZAH-ray)* to braise, cook slowly in liquid

brasato/a *(brah-ZAH-toh/-tah)* braised

brasato, il *(brah-ZAH-toh)* braised beef in red wine

bravo/a *(BRAH-voh/-vah)* good, clever, skillful

bresaola, la *(bray-ZAH-oh-lah)* dried salted beef

breve *(BREH-vay)* short, brief

brezza, la *(BRAYD-dzah)* breeze

bricco, il *(BREEK-koh)* (i brichi) jug

briciolata *(bree-choh-LAH-tah)* toasted breadcrumbs; sauce of olive oil, black pepper, toasted breadcrumbs

brillante *(breel-LAHN-tay)* brilliant

brioche, la *(bree-OHSH)* eggy, buttery breakfast bread

brocca, la *(BROHK-kah)* (le broche) jug

broccolo, il *(BROHK-koh-loh)* (i broccoli) broccoli

    broccoli alla romana *(BROHK-koh-lee AHL-lah roh-MAH-nah)* broccoli cooked in olive oil and wine

brodetto, il *(broh-DAYT-toh)* light broth

    brodetto di pesce, il *(broh-DAYT-toh dee PAYSH-shay)* fish stew

brodo, il *(BROH-doh)* (i brodi) broth, bouillon, soup, stock

    brodo di manzo, il *(BROH-doh dee MAHN-dzoh)* beef broth

    brodo di pollo, il *(BROH-doh dee POHL-loh)* chicken broth

bronchite, la *(brohn-KEE-tay)* bronchitis

bruciare *(broo-CHAH-ray)* to burn

bruidda, la *(broo-EED-dah)* fish soup

bruma, la *(BROO-mah)* mist, haze

bruno/a *(BROO-noh/-nah)* brown, dark, dark-haired

bruschetta, la *(broos-KAYT-tah)* sliced, toasted bread rubbed with garlic and topped with flavorings

bruscitt, il *(broo-SHEET)* stewed beef, usually served with cabbage or potatoes

bruti ma buoni, i *(BROO-tee mah BWOH-nee)* meringue-like cookie with hazelnuts

brutto/a *(BROOT-toh/-tah)* bad, ugly

Bruxelles *(brew-SEL)* Brussels

buca, la *(BOO-kah)* hole

    buca delle lettere, la *(BOO-kah DAYL-lay LET-tay-ray)* mail box

bucatini, i *(boo-kah-TEE-nee)* thick, tube-like spaghetti

buccellato di Lucca, il *(boot-chayl-LAH-toh dee LOOK-kah)* ring-shaped cake with raisins and anise

buddista, il/la *(bood-DEES-tah)* Buddhist

budino, il *(boo-DEE-noh)* (i budini) pudding

bufera, la *(boo-FEH-rah)* (le bufere) storm

buffo/a *(BOOF-foh/-fah)* funny, amusing

bugiardo/a, il/la *(boo-JAHR-doh/-dah)* liar

buonissimo *(bwohn-EES-see-moh)* the best

buono/a *(BWOH-noh/-nah)* good

burro, il *(BOOR-roh)* butter

burro e salvia *(BOOR-roh ay SAHL-vyah)* (pizza) with sage and butter, no tomato sauce

burro per labbra, il *(BOOR-roh payr LAHB-brah)* lip balm

busecca, la *(boo-SAYK-kah)* tripe; tripe, bean, vegetable soup

bussare *(boos-SAH-ray)* to knock

bussola, la *(BOO-soh-lah)* compass

busta, la *(BOOS-tah)* envelope

busta portatrucco, la *(BOOS-tah pohr-tah-TROOK-koh)* make-up bag

C

C, c *(chee)* C, c

cabina, la *(kah-BEE-nah)* (airplane) cabin; cubicle

cabina de prova, la *(kah-BEE-nah dee PROH-vah)* changing room

cabina telefonica, la *(kah-BEE-nah tay-lay-FOH-nee-kah)* phone booth

cabriolet, il *(kah-bree-oh-LEH)* convertible (car)

cacao, il *(kah-KAH-oh)* cocoa

caccia, la *(KAHT-chah)* hunting

cacciagione, la *(kaht-chah-JOH-nay)* game (food)

cacciatora, alla *(AHL-lah kaht-chah-TOH-ray)* cooked with white wine, garlic, rosemary, anchovy paste, hot peppers

cacciavite, il *(kaht-chah-VEE-tay)* screwdriver

cacciavite a croce/a stella, il *(kaht-chah-VEE-tay ah KROH-chay/ah STAYL-lah)* philips screwdriver

cacciucco, il *(kaht-CHOOK-koh)* spiced fish soup

cachi, il *(KAH-kee)* (i cachi) persimmon

cacio, il *(KAH-choh)* sheep's-milk cheese, smaller, younger and softer than pecorino

cacio e pepe, il *(KAH-choh ay PAY-pay)* sheep cheese and black pepper

cacioricotta, la *(kah-choh-ree-KOHT-tah)* cheese, firmer than ricotta

caciotta, la *(kah-CHOHT-tah)* soft, mild cheese

cadere *(kah-DAY-ray)* to fall

caffè, il *(kah-FEH)* (i caffi) coffee; coffee shop (with coffee, alcohol, maybe some food)

caffè americano, il *(kah-FEH ah-may-ree-KAH-noh)* espresso diluted with hot water, "American-like"

caffè corretto, il *(kah-FEH kohr-RET-toh)* coffee with a shot of alcohol

caffè freddo, il *(kah-FEH FRAYD-doh)* iced coffee

caffè latte, il *(kah-FEH LAHT-tay)* steamed milk with coffee

caffè machiato, il *(kah-FEH mah-KYAH-toh)* coffee "stained" with steamed milk foam

caffè solubile, il *(kah-FEH soh-LOO-bee-lay)* instant coffee

caffeina, la *(kahf-fay-EE-nah)* caffeine

caffettiera, la *(kahf-fayt-TYEH-rah)* coffeemaker, coffeepot

calamaretto, il *(kah-lah-mah-RET-toh)* (i calamaretti) baby squid

calamaro, il *(kah-lah-MAH-roh)* (i calamari) squid

calamita, la *(kah-lah-MEE-tah)* (le calamite) magnet

calcio, il *(KAHL-choh)* soccer

dare un calcio *(DAH-ray oon KAHL-choh)* to kick

calcolare *(kahl-koh-LAH-ray)* to calculate

calcolatrice, la *(kahl-koh-lah-TREE-chay)* calculator

caldo/a *(KAHL-doh/-dah)* hot, warm

caldo, il *(KAHL-doh)* heat

calendario, il *(kah-layn-DAH-ryoh)* (i calendari) calendar

caliginoso/a *(kah-lee-jee-NOH-soh/-sah)* foggy

calle, la *(KAHL-lay)* narrow Venetian street

caloria, la *(kah-loh-REE-ah)* (le calorie) calorie

calpestare *(kahl-pays-TAH-ray)* to trample on

non calpestare l'erba *(nohn kahl-pays-TAH-ray LEHR-bah)* keep off the grass

vietato calpestare le aiuole *(vyay-TAH-toh kahl-pays-TAH-ray lay ah-YWOH-lay)* keep off the flower beds

calza, la *(KAHL-tsah)* sock

calze, le *(KAHL-tsay)* stockings

calzino, il *(kahl-TSEE-noh)* (i calzini) sock (short)

calzoncini, i *(kahl-tsohn-CHEE-nee)* shorts

calzone, il *(kahl-TSOH-nay)* (i calzoni) savory turnover made with pizza dough

cambiare *(kahm-BYAH-ray)* to exchange, to change

cambio, il *(KAHM-byoh)* (i cambi) exchange, change, currency exchange office, gears

cambio automatico, il *(KAHM-byoh ow-toh-MAH-tee-koh)* automatic transmission

cambio valuta, la *(KAHM-byoh vah-LOO-tah)* currency exchange

camera, la *(KAH-may-rah)* (le camere) room

camera da letto, la *(KAH-may-rah dah LET-toh)* bedroom

camera d'aria, la *(KAH-may-rah DAHR-yah)* innertube

camera doppia, la *(KAH-may-rah DOHP-pyah)* (le camere doppie) double room

camera singola, la *(KAH-may-rah SEEN-goh-lah)* (le camere singole) single room

camera tripla, la *(KAH-may-rah TREEP-lah)* (le camere triple) triple room

camerata, la *(kah-may-RAH-tah)* dormitory

cameriera, la *(kah-may-RYEH-rah)* waitress

cameriere, il *(kah-may-RYEH-ray)* waiter

camicetta, la *(kah-mee-CHET-tah)* (le camicette) blouse

camicia, la *(kah-MEE-chah)* (le camicie) shirt

in camicia *(een kah-MEE-chah)* poached (egg)

camion, il *(KAH-myohn)* truck

camioncino, il *(kahm-yohn-CHEE-noh)* van

cammeo, il *(kahm-MEH-oh)* cameo

camminare *(kahm-mee-NAH-ray)* to walk

camomilla, la *(kah-moh-MEEL-lah)* camomile

campagna, la *(kahm-PAHN-nyah)* countryside

campagnia, la *(kahm-pahn-NYEE-ah)* company

campanile, il *(kahm-pah-NEE-lay)* bell tower

Campari *(kahm-PAH-ree)* bitters with orange peel, herbs

campeggiare *(kahm-payd-JAH-ray)* to camp

campeggio, il *(kahm-PAYD-joh)* camp site

campionato, il *(kahm-pyoh-NAH-toh)* championships

campo, il *(KAHM-poh)* (i campi) field, court

campo da golf, il *(KAHM-poh dah gohlf)* golf course

campo da tennis, il *(KAHM-poh dah TEN-nees)* tennis court

Canada, il *(kah-nah-DAH)* Canada

canale, il *(kah-NAH-lay)* channel, canal

cancella *(kahn-CHEL-lah)* cancel (ATM)

cancellare *(kahn-chayl-LAH-ray)* to cancel

cancello, il *(kahn-CHEL-loh)* gate

candela, la *(kahn-DAY-lah)* candle, spark plug

cane, il *(KAH-nay)* (i cani) dog

cane guida, il *(KAH-nay GWEE-dah)* guide dog

canederli, i *(kah-NAY-dayr-lee)* dumplings made with stale bread, bacon, and other ingredients

cannaroni, i *(kahn-nah-ROH-nee)* wide pasta tubes

cannella, la *(kahn-NEL-lah)* cinnamon

cannelloni, i *(kahn-nayl-LOH-nee)* dough tubes filled with meat, vegetables or cheese, baked in a white sauce

cannolo, il *(kahn-NOH-loh)* (i cannoli) cream horn

canottaggio, il *(kah-noht-TAHD-joh)* canoeing, rowing

cantante, il/la *(kahn-TAHN-tay)* singer

cantare to sing *(kahn-TAH-ray)*

cantarelli, i *(kahn-tah-RAYL-lee)* chanterelle mushrooms

cantina, la *(kahn-TEE-nah)* winery

cantucci, i *(kahn-TOOT-chee)* hazelnut or almond biscotti (hard cookies for dunking)

canzone, la *(kahn-TSOH-nay)* (le canzoni) song

caos, il *(KAH-ohs)* chaos

capanna, la *(kah-PAHN-nah)* (le capanne) hut

caparra, la *(kah-PAHR-rah)* deposit

capella, la *(kahp-PEL-lah)* chapel

capelli, i *(kah-PAYL-lee)* hair

capelli d'angelo, i *(kah-PAYL-lee DAHN-jay-loh)* angel hair pasta

capire *(kah-PEE-ray)* to understand

capiamo *(kah-PYAH-moh)* we understand

Capisce? *(kah-PEESH-shay)* Do you understand? (form. sing.)

capisco *(kah-PEES-koh)* I understand

Non capisco *(nohn kah-PEES-koh)* I don't understand

capo, il *(KAH-poh)* leader

capocollo, il *(kah-poh-KOHL-loh)* dry pork sausage made with head, neck, shoulder meat

capocuoco/a, il/la *(kah-poh-KWOH-koh/-kah)* head cook or chef

Capodanno, il *(kah-poh-DAHN-noh)* New Year's Day

capolinea, il *(kah-poh-LEE-nay-ah)* (i capilinea) terminus, end of the line

caponata, la *(kah-poh-NAH-tah)* appetizer, side dish or topping of eggplant and other vegetables with olive oil and spices

cappa, la *(KAHP-pah)* (le cappe) cape, cloak

cappa santa, la *(KAHP-pah SAHN-tah)* (le cappe sante) scallop

cappellacci di zucca, i *(kahp-payl-LAHT-chee dee TSOOK-kah)* pasta filled with squash and cheese

cappelletti, i *(kahp-payl-LAYT-tee)* ring-shaped ravioli stuffed with meat

cappello, il *(kahp-PEL-loh)* (i cappelli) hat

cappero, il *(KAHP-pay-roh)* (i capperi) caper

cappone, il *(kahp-POH-nay)* (i capponi) capon

cappon magro, il *(kahp-POHN MAH-groh)* elaborate seafood and vegetable salad

cappotto, il *(kahp-POHT-toh)* (i cappotti) coat, overcoat

cappuccino, il *(kahp-poot-CHEE-noh)* (i cappuccini) cappuccino

capra, la *(KAH-prah)* (le capre) goat, goat's cheese

caprese, il *(kah-PRAY-say)* tomato, basil mozzarella salad or pizza

capretto, il *(kah-PRAYT-toh)* (i capretti) kid goat

capricciosa, la *(kah-preet-CHOH-sah)* cook's specialty pizza; mushroom, artichoke, olive pizza

capriccioso, il *(kah-preet-CHOH-soh)* mixed salad

caprino, il *(kah-PREE-noh)* cheese from goat's milk, can be soft and creamy (fresco) or aged and tangy (stagionato)

carabinieri, i *(kah-rah-bee-NYEH-ree)* military police

caraffa, la *(kah-RAHF-fah)* (le caraffe) carafe

caramella, la *(kah-rah-MEL-lah)* (le caramelle) candy

carboidrato, il *(kahr-boh-ee-DRAH-toh)* (i carboidrati) carbohydrate

carbonara *(kahr-boh-NAH-rah)* sauce of cheese, eggs, butter or olive oil, ham or bacon

carcere, il *(KAHR-chay-ray)* jail

carciofo, il *(kahr-CHOH-foh)* (i carciofi) artichoke

carciofi alla giudea, i *(kahr-CHOH-fee AHL-lah joo-DEH-ah)* deep-fried artichoke

carciofi alla romana, i *(kahr-CHOH-fee AHL-lah roh-MAH-nah)* cooked artichokes stuffed with garlic, salt, olive oil, mint, parsley

cardigan, il *(KAHR-dee-gahn)* cardigan

cardinale, il *(kahr-dee-NAH-lay)* cardinal

cardiopalmo, il *(kahr-dyoh-PAHL-moh)* (i cardiopalmi) palpitation

cardoncelli, i *(kahr-dohn-CHEL-lee)* type of wild mushroom

carenza, la *(kah-REN-tsah)* shortage

caricabatteria, il *(kah-ree-kah-baht-tay-REE-ah)* battery charger

carico, il *(KAH-ree-koh)* charge (elec.)

carità, la *(kah-ree-TAH)* charity

carnaroli, i *(kahr-nah-ROH-lee)* medium-grained rice used for risotto

carne, la *(KAHR-nay)* meat

carne ai ferri, la *(KAHR-nay AH-ee FEHR-ree)* grilled meat

carne di cavallo, la *(KAHR-nay dee kah-VAHL-loh)* horse meat

carne equina, la *(KAHR-nay ay-KWEE-nah)* horse meat

carne suina, la *(KAHR-nay SWEE-nah)* pork

carne tritata, il *(KAHR-nay tree-TAH-tah)* mince meat

caro/a *(KAH-roh/-rah)* expensive

carota, la *(kah-ROH-tah)* (le carote) carrot

carpa, la *(KAHR-pah)* (le carpe) carp

carpaccio, il *(kahr-PAHT-choh)* thinly sliced raw beef tenderloin with tangy dressing

carpentiere, il *(kahr-payn-TYEH-ray)* carpenter

carrello, il *(kahr-REL-loh)* cart, dolly, trolley

carrettiera *(kahr-rayt-TYEH-rah)* sauce of tuna, mushroom, tomato, pepper

alla carrettiera *(AHL-lah kahr-rayt-TYEH-rah)* with hot peppers, pork

carro, il *(KAHR-roh)* cart, wagon

carrozza, la *(kahr-ROHT-tsah)* carriage, train car

carrozza ristorante, la *(kahr-ROHT-tsah rees-toh-RAHN-tay)* dining car

carrozzina, la *(kahr-roht-TSEE-nah)* baby carriage

carta, la *(KAHR-tah)* (le carte) card, map, paper, menu

carta bancomat, la *(KAHR-tah BAHN-koh-maht)* ATM card

carta da lettere, la *(KAHR-tah dah LET-tay-ray)* writing paper

carta da musica, la *(KAHR-tah dah MOO-zee-kah)* "sheet music"—very wide, thin, crispy flatbread

carta di credito, la *(KAHR-tah dee KRAY-dee-toh)* credit card

carta d'identità, la *(KAHR-tah dee-dayn-tee-TAH)* identity card

carta d'imbarco, la *(KAHR-tah deem-BAHR-koh)* boarding pass

carta igienica, la *(KAHR-tah ee-JEN-ee-kah)* toilet paper

carta telefonica, la *(KAHR-tah tay-lay-FOH-nee-kah)* phone card

carte, le *(KAHR-tay)* cards

cartello, il *(kahr-TEL-loh)* sign, notice

cartina, la *(kahr-TEE-nah)* map

cartoccio, il *(kahr-TOHT-choh)* food wrapped in parchment paper or aluminum foil and baked

cartoleria, la *(kahr-toh-lay-REE-ah)* stationery store

cartolina, la *(kahr-toh-LEE-nah)* (le cartoline) postcard

cartuccia, la *(kahr-TOOT-chah)* cartridge, refill

casa, la *(KAH-sah)* (le case) house, home

casalingo/a, il/la *(kah-sah-LEEN-goh/–gah)* homemaker

cascata, la *(kahs-KAH-tah)* waterfall

cascina, la *(kahsh-SHEE-nah)* farmstead

casco, il *(KAHS-koh)* helmut

caseificio, il *(kah-zay-ee-FEE-choh)* creamery

casino, il *(kah-SEE-noh)* brothel

casinò, il *(kah-zee-NOH)* casino

casoncelli, i *(kah-sohn-CHAYL-lee)* similar to ravioli, pasta stuffed with a mixture of bread crumbs, egg, cheese and meat or of sausage, spinach, garlic and pear, often served with butter and sage sauce

cassa, la *(KAHS-sah)* (le casse) cash register

cassaforte, la *(kahs-sah-FOHR-tay)* safe

cassata siciliana, la *(kahs-SAH-tah see-chee-LYAH-nah)* sponge cake with sweet cream cheese, chocolate, candied fruit

casseruola, la *(kahs-say-RWOH-lah)* saucepan

cassetta, la *(kahs-SAYT-tah)* cassette (le cassette)

cassetta delle lettere, la *(kahs-SAYT-tah DAYL-lay LET-tay-ray)* mailbox

cassetto, il *(kahs-SAYT-toh)* drawer

cassettone, il *(kahs-sayt-TOH-nay)* chest of drawers

cassiere/a, il/la *(kahs-SYEH-ray/–rah)* cashier

castagna, la *(kahs-TAHN-nyah)* (le castagne) chestnut

castagnaccio, il *(kahs-tahn-NYAHT-choh)* (i castagnacci) chestnut cake

castello, il *(kahs-TEL-loh)* (i castelli) castle

castelmagno, il *(kah-stayl-MAHN-nyoh)* a crumbly, somewhat-blue cheese

casunzei, i *(kah-soon-TSAY-ee)* a stuffed pasta

catacomba, la *(kah-tah-KOHM-bah)* (le catacombe) catacomb

catapulta, la *(kah-tah-POOL-tah)* catapult

catastrofe, la *(kah-TAHS-troh-fay)* catastrophe

catena, la *(kah-TAY-nah)* (le catene) chain, necklace

catena di montagne, la *(kah-TAY-nah dee mohn-TAHN-nyay)* mountain range

catene da neve, le *(kah-TAY-nay dah NAY-vay)* snow chains

cattedrale, la *(kaht-tay-DRAH-lay)* (le cattedrali) cathedral

cattivo/a *(kaht-TEE-voh/-vah)* bad

cattolico/a *(kaht-TOH-lee-koh/-kah)* Catholic

causa, la *(KOW-zah)* cause, reason

causare *(kow-ZAH-ray)* to cause

cautela, la *(kow-TEH-lah)* caution

cauzione, la *(kowt-TSYOH-nay)* security deposit

caval *(kah-VAHL)* horsemeat (in food listing)

cavalcare *(kah-vahl-KAH-ray)* to ride horse

cavallino, il *(kah-vahl-LEE-noh)* pony

cavallo, il *(kah-VAHL-loh)* horse

andare a cavallo *(ahn-DAH-ray ah kah-VAHL-loh)* horse riding

cavatelli, i *(kah-vah-TEL-lee)* small pasta shells

caviale, il *(kah-VYAH-lay)* caviar

caviglia, la *(kah-VEEL-lyah)* ankle (le caviglie)

cavo, il *(KAH-voh)* cable

cavoletti di Bruxelles, i *(kah-voh-LET-tee dee broo-SEL)* Brussels sprouts

cavolfiore, il *(kah-vohl-FYOH-ray)* (i cavolfiori) cauliflower

cavolino di Bruxelles, il *(kah-voh-LEE-noh dee broo-SEL)* (i cavolini) Brussels sprout

cavolo, il *(KAH-voh-loh)* (i cavoli) cabbage

cazzmar, il *(KAHT-zmahr)* sausage made of lamb or goat entrails

c'è *(cheh)* there is (=there exists)

cece, il *(CHAY-chay)* (i ceci) chickpea, garganzo bean

ceci, i *(CHAY-chee)* chickpeas, garbanzo beans

cedere *(CHEH-day-ray)* to yield, to give in

cefalo, il *(CHEH-fah-loh)* mullet (fish)

celebrare *(chay-lay-BRAH-ray)* to celebrate

celebrazione, la *(chay-lay-braht-TSYOH-nay)* celebration

celibe, il *(CHEH-lee-bay)* (i celibi) single man

cellulare, il *(chayl-loo-LAH-ray)* cell phone

  numero di cellulare, il *(NOO-may-roh dee chayl-loo-LAH-ray)* cell phone number

cembalo, il *(CHEM-bah-loh)* harpsichord

cena, la *(CHAY-nah)* (le cene) dinner, supper

centesimo, il *(chen-TEH-zee-moh)* (i centesimi) cent

centimetro, il *(chen-TEE-may-troh)* (i centimetri) centimeter

cento *(CHEN-toh)* hundred

centrale *(chen-TRAH-lay)* central

centro, il *(CHEN-troh)* (i centri) center

  centro commerciale, il *(CHEN-troh kohm-mayr-CHAH-lay)* shopping center

  centro della città, il *(CHEN-troh DAYL-lah cheet-TAH)* center of town, downtown

  centro storico, il *(CHEN-troh STOH-ree-koh)* old city

cercare *(chayr-KAH-ray)* to look for

  cerca *(CHAYR-kah)* you look for, he/she/it looks for

cerchiamo *(chayr-KYAH-moh)* we look for

cerco *(CHAYR-koh)* I look for

cereale, il *(chay-ray-AH-lay)* (i cereali) cereal

cerniera, la *(chayr-NYEH-rah)* zipper

cerotto, il *(chay-ROHT-toh)* (i cerotti) Band-aids

certamente *(chayr-tah-MAYN-tay)* certainly, surely

certificato, il *(chayr-tee-fee-KAH-toh)* certificate

certo *(CHEHR-toh)* of course, certainly

cervella, le *(chayr-VEL-lah)* brains (food)

cervello, il *(chayr-VEL-loh)* (i cervelli) brain

cervo, il *(CHEHR-voh)* (i cervi) deer, venison

cestino, il *(chays-TEE-noh)* (i cestini) basket

  cestino per la cartaccia, il *(chays-TEE-noh payr lah kahr-TAHT-chah)* (i cestini) wastebasket

cetriolino, il *(chay-tree-oh-LEE-noh)* (i cetriolini) pickle

cetriolo, il *(chay-tree-OH-loh)* (i cetrioli) cucumber

che *(kay)* who, which, that, what

chi *(kee)* who

chiamare *(kyah-MAH-ray)* to call

  chiami! *(KYAH-mee)* call!

chiamata, la *(kyah-MAH-tah)* phone call

chiami! *(KYAH-mee)* call!

Chianti *(KYAHN-tee)* robust red wine of Tuscany

chiaro/a *(KYAH-roh/-rah)* clear, light-colored

chiave, la *(KYAH-vay)* (le chiavi) key

chicco, il *(KEEK-koh)* (i chicchi) grain, bean, grape, bead

chiedere *(KYEH-day-ray)* to ask

chiesa, la *(KYEH-zah)* (le chiese) church

chilo, il *(KEE-loh)* (i chili) kilogram

chilometro, il *(kee-LOH-may-troh)* (i chilometri) kilometer

chimica, la *(KEE-mee-kah)* chemistry

chinulille, le *(kee-noo-LEEL-lay)* sweet, fried ricotta ravioli

chiocciola, la *(KYOHT-choh-lah)* spiral, @-symbol

chiodino, il *(kyoh-DEE-noh)* small, wild mushrooms

chiodo di garofano, il *(KYOH-doh dee gah-ROH-fah-noh)* (i chiodi) clove

chiostro, il *(KYOHS-troh)* cloister

chiropratico/a, il/la *(kee-roh-PRAH-tee-koh/-kah)* chiropractor

chirurgia, la *(kee-roor-JEE-ah)* surgery

chissà *(kees-SAH)* Who knows.

chitarra, la *(kee-TAHR-rah)* guitar

chiudere *(KYOO-day-ray)* to close

chiuso/a *(KYOO-soh/-sah)* closed, shut

chiusura, il **giorno di** *(JOHR-noh dee kyoo-SOO-rah)* closing day

ci *(chee)* us

ciabatta, la *(chah-BAHT-tah)* a broad, flat yeast bread

cialzons, i *(chahl-TSOHNS)* a stuffed pasta

ciambella, la *(chahm-BEL-lah)* ring-shaped cake

ciambelle al mosto, le *(chahm-BEL-lay ahl MOHS-toh)* fried, sweetened bread dough made with grape must

ciammotta, la *(chahm-MOHT-tah)* a mix of vegetables that have been sautéed in olive oil

cianfotta, la *(chahn-FOHT-tah)* a summer vegetable stew

ciao *(chow)* hi, bye

ciascuno/a *(chahs-KOO-noh/-nah)* each

ciaudedda, la *(chah-oo-DAYD-dah)* a hearty vegetable stew

cibo, il *(CHEE-boh)* food

cibo da bebè, il *(CHEE-boh dah bay-BEH)* baby food

ciceri e tria, i *(chee-CHAY-ree ay TREE-ah)* pasta with chickpeas

ciclismo, il *(chee-KLEEZ-moh)* cycling

ciclista, il/la *(chee-KLEES-tah)* cyclist

ciclomotore, il *(chee-kloh-moh-TOH-ray)* moped

ciclopista, la *(chee-kloh-PEES-tah)* bike path

cicoria, la *(chee-KOHR-yah)* chicory

cidi, il *(chee-DEE)* CD

cielo, il *(CHEH-loh)* sky

ciliegia, la *(chee-LYED-jah)* (le ciliege) cherry

cima, la *(CHEE-mah)* peak

cima (alla) genovese, la *(CHEE-mah [AHL-lah] jay-noh-VAY-say)* cold veal roll filled with calf's brains, sweetbreads

cime di rapa, le *(CHEE-may dee RAH-pah)* turnip greens or broccoli rabe

cimelio, il *(chee-MEL-yoh)* (i cimeli) relic

cimitero, il *(chee-mee-TEH-roh)* cemetery

cin cin! *(cheen-CHEEN)* cheers!

cinema, il *(CHEE-nay-mah)* cinema, movie theater

cinghia, la *(CHEEN-gyah)* belt

cinghia della ventola, la *(CHEEN-gyah DAYL-lah VEN-toh-lah)* fanbelt

cinghiale, il *(cheen-GYAH-lay)* (i cinghiali) wild boar

cinquanta *(cheen-KWAHN-tah)* fifty

cinquantacinque *(cheen-kwahn-tah-CHEEN-kway)* fifty-five

cinquantadue *(cheen-kwahn-tah-DOO-ay)* fifty-two

cinquantanove *(cheen-kwahn-tah-NOH-vay)* fifty-nine

cinquantaquattro *(cheen-kwahn-tah-KWAHT-troh)* fifty-four

cinquantasei *(cheen-kwahn-tah-SEH-ee)* fifty-six

cinquantasette *(cheen-kwahn-tah-SET-tay)* fifty-seven

cinquantatré *(cheen-kwahn-tah-TRAY)* fifty-three

cinquantotto *(cheen-kwahn-TOHT-toh)* fifty-eight

cinquantuno *(cheen-kwahn-TOO-noh)* fifty-one

cinque *(CHEEN-kway)* five

cinquecento *(cheen-kway-CHEN-toh)* five hundred

cintura, la *(cheen-TOO-rah)* belt

cintura di sicurezza, la *(cheen-TOO-rah dee see-koo-RAYT-tsah)* seatbelt

cioccolata, la *(chohk-koh-LAH-tah)* chocolate

cioccolata calda, la *(chohk-koh-LAH-tah KAHL-dah)* hot chocolate

cioccolato, il *(chohk-koh-LAH-toh)* chocolate

cioccolato al latte, il *(chohk-koh-LAH-toh ahl LAHT-tay)* milk chocolate

cioccolato fondente, il *(chohk-koh-LAH-toh fohn-DEN-tay)* cooking chocolate

cipolla, la *(chee-POHL-lah)* (le cipolle) onion

cipollata, la *(chee-pohl-LAH-tah)* onion soup

cipolle, le *(chee-POHL-lay)* onions

cipolle ripiene, le *(chee-POHL-lay ree-PYEH-nay)* baked stuffed onions

cipollina, la *(chee-pohl-LEE-nah)* (le cipolline) spring onion

cipresso, il *(chee-PRES-soh)* cypress

circo, il *(CHEER-koh)* circus, circle-like arena

ci sono *(chee SOH-noh)* there are, there exist

città, la *(cheet-TAH)* (le città) city

cittadella, la *(cheet-tah-DEL-lah)* citadel

cittadinanza, la *(cheet-tah-dee-NAHN-tsah)* citizenship

ciuccio, il *(CHOOT-choh)* (i ciucci) pacifier

ciucciotto, il *(choot-CHOHT-toh)* pacifier

classe, la *(KLAHS-say)* class

classe business, la *(KLAHS-say BEEZ-nays)* business class

classe turistica, la *(KLAHS-say too-REES-tee-kah)* economy class

di prima classe *(dee PREE-mah KLAHS-say)* first-class

di seconda classe *(dee say-KOHN-dah KLAHS-say)* second-class

classico/a *(KLAHS-see-koh/-kah)* classical

claustrofobia, la *(klows-troh-foh-BEE-ah)* claustrophobia

clementina, la *(klay-mayn-TEE-nah)* (le clementine) clementine orange

cliente, il/la *(klee-EN-tay)* client, customer

clima, il *(KLEE-mah)* (i clime) climate

climatizzazione, la *(klee-mah-teed-dzaht-TSYOH-nay)* air conditioning

cocomero, il *(koh-KOH-may-roh)* (i cocomeri) watermelon (south)

coda, la *(KOH-dah)* waiting line, queue, traffic jam

codice postale, il *(KOH-dee-chay pohs-TAH-lay)* zip code, postal code

codice segreto, il *(KOH-dee-chay say-GRAY-toh)* PIN, personal identification number

cognato/a, il/la *(kohn-NYAH-toh/-tah)* brother-/sister-in-law

cognome, il *(kohn-NYOH-may)* surname, last name, family name

coincidenza, la *(koh-een-chee-DEN-tsah)* (transportation) connection, coincidence

colazione, la *(koh-laht-TSYOH-nay)* (le colazioni) breakfast

colesterolo, il *(koh-lays-tay-ROH-loh)* cholesterol

collana, la *(kohl-LAH-nah)* (le collane) necklace

collant, il *(koh-LAH)* pantyhose

collare, il *(kohl-LAH-ray)* collar

collega, il/la *(kohl-LEH-gah)* colleague

collegamento, il *(kohl-lay-gah-MAYN-toh)* connection

collegio universitario, il *(kohl-LEH-joh oo-nee-vayr-see-TAH-ryoh)* college

collera, la *(KOHL-lay-rah)* anger

collier, il *(koh-LYAY)* necklace

collina, la *(kohl-LEE-nah)* hill

collirio, il *(kohl-LEE-ryoh)* eye drops

collo, il *(KOHL-loh)* neck

colloquio, il *(kohl-LOH-kwyoh)* interview

collutorio, il *(kohl-loo-TOH-ryoh)* mouthwash

colomba, la *(koh-LOHM-bah)* dove, dove-shaped cake

colombo, il *(koh-LOHM-boh)* (i colombi) pigeon

colonna, la *(koh-LOHN-nah)* (le colonne) column

colore, il *(koh-LOH-ray)* (i colori) color

colpa, la *(KOHL-pah)* fault, blame

colpevole *(kohl-PAY-voh-lay)* guilty

coltello, il *(kohl-TEL-loh)* (i coltelli) knife

coltivatore/trice, il/la *(kohl-tee-vah-TOH-ray/TREE-chay)* farmer

come *(KOH-may)* how

come sta? *(KOH-may stah?)* How are you?

come va? *(KOH-may vah?)* How's it going?

cominciare *(koh-meen-CHAH-ray)* to begin

comitiva, la *(koh-mee-TEE-vah)* group, party

commedia, la *(kohm-MEH-dyah)* theatrical play

commedia comica, il *(kohm-MEH-dyah KOH-mee-kah)* comedy

commercio, il *(kohm-MEHR-choh)* trade, commerce

commesso/a, il/la *(kohm-MAYS-soh/-sah)* salesperson

commissione, la *(kohm-mees-SYOH-nay)* order, commission, errand

comodino, il *(koh-moh-DEE-noh)* bedside table

comodo/a *(KOH-moh-doh/-dah)* comfortable, handy, convenient

compact disc, il *(KUM-pahkt deesk)* compact disc

compagnia, la *(kohm-pahn-NYEE-ah)* company

compagno/a, il/la *(kohm-PAHN-nyoh/-nyah)* campanion

compenso, il *(kohm-PEN-soh)* fee, payment, compensation

compito/a *(kohm-PEE-toh/-tah)* well-mannered, polite

compleanno, il *(kohm-play-AHN-noh)* birthday

complesso/a *(kohm-PLES-soh/-sah)* complex

completamente *(kohm-play-tah-MAYN-tay)* completely

completo/a *(kohm-PLEH-toh/-tah)* full, no vacancy, complete

comporre *(kohm-POHR-ray)* to compose

comprare *(kohm-PRAH-ray)* to buy

compra *(KOHM-prah)* You buy (form. sing.)

compriamo *(kohm-PRYAH-moh)* we buy

compro *(KOHM-proh)* I buy

compratore/trice, il/la *(kohm-prah-TOH-ray/-TREE-chay)* buyer, purchaser

comprendere *(kohm-PREN-day-ray)* to understand

compreso/a *(kohm-PRAY-soh/-sah)* included

computer, il *(kom-PYOO-ter)* computer

computer portatile, il *(kom-PYOO-ter pohr-TAH-tee-lay)* laptop

comunicare *(koh-moo-nee-KAH-ray)* to comunicate

comunicazione, la *(koh-moo-nee-kaht-TSYOH-nay)* communication

comunione, la *(koh-moo-NYOH-nay)* communion

con *(kohn)* with

concerto, il *(kohn-CHEHR-toh)* concert

conchiglia, la *(kohn-KEEL-lyah)* (le conchiglie) pasta shell

concludere *(kohn-KLOO-day-ray)* to conclude

condimento, il *(kohn-dee-MAYN-toh)* dressing

condizionamento, il *(kohn-deet-tsyoh-nah-MAYN-toh)* conditioning

condizionamento d'aria, il *(kohn-deet-tsyoh-nah-MAYN-toh DAHR-yah)* air conditioning

condurre *(kohn-DOOR-ray)* to lead (=to conduct)

conferenza, la *(kohn-fay-REN-tsah)* lecture

conferma, la *(kohn-FAYR-mah)* confirmation

confermare *(kohn-fayr-MAH-ray)* to confirm

confessione, la *(kohn-fays-SYOH-nay)* religious confession

confetto, il *(kohn-FET-toh)* (i confetti) sugar-coated almond

confettura, la *(kohn-fayt-TOO-rah)* jam, marmalade

confine, il *(kohn-FEE-nay)* border

confluenza, la *(kohn-floo-EN-tsah)* confluence

confondere *(kohn-FOHN-day-ray)* to confuse, to confound

confusione, la *(kohn-foo-ZYOH-nay)* confusion

confuso/a *(kohn-FOO-zoh/-zah)* confused, muddled

congelare *(kohn-jay-LAH-ray)* to freeze

congelato/a *(kohn-jay-LAH-toh/-tah)* frozen

congestione, la *(kohn-jays-TYOH-nay)* congestion

congiuntivite, la *(kohn-joon-tee-VEE-tay)* conjunctivitis, pink eye

coniglio, il *(koh-NEEL-lyoh)* (i conigli) rabbit

cono, il *(KOH-noh)* (i coni) cone (ice cream)

conoscente, il/la *(koh-nohsh-SHEN-tay)* acquaintance

conoscere *(koh-NOHSH-shay-ray)* to know, to be acquainted with

conserva, la *(kohn-SEHR-vah)* preserve (such as tomato, mushroom, or tuna), typically stored in olive oil

consigliare *(kohn-seel-LYAH-ray)* to recommend

consimile *(kohn-SEE-mee-lay)* similar

consolato, il *(kohn-soh-LAH-toh)* consulate

consumare *(kohn-soo-MAH-ray)* to consume, to wear out

contabile, il/la *(kohn-TAH-bee-lay)* bookkeeper, accountant

contante, i *(kohn-TAHN-tay)* cash
in contanti *(een kohn-TAHN-tay)* (pay) with cash

contare *(kohn-TAH-ray)* to count

contenere *(kohn-tay-NAY-ray)* to contain

contenitore, il *(kohn-tay-nee-TOH-ray)* container

contento/a *(kohn-TEN-toh/-tah)* happy, satisfied, pleased

continuato, l' orario *m (oh-RAH-ryoh kohn-tee-noo-AH-toh)* continuous hours, no pause

conto, il *(KOHN-toh)* (i conti) bill, check, account

contorni, i *(kohn-TOHR-nee)* side dishes

contorno, il *(kohn-TOHR-noh)* (i contorni) side dish, side order of vegetables

contraccettivo, il *(kohn-traht-chayt-TEE-voh)* (i contraccettivi) contraceptive

contrada, la *(kohn-TRAH-dah)* quarter, district, street

contraddire *(kohn-trahd-DEE-ray)* to contradict

contrafforte, il *(kohn-trahf-FOHR-tay)* buttress

contrario/a *(kohn-TRAH-ryoh)* contrary, opposite, adverse

contratto, il *(kohn-TRAHT-toh)* contract

contro *(KOHN-troh)* against

controfiletto, il *(kohn-troh-fee-LAYT-toh)* sirloin

controllare *(kohn-trohl-LAH-ray)* to check

controllo passaporti, il *(kohn-TROHL-loh pahs-sah-POHR-tee)* passport control

controllore, il *(kohn-trohl-LOH-ray)* ticket collector, customs officer

contusione, la *(kohn-too-ZYOH-nay)* bruise

convalidare *(kohn-vah-lee-DAH-ray)* to validate

convento, il *(kohn-VEN-toh)* convent, monastery

convertire *(kohn-vayr-TEE-ray)* to convert

convertitore, il *(kohn-vayr-tee-TOH-ray)* electrical converter

convincere *(kohn-VEEN-chay-ray)* to convince

convitato/a, il/la *(kohn-vee-TAH-toh/-tah)* guest

coperta, la *(koh-PEHR-tah)* (le coperte) blanket

coperto, il *(koh-PEHR-toh)* (i coperti) cover charge

prezzo del coperto, il *(PRET-tsoh dayl koh-PEHR-toh)* cover charge

copertura, la *(koh-payr-TOO-rah)* (le coperture) covering

copia, la *(KOH-pyah)* (le copie) copy

copiare *(koh-PYAH-ray)* to copy

copiatrice, la *(koh-pyah-TREE-chay)* photocopier

coppa, la *(KOHP-pah)* (le coppe) cup (e.g., of ice cream), large pork sausage

Coppa del Mondo, la *(KOHP-pah dayl MOHN-doh)* World Cup

coprire *(koh-PREE-ray)* to cover

corda, la *(KOHR-dah)* rope

cordone, il *(kohr-DOH-nay)* cord

cornetto, il *(kohr-NAYT-toh)* (i cornetti) croissant, cone

coro, il *(KOH-roh)* chorus, choir

corpo, il *(KOHR-poh)* body

corposo/a *(kohr-POH-soh/-sah)* full-bodied (wine)

correggere *(kohr-RED-jay-ray)* to correct

corrente, la *(kohr-REN-tay)* current

correre *(KOHR-ray-ray)* to run

correttamente *(kohr-rayt-tah-MAYN-tay)* correctly, properly

corridoio, il *(kohr-ree-DOH-yoh)* (i corridoi) aisle

corriere, il *(kohr-RYEH-ray)* courier, messenger

corrispondere *(kohr-rees-POHN-day-ray)* to correspond

corrompere *(kohr-ROHM-pay-ray)* to bribe, to corrupt

corsa, la *(KOHR-sah)* route, race

corsa semplice *(KOHR-sah SEM-plee-chay)* one-way

corso, il *(KOHR-soh)* avenue, main street

corte, la *(KOHR-tay)* court

cortile, il *(kohr-TEE-lay)* courtyard

corto/a *(KOHR-toh/-tah)* short

cosa, la *(KOH-sah)* (le cose) thing, object

qualche cosa *(KWAHL-kay KOH-sah)* something

coscia, la *(KOHSH-shah)* (le cosce) leg (meat), thigh

cosciotto, il *(kohsh-SHOHT-toh)* (i cosciotti) leg (meat)

così *(koh-SEE)* like so

costa, la *(KOHS-tah)* coast

costare *(kohs-TAH-ray)* to cost

costata, la *(kohs-TAH-tah)* (le costate) large chop of meat, steak

costata al prosciutto, la *(kohs-TAH-tah ahl proh-SHOOT-toh)* stuffed chop

costata di manzo alla pizzaiola, la *(kohs-TAH-tah dee MAHN-dzoh AHL-lah peet-tsah-YOH-la)* beef with tomatoes, garlic, oregano

costiera, la *(kohs-TYEH-rah)* coastline

costine, le *(kohs-TEE-nay)* spare ribs

costine maiale, le *(kohs-TEE-nay mah-YAH-lay)* grilled pork spare ribs

costipato/a *(kohs-tee-PAH-toh/-tah)* constipated

costipazione, la *(kohs-tee-paht-TSYOH-nay)* constipation, bad cold

costo, il *(KOHS-toh)* cost

costola, la *(KOHS-toh-lah)* (le costole) rib

costoletta, la *(kohs-toh-LAYT-tah)* cutlet

costume da bagno, il *(kohs-TOO-may dah BAHN-nyoh)* (i costumi) swim suit, swim trunks

cotechino, il *(koh-tay-KEE-noh)* salami-like pork sausage that must be cooked, usually boiled

cotechino in galera, il *(koh-tay-KEE-noh een gah-LEH-rah)* pork sausage and beef meat roll

cotenna, la *(koh-TAYN-nah)* bacon rind

cotoletta, la *(koh-toh-LAYT-tah)* (le cotolette) (breaded and fried) veal cutlet or pork chop

cotoletta alla bolognese, la *(koh-toh-LAYT-tah AHL-lah boh-lohn-NYAY-say)* like veal parmesan, breaded veal cutlets with ham and tomato sauce

cotoletta alla milanese, la *(koh-toh-LAYT-tah AHL-lah mee-lah-NAY-say)* like Wiener schnitzel, breaded veal cutlet fried in butter

cotone, il *(koh-TOH-nay)* cotton

cotto/a *(KOHT-toh/-tah)* cooked

ben cotto/a *(ben KOHT-toh/-tah)* well-done

cotto a vapore *(KOHT-toh ah vah-POH-ray)* steamed

non troppo cotto/a *(nohn TROHP-poh KOHT-toh/-tah)* medium rare

poco cotto/a *(POH-koh KOHT-toh/-tah)* rare

cozza, la *(KOHT-tsah)* (le cozze) mussel

cozze, le *f pl* *(KOHT-tsay)* mussels

cranio, il *(KRAHN-yoh)* skull

cravatta, la *(krah-VAHT-tah)* (le cravatte) necktie

cravattino, il *(krah-vaht-TEE-noh)* bow tie

credere *(KRAY-day-ray)* to believe

crema, la *(KREH-mah)* (le creme) cream, custard, cream soup, vanilla (ice cream)

crema da barba, la *(KREH-mah dah BAHR-bah)* shaving cream

crema de cacao, la *(KREH-mah day kah-KOW)* crème de cacao

crema di legumi, la *(KREH-mah dee lay-GOO-mee)* vegetable cream soup

crema inglese, la *(KREH-mah een-GLAY-say)* custard

crema solare, la *(KREH-mah soh-LAH-ray)* suntan cream

crema solare protettiva, la *(KREH-mah soh-LAH-ray proh-tayt-TEE-vah)* sunscreen

cren, il *(kren)* horseradish

crescenza, la *(kraysh-SHEN-tsah)* a creamy, rich fresh cheese of uncooked cow's milk

crescere *(KRAYSH-shay-ray)* to increase, to grow

crespella, la *(krays-PEL-lah)* an Italian crêpe

cripta, la *(KREEP-tah)* crypt

cristiano/a *(krees-TYAH-noh/-ah)* Christian

cristo, il *(KREES-toh)* Christ

Croazia, la *(kroh-AHT-tsyah)* Croatia

crocchetta, la *(krohk-KAYT-tah)* (le crocchette) croquette, fried mashed potato/egg mixture

croce, la *(KROH-chay)* cross

crocifisso, il *(kroh-chee-FEES-soh)* crucifix

crostacei, i *(krohs-TAH-chay-ee)* shellfish

crostaceo, il *(krohs-TAH-chay-oh)* (i crostacei) shellfish

crostata, la *(krohs-TAH-tah)* (le crostate) fruit pie, tart, crust

crostino, il *(krohs-TEE-noh)* (i crostini) small toasted bread slices with toppings, canapé

crostoli, i *(krohs-TOH-lee)* fried strips of sweet dough

crudo/a *(KROO-doh/-dah)* rare (meat), raw

crumiri, i *(kroo-MEE-ree)* crescent-shaped cookies of flour and corn meal

crusca, la *(KROOS-kah)* bran

cruscotto, il *(kroos-KOHT-toh)* dashboard

cubetto, il *(koo-BAYT-toh)* cube

cuccetta, la *(koot-CHAYT-tah)* couchette, berth (train)

cucchiaino, il *(kook-kyah-EE-noh)* (i cucchiaini) teaspoon

cucchiaio, il *(kook-KYAH-yoh)* (i cucchiai) spoon

cucciolo, il *(KOOT-choh-loh)* puppy

cucina, la *(koo-CHEE-nah)* kitchen

  cucina tradizionale, la *(koo-CHEE-nah trah-dee-tsyoh-NAH-lay)* traditional cooking

cucinare *(koo-chee-NAH-ray)* to cook

cucire *(koo-CHEE-ray)* to sew

cugino/a, il/la *(koo-JEE-noh/-nah)* (i cugini/le cugine) cousin

culaccio, il *(koo-LAHT-choh)* rump (food)

culatello, il *(koo-lah-TAYL-loh)* high-quality cold-cut ham

culla, la *(KOOL-lah)* cot, cradle

cultura, la *(kool-TOO-rah)* culture

cumino, il *(koo-MEE-noh)* cumin

cuocere *(KWOH-chay-ray)* to cook

cuoco/a, il/la *(KWOH-koh/-kah)* cook, chef

cuoio, il *(KWOH-yoh)* leather

cuore, il *(KWOH-ray)* (i cuori) heart

cupola, la *(KOO-poh-lah)* cathedral dome

curapipe, il *(koo-rah-PEE-pay)* pipe cleaner

curry, il *(KOOR-ree)* curry

cuscino, il *(koosh-SHEE-noh)* pillow, cushion

cuscus, il *(koos-KOOS)* couscous

cutturiddi, i *(koot-too-REED-dee)* lamb casserole

Cynar aperitif made from artichokes

D

D, d *(dee)* D, d

d' *(d)* from

da *(dah)* from, since, to

dall'altra parte *(dahl-LAHL-trah PAHR-tay)* on the opposite side

dama, la *(DAH-mah)* lady

danno, il *(DAHN-noh)* damage

dare *(DAH-ray)* to give

  da *(dah)* you give (form. sing.)

  dai *(DAH-ee)* you give (inf. sing.)

  diamo *(DYAH-moh)* we give

  do *(doh)* I give

  dare la precedenza *(DAH-ray lah pray-chay-DEN-tsah)* to yield (auto)

da solo/a *(dah SOH-loh/-lah)* alone

d'asporto *(dahs-POHR-toh)* "to go" (food), takeout

data, la *(DAH-tah)* (le date) date

  data di arrivo *(DAH-tah dee ahr-REE-voh)* date of arrival

  data di nascita, la *(DAH-tah dee NAHSH-shee-tah)* date of birth

  data di partenza, la *(DAH-tah dee pahr-TEN-tsah)* date of departure

datteri, i *(DAHT-tay-ree)* dates (fruit)

  datteri de mare, i *(DAHT-tay-ree day MAH-ray)* mussels

dattero, il *(DAHT-tay-roh)* (i datteri) date (fruit)

davanti *(dah-VAHN-tee)* in front of

dea, la *(DEH-ah)* goddess

debole *(DAY-boh-lay)* weak

decade, la *(DEH-kah-day)* ten days

decaffeinato/a *(day-kahf-fay-ee-NAH-toh/-tah)* decaffeinated

decidere *(day-CHEE-day-ray)* to decide

decongestionante, il *(day-kohn-jays-tyoh-NAHN-tay)* decongestant

decurtazione, la *(day-koor-taht-TSYOH-nay)* reduction

deficienza, la *(day-fee-CHEN-tsah)* deficiency

deficit, il *(DEH-fee-cheet)* deficit

degustazione, la *(day-goos-taht-TSYOH-nay)* wine tasting, sampling

delfino, il *(dayl-FEE-noh)* (i delfini) dolphin

delicato/a *(day-lee-KAH-toh/-tah)* delicate, fine

delizioso/a *(day-leet-TSYOH-soh/-sah)* delicious

del pomeriggio *(dayl poh-may-REED-joh)* in the afternoon

democrazia, la *(day-moh-kraht-TSEE-ah)* democracy

denaro, il *(day-NAH-roh)* money

dentaruolo, il *(dayn-tah-RWOH-loh)* teething ring

dente, il *(DEN-tay)* (i denti) tooth
  al dente *(ahl DEN-tay)* (state of cooked pasta) still firm

dentiera, la *(dayn-TYEH-rah)* dentures

dentifricio, il *(dayn-tee-FREE-choh)* (i dentifrici) toothpaste

dentista, il/la *(dayn-TEES-tah)* dentist

dentro *(DAYN-troh)* inside

deodorante, il *(day-oh-doh-RAHN-tay)* (i deodoranti) deodorant

deperibile *(day-pay-REE-bee-lay)* perishable

depositare *(day-poh-zee-TAH-ray)* to deposit

deposito, il *(day-POH-zee-toh)* deposit

deposito bagagli, il *(day-POH-zee-toh bah-GAHL-lyee)* baggage deposit

desiderare *(day-see-day-RAH-ray)* to desire, to wish
  desidera *(day-ZEE-day-rah)* You would like (form. sing.), he/she/it would like
  desidero *(day-ZEE-day-roh)* I would like

desinare *(day-zee-NAH-ray)* to dine

destinazione, la *(days-tee-naht-TSYOH-nay)* destination

destra *(DES-trah)* right

detergente, il *(day-tayr-JEN-tay)* detergent

detersivo, il *(day-tayr-SEE-voh)* laundry detergent

detestare *(day-tays-TAH-ray)* to detest, to hate

deve *(DAY-vay)* you must (form. sing.)

deviazione, la *(day-vee-aht-TSYOH-nay)* detour, deviation

devo *(DAY-voh)* I must

di *(dee)* of, from, by
  di lusso *(dee LOOS-soh)* luxurious
  di meno *(dee MAY-noh)* less
  di nuovo *(dee NWOH-voh)* again
  di più *(dee pyoo)* more

di seconda mano *(dee say-KOHN-dah MAH-noh)* second-hand

diabete, il *(dee-ah-BEH-tay)* diabetes

diabetico/a *(dee-ah-BEH-tee-koh/-kah)* diabetic

diarrea, la *(dee-ahr-REH-ah)* diarrhea

diavola *(DYAH-voh-lah)* (pizza) with spicy sausage

diavolicchio, il *(dyah-voh-LEEK-kyoh)* "little devil" hot peppers

dica, mi *(mee DEE-kah)* tell me, =May I help you?

dicembre, il *(dee-CHEM-bray)* December

diciannove *(dee-chahn-NOH-vay)* nineteen

diciassette *(dee-chahs-SET-tay)* seventeen

diciotto *(dee-CHOHT-toh)* eighteen

dieci *(DYEH-chee)* ten

diesel, il *(DEE-zul)* diesel

dieta, la *(DYEH-tah)* diet

dietro *(DYEH-troh)* behind

difettoso/a *(dee-fayt-TOH-soh/-sah)* defective

differente (da) *(deef-fay-REN-tay [dah])* different (from)

differenza, la *(deef-fay-REN-tsah)* difference

difficile *(deef-FEE-chee-lay)* difficult

digestivo, il *(dee-jays-TEE-voh)* (i digestivi) after-dinner liqueur

digitale *(dee-jee-TAH-lay)* digital

dimensione, la *(dee-mayn-SYOH-nay)* (le dimensioni) size

dimenticare *(dee-mayn-tee-KAH-ray)* to forget

dio, il *(DEE-oh)* (gli dei) God, god

dipendente, il/la *(dee-payn-DEN-tay)* dependant, employee

dipendere *(dee-PEN-day-ray)* to depend

dire *(DEE-ray)* to say

diretto/a *(dee-RET-toh/-tah)* direct (e.g., train)

direttore/direttrice, il/la *(dee-rayt-TOH-ray/-TREE-chay)* manager, director (=anyone in charge)

direzione, la *(dee-rayt-TSYOH-nay)* direction

dirigere *(dee-REE-jay-ray)* to direct, to manage

diritto/a *(dee-REET-toh/-tah)* straight, direct

disabile *(dees-AH-bee-lay)* disabled

disagevole *(dee-zah-JAY-voh-lay)* uncomfortable, difficult

disagio, il *(dee-ZAH-joh)* discomfort, difficulty, awkwardness

disappunto, il *(dee-zahp-POON-toh)* disappointment

discendere *(deesh-SHAYN-day-ray)* to descend

dischetto, il *(dees-KAYT-toh)* computer disk

disco orario, il *(DEES-koh oh-RAHR-yoh)* (i dischi orari) parking disk

discutere *(dees-KOO-tay-ray)* to discuss

disfare *(dees-FAH-ray)* to undo

disgustare *(deez-goos-TAH-ray)* to disgust

disidratato/a *(dee-zee-drah-TAH-toh/-tah)* dehydrated

disidratazione, la *(dee-zee-drah-taht-TSYOH-nay)* dehydration

disinfettante, il *(dee-zeen-fayt-TAHN-tay)* disinfectant

disinserire *(dee-zeen-say-REE-ray)* to disconnect

disoccupato/a *(deez-ohk-koo-PAH-toh/-tah)* unemployed

dispiacere *(dees-pyah-CHAY-ray)* to be sorry

disponibile *(dees-poh-NEE-bee-lay)* available

disponibilità, la *(dees-poh-nee-bee-lee-TAH)* availability, helpfulness

distributore, il *(dees-tree-boo-TOH-ray)* dispenser, distributor

distributore automatico, il *(dees-tree-boo-TOH-ray ow-toh-MAH-tee-koh)* self-service station

distributore automatico di biglietti, il *(dees-tree-boo-TOH-ray ow-toh-MAH-tee-koh dee beel-LYAYT-tee)* ticket machine

distributore di benzina, il *(dees-tree-boo-TOH-ray dee bayn-DSEE-nah)* gas station, gas pump

disturbo, il *(dees-TOOR-boh)* (i disturbi) trouble, inconvenience

disturbi cardiaci, i *(dees-TOOR-bee kahr-DYAH-chee)* heart condition

disturbi da fuso orario, i *(dees-TOOR-bee dah FOO-soh oh-RAHR-yoh)* jet lag

ditale, il *(dee-TAH-lay)* (i ditali) thimble

ditali, i *(dee-TAH-lee)* thimble-shaped pasta

dito, il *(DEE-toh)* (le dita) finger

dito del piede, il *(DEE-toh dayl PYEH-day)* toe

ditta, la *(DEET-tah)* company, firm

divenire *(dee-vay-NEE-ray)* to become

diverso/a (da) *(dee-VEHR-soh/-sah [dah])* diverse, different (from), various

divertimento, il *(dee-vayr-tee-MAYN-toh)* fun, pastime, amusement

divertirsi *(dee-vayr-TEER-see)* to enjoy oneself

dividere *(dee-VEE-day-ray)* to divide

divieto, il *(dee-VYEH-toh)* prohibition (forbidden, prohibited)

   divieto di accesso *(dee-VYEH-toh dee aht-CHES-soh)* no entry

   divieto di sorpasso *(dee-VYEH-toh dee sohr-PAHS-soh)* no passing

   divieto di sostare *(dee-VYEH-toh dee sohs-TAH-ray)* no parking

divorziato/a *(dee-vohr-TSYAH-toh/-tah)* divorced

doccia, la *(DOHT-chah)* (le docce) shower

documenti, i *(doh-koo-MAYN-tee)* papers

documento, il *(doh-koo-MAYN-toh)* (i documenti) document

   documento d'identità, il *(doh-koo-MAYN-toh dee-dayn-tee-TAH)* identification

dodici *(DOH-dee-chee)* twelve

dogana, la *(doh-GAH-nah)* customs

dolce *(DOHL-chay)* mild, sweet, soft

dolce, il *(DOHL-chay)* (i dolci) dessert, sweet

dolcelatte, il *(dohl-chay-LAH-tay)* sweet, soft blue cheese

dolciumi, i *(dohl-CHOO-mee)* candy, sweets

dolere *(doh-LAY-ray)* to ache, to hurt

dollaro, il *(DOHL-lah-roh)* (i dollari) dollar

Dolomiti, le *(doh-loh-MEE-tee)* the Dolomites

dolore, il *(doh-LOH-ray)* (i dolori) hurt, pain

   dolori mestruali, i *(doh-LOH-ree mays-troo-AH-lee)* menstrual pain

doloroso/a *(doh-loh-ROH-soh/-sah)* painful

domanda, la *(doh-MAHN-dah)* question

domani *(doh-MAH-nee)* tomorrow

   domani mattina *(doh-MAH-nee maht-TEE-nah)* tomorrow morning

   domani pomeriggio *(doh-MAH-nee poh-may-REED-joh)* tomorrow afternoon

   domani sera *(doh-MAH-nee SAY-rah)* tomorrow evening

domenica, la *(doh-MAY-nee-kah)* Sunday

donna, la *(DOHN-nah)* (le donne) woman

   donna d'affari, la *(DOHN-nah dahf-FAH-ree)* businesswoman

donne, le *(DOHN-nay)* women

dono, il *(DOH-noh)* (i doni) gift, present

dopo *(DOH-poh)* after

   dopobarba, la *(doh-poh-BAHR-bah)* (le dopobarbe) aftershave

dopodomani *(doh-poh-doh-MAH-nee)* day after tomorrow

dopopranzo *(doh-poh-PRAND-zoh)* afternoon

doppio/a *(DOHP-pyoh/-pyah)* double

doppione, il *(dohp-PYOH-nay)* (i doppioni) duplicate, copy

dorato/a *(doh-RAH-toh/-tah)* golden (color), gilded

dormire *(dohr-MEE-ray)* to sleep

dormita, la *(dohr-MEE-tah)* sleep

dorso, il *(DOHR-soh)* back

dose, la *(DOH-zay)* dose

dottore/dottoressa, il/la *(doht-TOH-ray/doht-toh-RAYS-sah)* "doctor" (=someone with a university degree)

dov'è *(doh-VEH)* where is

dove *(DOH-vay)* where

dovere *(doh-VAY-ray)* must, to have to

dovunque *(doh-VOON-kway)* wherever

dozzina, la *(dohd-DZEE-nah)* dozen

drago, il *(DRAH-goh)* (i draghi) dragon

dramma, il *(DRAHM-mah)* drama

dritta *(DREET-tah)* right, right side

dritto *(DREET-toh)* straight, direct, straight ahead

droga, la *(DROH-gah)* (le droghe) drug

drogheria, la *(droh-gay-REE-ah)* (le drogherie) grocery store

ducale *(doo-KAH-lay)* ducal

due *(DOO-ay)* two

duecento *(doo-ay-CHEN-toh)* two hundred

duepezzi, i *(doo-ay-PET-tsee)* bikini, two-piece

duomo, il *(DWOH-moh)* (i duomi) cathedral

duplicare *(doo-plee-KAH-ray)* to duplicate

dura *(DOO-rah)* (it) lasts

durante *(doo-RAHN-tay)* during

durata, la *(doo-RAH-tah)* duration, length (time)

duro/a *(DOO-roh/-rah)* hard, stiff, tough

E

E, e *(ay)* E, e

e *(ay)* and

è *(eh)* you are, he is, she is

ebreo/a *(ay-BREH-oh/-ah)* Jewish

eccellente *(ayt-chel-LEN-tay)* excellent

eccessivo/a *(ayt-chays-SEE-voh/-vah)* excessive

eccezionale *(ayt-chayt-tsyoh-NAH-lay)* exceptional

eccezione, l' *f* *(ayt-chayt-TSYOH-nay)* exception

ecchimosi, l' *f* *(ayk-KEE-moh-zee)* bruise

ecco *(EK-koh)* here!, there is/are!

economico/a *(ay-koh-NOH-mee-koh/-kah)* cheap

eczema, l' *m (ayk-DZEH-mah)* eczema

edicola, l' *f (ay-DEE-koh-lah)* (le edicole) newstand

edificio, l' *m (ay-dee-FEE-choh)* (gli edifici) building

effetto, l' *m (ayf-FET-toh)* (gli effetti) effect, result

elastico, l' *m (ay-LAHS-tee-koh)* elastic

elegante *(ay-lay-GAHN-tay)* elegant, smart

elenco telefonico, l' *m (ay-LEN-koh tay-lay-FOH-nee-koh)* phone book

elettricista, l'/l' *m/f (ay-layt-tree-CHEES-tah)* electrician

elettricità, l' *f (ay-layt-tree-chee-TAH)* electricity

elettrodomestici *(ay-layt-troh-doh-MES-tee-chee)* electronics store

elezione, l' *f (ay-layt-TSYOH-nay)* election

email, l' *m (EE-mayl)* e-mail

emergenza, l' *f (ay-mayr-JEN-tsah)* emergency

emicrania, l' *f (ay-mee-KRAHN-yah)* migraine

emorroidi, le *(ay-mohr-ROH-ee-dee)* hemorrhoids

emotivo/a *(ay-moh-TEE-voh/-vah)* emotional

EMS *(ay-em-es)* international express mail

energia, l' *f (ay-nayr-JEE-ah)* energy

enorme *(ay-NOHR-may)* enormous

enoteca, l' *f (ay-noh-TEH-kah)* (le enoteche) liquor store, wine shop

entrare *(ayn-TRAHR-ray)* to enter

non entrare *(nohn ayn-TRAHR-ray)* no entry

entrata, l' *f (ayn-TRAH-tah)* (le entrate) admission, entrance

entro *(AYN-troh)* within

epatite, l' *f (ay-pah-TEE-tay)* hepatitis

epicentro, l' *m (ay-pee-CHEN-troh)* epicenter

epilessia, l' *f (ay-pee-lays-SEE-ah)* epilepsy

equo/a *(EK-woh/-wah)* fair, equitable

era *(EH-rah)* it was

erba, l' *f (EHR-bah)* (le erbe) herb

erbazzone, l' *m (ayr-baht-TSOH-nay)* vegetable tart with greens and cheese

erborista, l'/l' *m/f (ayr-boh-REES-tah)* herbalist

eritema solare, l' *m (ay-ree-TEM-ah soh-LAH-ray)* sunburn

ero *(EH-roh)* I was

errato/a *(ayr-RAH-toh/-tah)* wrong, incorrect

errore, l' *m (ayr-ROH-ray)* (gli errori) mistake

ES (train) *(ay-es)* (=Eurostar Italia) very fast train

esame, l' *m (ay-ZAH-may)* test, exam

esaminare *(ay-zah-mee-NAH-ray)* to examine, to consider

esattamente *(ay-zaht-tah-MAYN-tay)* exactly

esaurire *(ay-zow-REE-ray)* to use up, to exhaust

escludere *(ays-KLOO-day-ray)* to exclude

escluso/a *(ays-KLOO-zoh/-zah)* excluded

escursione, l' *f (ays-koor-SYOH-nay)* excursion

  escursione a piedi, l' *f (ays-koor-SYOH-nay ah PYEH-dee)* hike

esegui *(ays-AY-gwee)* (ATM) proceed, enter, execute

esempio, l' *m (ay-ZEM-pyoh)* example

esperienza, l' *f (ays-pay-RYEN-tsah)* experience

esperto/a, l'/l' *m/f (ays-PER-toh/-tah)* expert

esposizione, l' *f (ays-poh-zeet-TSYOH-nay)* exhibition

espresso *(ays-PRES-soh)* fast train, only major stops

espresso, l' *m (ays-PRES-soh)* (gli espressi) espresso, strong black coffee

essere *(ES-say-ray)* to be

  é *(eh)* you are (form. sing.), he/she/it is

  sei *(SAY-ee)* you are (inf. sing.)

  siamo *(SYAH-moh)* we are

  siete *(SYAY-tay)* you are (inf. pl.)

  sono *(SOH-noh)* I am, they are, you are (form. pl.)

esso/a *(AYS-soh/-sah)* it (subject)

est *(est)* east

estate, l' *f (ays-TAH-tay)* (le estati) summer

esterno/a *(ays-TEHR-noh/-nah)* exterior, outer

estero/a *(ES-tay-roh/-rah)* foreign

  all' estero *(ahl-LES-tay-roh)* abroad

estetista, l'/l' *m/f (ays-tay-TEES-tah)* beautician

estrarre *(ays-TRAHR-ray)* to remove, to extract

età, l' *f (ay-TAH)* age

etichetta, l' *f (ay-tee-KAYT-tah)* label, luggage tag

etto, l' *m (ET-toh)* 100 grams

euro, l' *m* *(AY-oo-roh)* (gli euro)
euro

europeo/a *(ay-oo-roh-PEH-oh/-ah)*
European

Eurostar Italia *(ay-oo-roh-STAHR ee-TAHL-yah)* very fast train

evitare *(ay-vee-TAH-ray)* to avoid

F

F, f *(AYF-fay)* F, f

fa *(fah)* you do, do you do?

fabbrica, la *(FAHB-bree-kah)*
factory

facchino, il *(fahk-KEE-noh)* baggage porter

faccia, la *(FAHT-chah)* face

facciamo *(faht-CHYAH-moh)* we do

faccio *(FAHT-choh)* I do

facile *(FAH-chee-lay)* easy

facsimile, il *(fahk-SEE-mee-lay)* fax, copy

fagiano, il *(fah-JAH-noh)* (i fagiani)
pheasant

fagioli, i *(fah-JOH-lee)* dried beans
  fagioli alla toscana, i *(fah-JOH-lee AHL-lah tohs-KAH-nah)* slow-cooked beans with salt, black pepper and olive oil
  fagioli all'uccelletto, i *(fah-JOH-lee ahl-loot-chayl-LET-toh)* beans cooked in tomatoes and black olives

fagioli in umido, i *(fah-JOH-lee een OO-mee-doh)* beans cooked in tomato sauce and spices

fagiolini, i *(fah-joh-LEE-nee)*
green beans

fagiolino, il *(fah-joh-LEE-noh)* (i fagiolini) green bean

fagiolo, il *(fah-JOH-loh)* (i fagioli)
dried bean

faglia d'alloro, la *(FAHL-yah dahl-LOH-roh)* bay leaf

fai da te *(fah-ee-dah-TAY)* do-it-yourself, self-service

falesia, la *(fah-LEZ-yah)* cliff

fallire *(fahl-LEE-ray)* to fail, to go bankrupt

fallo, il *(FAHL-loh)* fault

falò, il *(fah-LOH)* bonfire

falsificare *(fahl-see-fee-KAH-ray)* to falsify, to fake, to forge

falso/a *(FAHL-soh/-sah)* forged, fake

fama, la *(FAH-mah)* fame

fame, la *(FAH-may)* hunger
  ho fame *(oh FAH-may)* I'm hungry

famiglia, la *(fah-MEEL-yah)* (le famiglie) family

famoso/a *(fah-MOH-soh/-sah)* famous

fanale, il *(fah-NAH-lay)* headlight, beacon

fango, il *(FAHN-goh)* mud

fantasia, la *(fahn-tah-ZEE-ah)* imagination, fancy

fantastico/a *(fahn-TAHS-tee-koh/-kah)* fantastic, terrific

farcito/a *(FAHR-chee-toh/-tah)* stuffed

fare *(FAH-ray)* to do, to make

  fa *(fah)* you do/make (form. sing.), he/she/it does/makes

  facciamo *(faht-CHAH-moh)* we do/make

  faccio *(FAHT-choh)* I do/make

  fanno *(FAHN-noh)* they do/make

  fare la barba *(FAH-rah lah BAHR-bah)* to shave

  fare l'autostop *(FAH-ray low-tohs-TOHP)* to hitchhike

  fare male *(FAH-ray MAH-lay)* to hurt

farfalla, la *(fahr-FAHL-lah)* (le farfalle) butterfly

farfalle, le *(fahr-FAHL-lay)* (le farfalli) butterfly-shaped pasta

farfallino, il *(fahr-fahl-LEE-noh)* (i farfallini) small, bow-shaped pasta

fari, i *(FAH-ree)* headlights

farina, la *(fah-REE-nah)* flour

farmacia, la *(fahr-mah-CHEE-ah)* (le farmacie) drugstore (medicine), pharmacy

farmacista, il/la *(fahr-mah-CHEES-tah)* pharmacist

farmaco, il *(FAHR-mah-koh)* (i farmaci) drug, medicine

faro, il *(FAH-roh)* (i fari) headlight

fascia, la *(FAHSH-shah)* (le fasce) bandage

fascismo, il *(fahsh-SHEEZ-moh)* facism

fatto/a *(FAHT-toh/-tah)* made

  fatto/a a mano *(FAHT-toh/-tah ah MAH-noh)* handmade

  fatto di *(FAHT-toh dee)* made of

  fatto/a in casa *(FAHT-toh/-tah een KAH-sah)* homemade

fattoria, la *(faht-toh-REE-ah)* farm, farmhouse

fattura, la *(faht-TOO-rah)* invoice

fava, la *(FAH-vah)* (le fave) broad bean

favata, la *(fah-VAH-tah)* bean and pork stew

fave, le *(FAH-vay)* broad beans (see fava)

favore, il *(fah-VOH-ray)* (i favori) favor

  per favore *(payr fah-VOH-ray)* please

fax, il *(fahks)* fax

faxare *(fahk-SAH-ray)* to fax

fazzoletto/fazzolettino (di carta), il *(faht-tsoh-LAYT-toh/faht-tsoh-layt-TEE-noh [dee KAHR-tah])* (i fazzoletti) facial tissue

febbraio, il *(fayb-BRAH-yoh)*
February

febbre, la *(FEB-bray)* fever
 febbre da fiene, la *(FEB-bray dah-FYEH-nay)* hay fever

federa, la *(FEH-day-rah)* pillowcase

fegato, il *(FAY-gah-toh)* (i fegati)
liver
 fegato alla veneziana, il *(FAY-gah-toh AHL-lah vay-nayt-TSYAH-nah)*
liver fried with onions

felice *(fay-LEE-chay)* happy

felino, il *(fay-LEE-noh)* a pork
salami, feline

felpa, la *(FAYL-pah)* (le felpe)
sweatshirt

ferita, la *(fay-REE-tah)* injury

ferito/a *(fay-REE-toh/-tah)* injured

fermare *(fayr-MAH-ray)* to stop
 fermarsi *(fayr-MAHR-see)* to stop,
to halt
 fermo! *(FAYR-moh)* stop!
 si ferma *(see FAYR-mah)* (it)
stops

fermata, la *(fayr-MAH-tah)* train or
bus stop

fermo posta, la *(FAYR-moh POHS-tah)* poste restante, general
delivery

ferramenta, la *(fayr-rah-MAYN-tah)*
hardware shop

ferri, ai *(AH-ee FEHR-ree)* grilled

ferro, il *(FEHR-roh)* iron
 ferro da stiro, il *(FEHR-roh dah STEE-roh)* clothes iron

ferrovia, la *(fayr-roh-VEE-ah)*
train station, railroad

Ferrovia dello Stato *(fayr-roh-VEE-ah DAYL-loh STAH-toh)*
Italian state train system

ferroviaria, la **stazione** *(stah-TSYOH-nay fayr-roh-VYAHR-yah)*
train station

ferry boat, il *(FEHR-ree BOH-oot)*
ferry

fesa, la *(FAY-zah)* rump of veal

festa, la *(FES-tah)* festival,
holiday

festeggiare *(fays-tayd-JAH-ray)*
to celebrate

festivo/a *(fays-TEE-voh/-vah)*
holiday

fetta, la *(FAYT-tah)* (le fette)
slice, strip

fettuccine, le *(fayt-toot-CHEE-nay)*
ribbon-shaped pasta
 fettuccine Alfredo, le *(fayt-toot-CHEE-nay ahl-FRAY-doh)*
noodle ribbons with
parmesan and cream
 fettuccine alla romana, le *(fay-toot-CHEE-nay AHL-lah roh-MAH-nah)* noodle ribbons
with tomato and meat
sauce

fiammiferi, i *(fyahm-MEE-fay-ree)*
matches

fiammifero, il *(fyahm-MEE-fay-roh)* (i fiammiferi) match
(fire)

fico, il *(FEE-koh)* (i fichi) fig

fidanzamento, il *(fee-dahn-tsah-MAYN-toh)* engagement

fidanzato/a, il/la *(fee-dahn-TSAH-toh/-tah)* fiance(e)

fieno, il *(FYEH-noh)* hay

febbre da fieno, il *(FEB-bray dah FYEH-noh)* hay fever

figlia, la *(FEEL-lyah)* (le figlie) daughter

figlio, il *(FEEL-lyoh)* (i figli) son

figura, la *(fee-GOO-rah)* figure, illustration

bella figura, la *(BEL-lah fee-GOO-rah)* good image

fila, la *(FEE-lah)* (le file) line, queue, traffic jam

filato, il *(fee-LAH-toh)* yarn, thread

filetto, il *(fee-LAYT-toh)* (i filetti) fillet

filetto al pepe verde, il *(fee-LAYT-toh ahl PAY-pay VAYR-day)* steak in creamy sauce seasoned with green peppercorns

film, il *(feelm)* movie

filo, il *(FEE-loh)* (i fili) thread, yarn, string

filo dentario, il *(FEE-loh dayn-TAHR-yoh)* dental floss

filoncino, il *(fee-lohn-CHEE-noh)* (i filoncini) breadstick

filovia, la *(fee-loh-VEE-ah)* trolley line, trolley bus

fine, la *(FEE-nay)* end

fine settimana, il *(FEE-nay sayt-tee-MAH-nah)* weekend

finestra, la *(fee-NES-trah)* (le finestre) window

finestrino, il *(fee-nays-TREE-noh)* window (auto, train)

finire *(fee-NEE-ray)* to finish, to end

finito/a *(fee-NEE-toh/-tah)* finished

fino a *(FEE-noh ah)* until

finocchio, il *(fee-NOHK-kyoh)* fennel

fiocchi di mais, i *(FYOHK-kee dee MAH-ees)* cornflakes

fioraio/a, il/la *(fyoh-RAH-yoh/-yah)* florist

fior di latte, il *(fyohr dee LAHT-tay)* mozzarella made from cow's milk

fiore, il *(FYOH-ray)* (i fiori) flower

fiori, i *(FYOH-ree)* flowers

fiori di zucca ripiene, i *(FYOH-ree dee TSOOK-kah ree-PYEH-nay)* stuffed and fried squash blossoms

fiorista, il/la *(fyoh-REES-tah)* florist

Firenze *(fee-REN-tsay)* Florence

firma, la *(FEER-mah)* signature

firmare *(feer-MAH-ray)* to sign

fisarmonica, la *(fee-zahr-MOH-nee-kah)* (le fisarmoniche) accordion

fissare *(fees-SAH-ray)* to fix, to book, to reserve

fisso/a *(FEES-soh/-sah)* fixed, permanent, constant

fiume, il *(FYOO-may)* river

flash, il *(flesh)* camera flash

flirtare *(fleer-TAH-ray)* to flirt

focaccia, la *(foh-KAHT-chah)* (le focacce) flatbread

foglia, la *(FOHL-lyah)* leaf

föhn, il *(fun)* hair-dryer

fondamenta, la *(fohn-dah-MAYN-tah)* (Venice) street along waterway

fondere *(FOHN-day-ray)* to melt

fondo/a *(FOHN-doh/-dah)* deep

fondo, il *(FOHN-doh)* bottom

fonduta, la *(fohn-DOO-tah)* cheese fondue

fontana, la *(fohn-TAH-nah)* (le fontane) fountain

fonte, la *(FOHN-tay)* spring

fontina, la *(fohn-TEE-nah)* rich, creamy cow's milk cheese

footing, il *(FOO-teeng)* jogging

forbici, le *(FOHR-bee-chee)* scissors

forchetta, la *(fohr-KAYT-tah)* (le forchette) fork

forcina, la *(fohr-CHEE-nah)* (le forcine) hairpin

foresta, la *(foh-RES-tah)* forest

forfora, la *(FOHR-fohr-ah)* dandruff

forma, la *(FOHR-mah)* shape

formaggeria, la *(fohr-mahd-jay-REE-ah)* cheese shop

formaggio, il *(fohr-MAHD-joh)* (i formaggi) cheese

formaggio fresco, il *(fohr-MAHD-joh FRAYS-koh)* cream cheese

quattro formaggi *(KWAHT-troh fohr-MAHD-jee)* (pizza) with four types of cheese

formare *(fohr-MAH-ray)* to form, to shape

formica, la *(fohr-MEE-kah)* (le formiche) ant

forno, il *(FOHR-noh)* oven

al forno *(ahl FOHR-noh)* baked

forno a microonde, il *(FOHR-noh ah mee-kroh-OHN-day)* microwave oven

foro, il *(FOH-roh)* forum

forse *(FOHR-say)* maybe

forte *(FOHR-tay)* loud, loudly, strong

fortezza, la *(fohr-TAYT-tsah)* (le fortezze) fortress

fortuna, la *(fohr-TOO-nah)* luck, chance

fortunato/a *(fohr-too-NAH-toh/-tah)* lucky

fossato, il *(fohs-SAH-toh)* moat, ditch

foto, la *(FOH-toh)* photo

fotocine, il **negozio di** *(nay-GOH-tsyoh dee foh-toh-CHEE-nay)* photo shop

fotocopia, la *(foh-toh-KOHP-yah)* (le fotocopie) photocopy

fotocopiare *(foh-toh-koh-PYAH-ray)* to photocopy

fotografare *(foh-toh-grah-FAH-ray)* to photograph

fotografia, la *(foh-toh-grah-FEE-ah)* photography

fotografo/a, il/la *(foh-TOH-grah-foh/-fah)* photographer

fra *(frah)* between

fra poco *(frah POH-koh)* soon

fragile *(FRAH-jee-lay)* fragile

fragola, la *(FRAH-goh-lah)* (le fragole) strawberry

fragole, le *(FRAH-goh-lay)* strawberries (see fragola)

franamento, il *(frahn-nah-MAYN-toh)* landslide

Francia, la *(FRAHN-chah)* France

francobollo, il *(frahn-koh-BOHL-loh)* (i francobolli) postage stamp

frappé, il *(frahp-PAY)* milk shake

fratello, il *(frah-TEL-loh)* (i fratelli) brother

frattaglie, le *(fraht-TAHL-yay)* offal, giblets

freccia, la *(FRAYT-chah)* turn signal

freddo/a *(FRAYD-doh/-dah)* cold

fregola, la *(FRAY-goh-lah)* pasta, similar to couscous

freno, il *(FRAY-noh)* brake

frequentato/a *(fray-kwayn-TAH-toh/-tah)* busy

frequente *(fray-KWEN-tay)* frequent

fresco/a *(FRAYS-koh/-kah)* cool, fresh

fresco, il *(FRAYS-koh)* fresco

fretta, la *(FRAYT-tah)* hurry

avere fretta *(ah-VAY-ray FRAYT-tah)* to be in a hurry

friggere *(FREED-jay-ray)* to fry

friggitoria, la *(freed-jee-toh-REE-ah)* fish-and-chip shop

frigo, il *(FREE-goh)* (i frighi) fridge

frigobar, il *(free-goh-BAHR)* mini-bar

frigorifero, il *(free-goh-REE-fay-roh)* refrigerator

fritole, le *(free-TOH-lay)* fried dough dessert

frittata, la *(free-TAH-tah)* (le frittate) omelette

frittatensuppe, la *(free-TAH-ten-zoo-puh)* thin pancake or omelet strips served in clear soup

frittella, la *(freet-TEL-lah)* (le frittelle) fritter

frittelle, le *(freet-TEL-lay)* round, fried yeast-dough pastries, fritters

fritto/a *(FREET-toh/-tah)* fried

fritto misto, il *(FREET-toh MEES-toh)* fried mix of small fish and shellfish

frizione, la *(freet-TSYOH-nay)* clutch (auto), massage

frizzante *(freed-DZAHN-tay)*
carbonated, fizzy

frollino, il *(frohl-LEE-noh)* candied-
fruit pastry

frugale *(froo-GAH-lay)* frugal

frullato di latte, il *(frool-LAH-toh dee
LAHT-tay)* milk shake

frutta, la *(FROOT-tah)* (le frutte)
fruit

  frutta secca, la *(FROOT-tah SAYK-
kah)* nuts, dried fruit

frutti di mare, i *(FROO-tee-dee
MAH-ray)* seafood, shellfish

fruttivendolo/a, il/la *(froot-tee-
VAYN-doh-loh/-lah)* greengrocer

fruttosio, il *(froot-TOHZ-yoh)*
fructose

FS *(EF-fay-ES-say)* (Ferrovia dello
Stato) state train system

fumaiolo, il *(foo-mah-YOH-loh)*
chimney

fumare *(foo-MAH-ray)* to smoke

fumare, il *(foo-MAH-ray)* smoking

fumato/a *(foo-MAH-toh/-tah)*
smoked

fumatori, i *(foo-mah-TOH-ree)*
smokers

fumicato/a *(foo-mee-KAH-toh/-tah)*
smoked

fumo, il *(FOO-moh)* smoking,
smoke

funerale, il *(foo-nay-RAH-lay)*
funeral

funghi, i *(FOON-gee)* mushrooms

funghi porcini arrosti, i
*(FOON-gee pohr-CHEE-nee ahr-
ROHS-tee)* porcini
mushrooms roasted with
garlic, parsley and chili
peppers

fungo, il *(FOON-goh)* (i funghi)
mushroom

funicolare, la *(foo-nee-koh-LAH-
ray)* funicular railway

funivia, la *(foo-nee-VEE-ah)* cable
car

funzionare *(foon-tsyoh-NAH-ray)*
to function, to act

  funziona *(foon-TSYOH-nah)* it
functions/works

  non funziona *(nohn foon-
TSYOH-nah)* it doesn't
function/work

fuoco, il *(FWOH-koh)* (i fuochi)
fire

fuori *(FWOH-ree)* outside

  fuori servizio *(FWOH-ree sayr-
VEET-tsyoh)* out of service

furgone, il *(foor-GOH-nay)* van

furto, il *(FOOR-toh)* theft

fusilli, i *(foo-SEEL-lee)* pasta
spirals

fusillo, il *(foo-SEEL-loh)* (i fussili)
pasta spiral

futuro, il *(foo-TOO-roh)* future

G

G, g *(jee)* G, g

gabinetto, il *(gah-bee-NAYT-toh)* (i gabinetti) bathroom, toilet

galani, i *(gah-LAH-nee)* delicate, crispy, sweetened ribbons of fried dough

galleria, la *(gah-lay-REE-ah)* tunnel
galleria d'arte, la *(gah-lay-REE-ah DAHR-tay)* art gallery

Galles, il *(GAHL-lays)* Wales

galletto, il *(gahl-LAYT-toh)* young chicken (rooster)

gallina, la *(gahl-LEE-nah)* (le galline) hen

gallo, il *(GAHL-loh)* (i galli) rooster

gallone, il *(gahl-LOH-nay)* (i galloni) gallon

gamba, la *(GAHM-bah)* (le gambe) leg

gambale, il *(gahm-BAH-lay)* legging

gambaletto, il *(gahm-bah-LAYT-toh)* (i gambaletti) knee-high sock

gamberetto, il *(gahm-bay-RAYT-toh)* (i gamberetti) shrimps

gambero, il *(GAHM-bay-roh)* (i gamberi) prawn, shrimp

gamberono, il *(gahm-bay-ROH-noh)* (i gamberoni) jumbo shrimp

garage, il *(gah-RAHZH)* garage

garantire *(gah-rahn-TEE-ray)* to guarantee

garantito/a *(gah-rahn-TEE-toh/-tah)* guaranteed

garganelli, i *(gahr-gahn-NEL-lee)* penne-sized, egg-based rolled pasta tubes

gas, il *(gahs)* gas, natural gas
con gas *(kohn gahs)* carbonated, fizzy (e.g., mineral water)

gasolio, il *(gah-ZOH-lyoh)* diesel

gassato/a *(gahs-SAH-toh/-tah)* carbonated, fizzy

gastroenterite, la *(gahs-troh-ayn-tay-REE-tay)* gastroenteritis

gattino, il *(gaht-TEE-noh)* (i gattini) kitten

gatto, il *(GAHT-toh)* (i gatti) cat

gay *(GAY-ee)* gay

gazolina, la *(gahd-dzoh-LEE-nah)* gasoline

gelata, la *(jay-LAH-tah)* frost

gelateria, la *(jay-lah-tay-REE-ah)* (le gelaterie) ice cream parlor

gelatina, la *(jay-lah-TEE-nah)* gelatine

gelato, il *(jay-LAH-toh)* (i gelati) ice cream

gelosia, la *(jay-loh-SEE-ah)* shutter

geloso/a *(jay-LOH-soh/-sah)* jealous

gemelli/e, i/le *(jay-MEL-lee/-lay)* twins

gemello/a, il/la *(jay-MEL-loh/-lah)* (i gemelli/le gemelle) twin

gemma, la *(JEM-mah)* gem, jewel

genealogia, la *(jay-nay-ah-loh-JEE-ah)* geneology

generale *(jay-nay-RAH-lay)* general

genere, il *(JAY-nay-ray)* kind, type, sort

genero, il *(JEH-nay-roh)* son-in-law

generoso/a *(jay-nay-ROH-soh/-sah)* generous, very strong (wine)

gengiva, la *(jayn-JEE-vah)* gum (mouth)

genitore/trice, il/la *(jay-nee-TOHR-ray/TREE-chay)* (i genitori) parent

gennaio, il *(jayn-NAH-yoh)* January

Genova *(JEN-oh-vah)* Genoa

genovese, il **pesto alla** *(PAYS-toh AHL-lah jay-noh-VAY-say)* sauce of olive oil, garlic, basil, pine nuts, parmesan

gente, la *(JEN-tay)* people

gentile *(jayn-TEE-lay)* kind, nice

Germania, la *(jayr-MAHN-yah)* Germany

germogli, i *(jayr-MOHL-lyee)* sprouts

Gesù *(jay-ZOO)* Jesus

  Gesù Bambino *(jay-ZOO bahm-BEE-noh)* the Christ child

gettare *(jayt-TAH-ray)* to throw

gettone, il *(jayt-TOH-nay)* (i gettoni) token

ghetto, il *(GAYT-toh)* (i ghetti) ghetto

ghiaccio, il *(GYAHT-choh)* ice

  cubetti di ghiaccio, i *(koo-BAYT-tee dee GYAHT-choh)* ice cubes

già *(jah)* already

giacca, la *(JAHK-kah)* (le giacche) jacket

giacere *(jah-CHAY-ray)* to lie (e.g., in bed)

giallo/a *(JAHL-loh/-lah)* yellow

gianduia, la *(jahn-DOO-ee-ah)* cold chocolate pudding, chocolate shavings (ice cream)

gianduiotto, il *(jahn-doo-ee-OHT-toh)* hazelnut chocolate wedges wrapped in tinfoil

Giappone, il *(jahp-POH-nay)* Japan

giardinaggio, il *(jahr-dee-NAHD-joh)* gardening

giardiniera, la *(jahr-dee-NYEH-rah)* pickled vegetable mix

giardino, il *(jahr-DEE-noh)* (i giardini) garden

  giardino zoologico, il *(jahr-DEE-noh dzoh-oh-LOH-jee-koh)* zoo

ginecologo/a, il/la *(jee-nay-KOH-loh-goh/-gah)* gynecologist

gingerino, il *(jeen-jayr-EE-noh)* aperitif, ginger-flavored

ginnastica, la *(jeen-NAHS-tee-kah)* gymnastics

ginocchiera, la *(jee-nohk-KYEH-rah)* (le ginocchiere) kneepad

ginocchio, il *(jee-NOHK-kyoh)* (le ginocchia) knee

giocare *(joh-KAH-ray)* to play

gioco, il *(JOH-koh)* (i giochi) game

gioco elettronico, il *(JOH-koh ay-layt-TROH-nee-koh)* computer game

gioielli, i *(joh-YEL-lee)* jewelry

giornale, il *(johr-NAH-lay)* (i giornali) newspaper

giornalista, il/la *(johr-nah-LEES-tah)* journalist

giornalmente *(johr-nahl-MAYN-tay)* daily

giorno, il *(JOHR-noh)* (i giorni) day

giorno di chiusura, il *(JOHR-noh dee kyoo-SOO-rah)* closing day

giorno feriale, il *(JOHR-noh fay-RYAH-lay)* (giorni feriali) week day

giorno festivo, il *(JOHR-noh fays-TEE-voh)* (giorni festivi) holiday

giorno lavorativo, il *(JOHR-noh lah-voh-rah-TEE-voh)* (giorni lavorativi) work day, week day

giovane *(JOH-vah-nay)* young

giovedì, il *(joh-vay-DEE)* Thursday

girare *(jee-RAH-ray)* to turn

girasole, il *(jee-rah-SOH-lay)* sunflower

girello, il *(jee-REL-loh)* (cut of meat) the eye of the round, top round

giro, il *(JEE-roh)* circle

gita, la *(JEE-tah)* (le gite) trip

giù *(joo)* down

giubbone, il *(joob-BOH-nay)* heavy coat

giubbotto di salvataggio, il *(joob-BOHT-toh dee sahl-vah-TAHD-joh)* life jacket

giudice, il *(JOO-dee-chay)* judge

giudò, il *(joo-DOH)* judo

giugno, il *(JOON-nyoh)* June

giusto/a *(JOOS-toh/-tah)* right, correct, fair

glassa, la *(GLAHS-sah)* icing

gli *(lyee)* the (plural of *lo* and masc. *l*)

glutine, il *(GLOO-tee-nay)* gluten

gnocchetti, gli *(nyohk-KET-tee)* smaller version of gnocchi, shell-shaped pasta

gnocchi, gli *(NYOHK-kee)* small potato or semolina dumplings

gnocco, lo *(NYOHK-koh)* (gli gnocchi) small dumpling from potato or semolina

gnoccho di pane, lo *(NYOHK-koh dee PAH-nay)* bread gnocchi

gnoccho di patate, lo *(NYOHK-koh dee pah-TAH-tay)* (gli gnocchi) potato dumpling

godere *(goh-DAY-ray)* to enjoy

gola, la *(GOH-lah)* throat

golfo, il *(GOHL-foh)* gulf

gomito, il *(GOH-mee-toh)* (i gomiti) elbow

gomma, la *(GOHM-mah)* (i gomme) tire (vehicle), eraser

gomma da masticare, la *(GOHM-mah dah mahs-tee-KAH-ray)* chewing gum

gondola, la *(GOHN-doh-lah)* gondola

gondoliere, il *(gohn-doh-LYEH-ray)* gondolier

gonfiore, il *(gohn-FYOH-ray)* swelling

gonna, la *(GOHN-nah)* (le gonne) skirt

gorgonzola, la *(gohr-gohn-DZOH-lah)* a pungent blue cheese

gotta, la *(GOHT-tah)* gout

governo, il *(goh-VEHR-noh)* government

grado, il *(GRAH-doh)* degree

graffetta, la *(grahf-FAYT-tah)* paper clip, staple

grammi, i *(GRAHM-mee)* grams

grammo, il *(GRAHM-moh)* (i grammi) gram

grana padano, la *(GRAH-nah pah-DAH-noh)* a cheese similar to Parmesan

granchio, il *(GRAHNK-yoh)* (i granchi) crab

grande *(GRAHN-day)* big

grande magazzino, il *(GRAHN-day mah-gahd-DZEE-noh)* department store

grandinata, la *(grahn-dee-NAH-tah)* hailstorm

grandine, la *(GRAHN-dee-nay)* hail

granita, la *(grah-NEE-tah)* semi-frozen, sweetened and flavored, flaked ice dessert

granseola, la *(grahn-say-OH-lah)* spider crab

grappa, la *(GRAHP-pah)* grape-based alcoholic drink

grasso/a *(GRAHS-soh/-sah)* fat

graticola, la *(grah-TEE-koh-lah)* grill

alla graticola *(AHL-lah grah-TEE-koh-lah)* barbequed

gratis *(GRAH-tees)* free

gratta e sosta *(GRAHT-tah ay SOHS-tah)* scratch and park

gratuito/a *(grah-TOO-ee-toh/-tah)* free, no cost

grave *(GRAH-vay)* grave, serious

grazie *(GRAHT-tsyay)* thank you

grigio/a *(GREE-joh/-jah)* gray

griglia, la *(GREEL-lyah)* grill

alla griglia *(AHL-lah GREEL-lyah)* grilled, broiled

grissino, il *(grees-SEE-noh)* (i grissini) thin, crisp breadstick

grosso/a *(GROHS-soh/-sah)* big, thick, heavy

grotta, la *(GROHT-tah)* cave

groviera, la *(groh-VYEH-rah)* gruyère (cheese)

gruppo, il *(GROOP-poh)* group, music band

guanciale, il *(gwahn-CHAH-lay)* pillow; unsmoked bacon, from pig's cheek

guanti, i *(GWAHN-tee)* gloves

guanto, il *(GWAHN-toh)* (i guanti) glove

guardare *(gwahr-DAH-ray)* to look, to watch

guarda *(GWAHR-dah)* you look (form. sing.)

guardando *(gwahr-DAHN-doh)* looking

guardiamo *(gwahr-DYAH-moh)* we look

guardo *(GWAHR-doh)* I look

guardaroba, il *(gwahr-dah-ROH-bah)* checkroom, cloakroom

guarire *(gwah-REE-ray)* to heal, to recover, to cure

guastarsi *(gwahs-TAHR-see)* to break down

guastato/a *(gwahs-TAH-toh/-tah)* broken down

guasto/a *(GWAHS-toh/-tah)* (it's) not working, broken

guerra, la *(GWEHR-rah)* war

guglia, la *(GOOL-lyah)* spire

guida, la *(GWEE-dah)* guide, guidebook

guida audio, la *(GWEE-dah OWD-yoh)* audioguide

guida turistica, la *(GWEE-dah too-REES-tee-kah)* guidebook

guidare *(gwee-DAH-ray)* to drive

guida *(GWEE-dah)* you drive (form. sing.)

guidiamo *(gwee-DYAH-moh)* we drive

guido *(GWEE-doh)* I drive

gusto, il *(GOO-stoh)* taste, flavor

gustoso/a *(goos-TOH-soh/-sah)* tasty

H

H, h *(AHK-kah)* H, h

ha *(ah)* you have

hamburger, l' *m (ahm-BOOR-gayr)* hamburger

ho *(oh)* I have

hot dog, l' *m (OT-dog)* hot dog

hotel, l' *m (oh-TEL)* hotel

I

I, i *(ee)* I, i

idea, l' *f (ee-DEH-ah)* idea

identificazione, l' *f (ee-dayn-tee-fee-kaht-TSYOH-nay)* identification

identità, l' *f* *(ee-dayn-tee-TAH)* identity

idiota, l'/l' *m/f* *(ee-DYOH-tah)* (gli idioti/le idiote) idiot

idratante, l' *m* *(ee-drah-TAHN-tay)* moisturizer

idraulico/a, l'/l' *m/f* *(ee-DROW-lee-koh)* plumber

ieri *(YEH-ree)* yesterday

igiene, l' *f* *(ee-JEH-nay)* hygiene

illegale *(eel-lay-GAH-lay)* illegal

imballaggio, l' *m* *(eem-bahl-LAHD-joh)* (gli imballaggi) packing (material)

imballare *(eem-bahl-LAH-ray)* to pack

imbarazzato/a *(eem-bah-raht-TSAH-toh/-tah)* embarassed

imbarcadero, l' *m* *(eem-bahr-kah-DEH-roh)* landing dock

imbarcare *(eem-bahr-KAH-ray)* to embark, to load

imbarco, l' *m* *(eem-BAHR-koh)* embarkation, boarding

imbucare *(eem-boo-KAH-ray)* to mail a letter

immacolato/a *(ee-mah-koh-LAH-toh/-tah)* immaculate, spotless

immediato/a *(eem-may-DYAH-toh/-tah)* immediate, prompt

immersione, l' *f* *(eem-mayr-SYOH-nay)* dive

immersione in apnea, l' *f* *(eem-mayr-SYOH-nay een ahp-NEH-ah)* snorkelling

immersione subacquea, l' *f* *(eem-mayr-SYOH-nay soo-BAHK-kway-ah)* scuba diving

immigrazione, l' *f* *(eem-mee-graht-TSYOH-nay)* immigration

impanato/a *(eem-pah-NAH-toh/-tah)* breaded

imparare *(eem-pah-RAH-ray)* to learn

impazzire *(eem-paht-TSEE-ray)* to go insane

imperfetto/a *(eem-payr-FET-toh/-tah)* imperfect, faulty, defective

impermeabile *(eem-payr-may-AH-bee-lay)* waterproof

impiegare *(eem-pyay-GAH-ray)* to employ

impiegato/a, l'/l' *m/f* *(eem-pyay-GAH-toh/-tah)* employee

imporre *(eem-POHR-ray)* to impose

importante *(eem-pohr-TAHN-tay)* important

importanza, l' *f* *(eem-pohr-TAHN-tsah)* importance, significance

importo, l' *m* *(eem-POHR-toh)* amount

impossibile *(eem-pohs-SEE-bee-lay)* impossible

imprenditrice, l' *f* *(eem-prayn-dee-TREE-chay)* businesswoman

imprudente *(eem-proo-DEN-tay)*
imprudent, careless, foolish

in *(een)* in

in bianco *(een BYAHN-koh)*
without tomato sauce, with
butter and Parmesan

in lista d'attesa *(een LEES-tah
daht-TAY-sah)* standby (ticket)

in loco *(een LOH-koh)* on the
spot

in ritardo *(een ree-TAHR-doh)* late

in sciopero *(een SHOH-pay-roh)*
on strike

in vendita *(een VAYN-dee-tah)* on
sale

inalatore, l' *m (ee-nah-lah-TOH-ray)*
inhaler

incerto/a *(een-CHEHR-toh/-tah)*
uncertain, doubtful

incidente, l' *m (een-chee-DEN-tay)*
accident

incinta *(een-CHEEN-tah)* pregnant

includere *(een-KLOO-day-ray)* to
include

incluso/a *(een-KLOO-zoh/-zah)*
included

incontrare *(een-kohn-TRAH-ray)* to
meet

incredibile *(een-kray-DEE-bee-lay)*
incredible

incrocio, l' *m (een-KROH-choh)* (gli
incroci) crossroads,
intersection

indelicato/a *(een-day-lee-KAH-
toh/-tah)* tactless, indiscreet

indicare *(een-dee-KAH-ray)* to
point, to show, to indicate

indietro *(een-DYEH-troh)* behind

indigestione, l' *f (een-dee-jays-
TYOH-nay)* indigestion

indiretto/a *(een-dee-RET-toh/-tah)*
indirect

indirizzo, l' *m (een-dee-REET-
tsoh)* address

indisposto/a *(een-dees-POHS-
toh/-tah)* indisposed

indivia, l' *f (een-DEEV-yah)*
endive

ind. suss. (train) intermediate
stop

indù *(een-DOO)* Hindu

industria, l' *f (een-DOOS-tryah)*
industry

inebriato/a *(ee-nay-bree-AH-toh/-
tah)* inebriated, intoxicated

infarto, l' *m (een-FAHR-toh)*
heart attack

infatti *(een-FAHT-tee)* in fact

infermiere/a, l'/l' *m/f (een-
fayr-MYEH-ray/-rah)* nurse

infermo/a *(een-FAYR-moh/-mah)*
infirm, ill

inferno, l' *m (een-FEHR-noh)* hell

infezione, l' *f (een-fayt-TSYOH-
nay)* infection

infiammazione, l' *f (een-fyahm-
maht-TSYOH-nay)*
inflammation

influenza, l' *f (een-floo-EN-tsah)* flu

informare *(een-fohr-MAH-ray)* to inform

informatica, l' *f (een-fohr-MAH-tee-kah)* IT, computer science

informazione, l' *f (een-fohr-maht-TSYOH-nay)* (le informazioni) information

infortunato/a *(een-fohr-too-NAH-toh/-tah)* injured

ingegnere, l' *m (een-jayn-NYEH-ray)* engineer

Inghilterra, l' *f (een-geel-TEHR-rah)* England

inglese *(een-GLAY-say)* English

ingorgo (del traffico), l' *m (een-GOHR-goh [dayl TRAHF-fee-koh])* (gli ingorghi) traffic jam

ingrediente, l' *m (een-gray-DYEN-tay)* (gli ingredienti) ingredient

ingresso, l' *m (een-GRES-soh)* (gli ingressi) admission, admittance, entrance

ingresso gratuito, l' *m (een-GRES-soh grah-TOO-ee-toh)* free admission

iniezione, l' *f (een-yet-TSYOH-nay)* injection

inizio, l' *m (ee-NEET-tsyoh)* beginning, start

innocente *(een-noh-CHEN-tay)* innocent

input, l' *m (EEN-poot)* input

inquinare *(een-kwee-NAH-ray)* to pollute

insaccati, gli *(een-sahk-KAH-tee)* sausages

insalata, l' *f (een-sah-LAH-tah)* (le insalate) salad

insalata caprese, l' *f (een-sah-LAH-tah kah-PRAY-say)* salad of tomato slices, mozzarella, and basil

insalata mista, l' *f (een-sah-LAH-tah MEES-tah)* mixed salad

insegnante, l'/l' *m/f (een-sayn-NYAHN-tay)* teacher

insetto, l' *m (een-SET-toh)* (gli insetti) insect

insieme *(een-SYEH-may)* together

insolazione, l' *f (een-soh-laht-TSYOH-nay)* sunstroke

insonnia, l' *f (een-SOHN-nyah)* insomnia

insopportabile *(een-sohp-pohr-TAH-bee-lay)* unbearable

installare *(eens-tahl-LAH-ray)* to install

insulina, l' *f (een-soo-LEE-nah)* insulin

integrale *(een-tay-GRAH-lay)* complete, full, whole

intelletto, l' *m (een-tayl-LET-toh)* intellect

intellettuale *(een-tayl-layt-too-AH-lay)* intellectual

intelligente *(een-tayl-lee-JEN-tay)* intelligent

intelligenza, l' *f (een-tayl-lee-JEN-tsah)* intelligence

intendere *(een-TEN-day-ray)* to intend, to understand

intento, l' *m (een-TEN-toh)* intention, purpose

intenzionale *(een-tayn-tsyoh-NAH-lay)* intentional, deliberate

intenzione, l' *f (een-tayn-TSYOH-nay)* intention

Inter City *(een-tayr-SEE-tee)* city-to-city train

interdizione, l' *f (een-tayr-deet-TSYOH-nay)* prohibition, ban

interessante *(een-tay-rays-SAHN-tay)* interesting

internazionale *(een-tayr-naht-tsyoh-NAH-lay)* international

Internet, l' *m (EEN-tehr-net)* Internet

Internet point, l' *m (EEN-tehr-net poynt)* Internet cafe

interprete, l'/l' *m/f (een-TEHR-pray-tay)* interpreter

interurbano/a *(een-tayr-oor-BAH-noh/-nah)* long-distance

intervallo, l' *m (een-tayr-VAHL-loh)* intermission, break

intervenire *(een-tayr-vay-NEE-ray)* to intervene

intervista, l' *f (een-tayr-VEES-tah)* interview

intimo/a *(EEN-tee-moh/-mah)* intimate, private

intossicazione alimentare, l' *f (een-tohs-see-kaht-TSYOH-nay ah-lee-mayn-TAH-ray)* food poisoning

inverno, l' *m (een-VEHR-noh)* winter

invitare *(een-vee-TAH-ray)* to invite

involtini, i *(een-vohl-TEE-nee)* stuffed meat or fish rolls

involtino, l' *m (een-vohl-TEE-noh)* (gli involtini) roulade; rolled and stuffed slices of meat or fish

io *(yoh)* I

Irlanda, l' *f (eer-LAHN-dah)* Ireland

isola, l' *f (EE-zoh-lah)* island

istruire *(ees-troo-EE-ray)* to teach, to instruct

istruttore/istrutrice, l'/l' *m/f (ees-troot-TOH-ray/ees-troo-TREET-chay)* instructor

Italia, l' *f (ee-TAHL-yah)* Italy

Italiano/a *(ee-tah-LYAH-noh/-nah)* Italian

itinerario, l' *m (ee-tee-nay-RAH-ryoh)* itinerary

I.V.A., l' *f (EE-vah)* sales tax

J

J, j *(ee-LOON-gah)* J, j

jazz, il *(jahz)* jazz

jeans, i *(jeenz)* jeans

jet lag, il *(jet lahg)* jet lag

jogging, il *(JOH-ging)* jogging

jota, la *(YOH-tah)* bean and pork soup

K

K, k *(KAHP-pah)* K, k

kasher *(kah-SHAYR)* kosher

ketchup, il *(KEH-chup)* ketchup

kiwi, il *(KEE-wee)* kiwi

L

L, l *(EL-lay)* L, l

la *(lah)* it *f* (direct object)

là *(lah)* there

labbra, le *(LAHB-brah)* lips

labbro, il *(LAHB-broh)* (le labbra) lip

ladro/a, il/la *(LAH-droh/-drah)* thief

lagnarsi *(lahn-NYAHR-see)* to complain

lago, il *(LAH-goh)* (i laghi) lake

lametta da barba, la *(lah-MAYT-tah dah BAHR-bah)* (le lamette) razor blade

lampada, la *(LAHM-pah-dah)* (le lampade) lamp

lampadina, la *(lahm-pah-DEE-nah)* (le lampadine) light bulb

lampone, il *(lahm-POH-nay)* (i lamponi) raspberry

lamponi, i *(lahm-POH-nee)* raspberries

lana, la *(LAH-nah)* wool

lanciare *(lahn-CHAH-ray)* to throw

lardo, il *(LAHR-doh)* lard, pork fat

largo/a *(LAHR-goh/-gah)* wide

largo, il *(LAHR-goh)* small city square

lasagne, le *(lah-ZAHN-nyay)* lasagna

  lasagne alla bolognese, le *(lah-ZAHN-nyay AHL-lah boh-lohn-NYAY-say)* lasagna with meat sauce

  lasagne con le verdure, le *(lah-ZAHN-nyay kohn lay vayr-DOO-ray)* vegetable lasagne

lasciare *(lahsh-SHAH-ray)* to leave

lassativi, i *(lahs-sah-TEE-vee)* laxatives

lato, il *(LAH-toh)* side

lattaiolo, il *(laht-tah-YOH-loh)* cinnamon custard

latte, il *(LAHT-tay)* milk, dairy

  latte di soia, il *(LAHT-tay dee SOH-yah)* soy milk

  latte scremato, il *(LAHT-tay skray-MAH-toh)* skim milk

latteria, la *(laht-tay-REE-ah)* dairy

lattuga, la *(laht-TOO-gah)* (le lattughe) lettuce

lauro, il *(LOW-roh)* bay, laurel

lavaggio a secco, il *(lah-VAHD-joh ah SAYK-koh)* dry cleaning

lavanderia, la *(lah-vahn-day-REE-ah)* laundry

lavanderia a gettone, la *(lah-vahn-day-REE-ah ah jayt-TOH-nay)* coin-operated laundry

lavapiatti, la *(lah-vah-PYAHT-tee)* dishwasher (machine)

lavare *(lah-VAH-ray)* to wash

lavarelli, i *(lah-vah-REL-lee)* lake bream (whitefish)

lavasecco, il *(lah-vah-SAYK-koh)* dry cleaner

lavatrice, la *(lah-vah-TREE-chay)* washing machine

lavorare *(lah-voh-RAH-ray)* to work

lavorare in proprio *(lah-voh-RAH-ray een PROH-pryoh)* to be self-employed

lavori in corso, i *(lah-VOH-ree een KOHR-soh)* roadwork

lavoro, il *(lah-VOH-roh)* job, work

lecca lecca, la *(LAYK-kah LAYK-kah)* lollipop

leggere *(LED-jay-ray)* to read

leggero/a *(layd-JEH-roh/-rah)* light (wine or food)

legna, la *(LAYN-nyah)* wood

legume, il *(lay-GOO-may)* legume

Lei *(LEH-ee)* you (form. sing.)

lei *(LEH-ee)* she

lentamente *(layn-tah-MAYN-tay)* slow, slowly

lenti a contatto, le *(LEN-tee ah kohn-TAHT-toh)* contact lenses

lenticchia, la *(layn-TEEK-kyah)* (le lenticchie) lentil

lenticchie, le *(layn-TEEk-kyay)* lentils

lento/a *(LEN-toh/-tah)* slow

lenzuolo, il *(len-TSWOH-loh)* (i lenzuoli) bedsheet

lepre, la *(LEP-ray)* (le lepri) hare

lesbica, la *(LEZ-bee-kah)* (le lesbiche) lesbian

lesione, la *(lay-ZYOH-nay)* injury, damage

lesso/a *(LAYS-soh/-sah)* boiled

lettera, la *(LET-tay-rah)* (le lettere) letter

letti separati, i *(LET-tee say-pay-RAH-tee)* twin beds

lettino, il *(layt-TEE-noh)* crib

letto, il *(LET-toh)* (i letti) bed

letto matrimoniale, il *(LET-toh mah-tree-mohn-NYAH-lay)* double bed

libero/a *(LEE-bay-roh/-rah)* available, vacant

libreria, la *(lee-bray-REE-ah)* (le librerie) bookstore

libretto, il *(lee-BRAYT-toh)* booklet

libretto di circolazione, il *(lee-BRAYT-toh dee cheer-koh-lah-TSYOH-nay)* title of car ownership

libro, il *(LEE-broh)* (i libri) book

licenza, la *(lee-CHEN-tsah)* permit

lido, il *(LEE-doh)* beach

lievito, il *(LYEH-vee-toh)* yeast

limetta, la *(lee-MAYT-tah)* lime, nail file

limite di velocità, il *(LEE-mee-tay dee vay-loh-chee-TAH)* speed limit

limonata, la *(lee-moh-NAH-tah)* lemonade

limone, il *(lee-MOH-nay)* (i limoni) lemon

linea, la *(LEE-nay-ah)* (transportation) line

linea aerea, la *(LEE-nay-ah ah-EH-ray-ah)* airline

lingua, la *(LEEN-gwah)* (le lingue) tongue, language

linguine, le *(leen-GWEE-nay)* thick flat spaghetti

liquido, il *(LEE-kwee-doh)* liquid, fluid

liquore, il *(lee-KWOH-ray)* (i liquori) liqueur

liscio/a *(LEESH-shoh/-shah)* simple, straight

lista, la *(LEES-tah)* list, menu

lista d'attesa, la *(LEES-tah daht-TAY-sah)* waiting list

lista dei vini, la *(LEES-tah DAY-ee VEE-nee)* wine list

litro, il *(LEE-troh)* (i litri) liter

L'IVA *f (LEE-vah)* sales tax

livido, il *(LEE-vee-doh)* bruise

lo *(loh)* it *m* (direct object)

locale *(loh-KAH-lay)* local

locale, il *(loh-KAH-lay)* (i locali) (train) local train, lots of stops, usually slow; bar, venue

locanda, la *(loh-KAHN-dah)* (le locande) inn, simple restaurant with local dishces

loggia, la *(LOHD-jah)* covered porch

logico/a *(LOH-jee-koh/-kah)* logical

Lombardia, la *(lohm-bahr-DEE-ah)* Lombardy

lombata, la *(lohm-BAH-tah)* (le lombate) loin steak

Londra *(LOHN-drah)* London

lontano/a *(lohn-TAH-noh/-nah)* far away

lonza, la *(LOHN-tsah)* pork loin

Loro *(LOH-roh)* you (form. pl.)

loro *(LOH-roh)* they

losanga, la *(loh-ZAHN-gah)* (le losanghe) lozenge

lozione, la *(loht-TSYOH-nay)* lotion

lucchetto, il *(look-KAYT-toh)* padlock

luce, la *(LOO-chay)* (le luci) light

luganega, la *(loo-GAH-nay-gah)* mild, lean pork sausage

luglio, il *(LOOL-lyoh)* July

lui *(LOO-ee)* he

lumaca, la *(loo-MAH-kah)* (le lumache) snail

lumache, le *(loo-MAH-kay)* snails
  lumache alle milanese, le *(loo-MAH-kay AHL-lay mee-lah-NAY-say)* snails with sauce (anchovy, fennel, wine)

luna, la *(LOO-nah)* moon
  luna di miele, la *(LOO-nah dee MYEH-lay)* honeymoon

lunedì, il *(loo-nay-DEE)* Monday

lunette, le *(loo-NAY-tay)* filled half-moon pasta

lungo/a *(LOON-goh/-gah)* long
  lungo percorrenza *(LOON-goh payr-kohr-RAYN-tsah)* long-distance

lungomare, il *(loon-goh-MAH-ray)* promenade

luogo, il *(LWOH-goh)* place
  luogo di nascita, il *(LWOH-goh dee NAHSH-shee-tah)* place of birth

lusso, il *(LOOS-soh)* luxury

M

M, m *(EM-may)* M, m

ma *(mah)* but

maccheroni, i *(mahk-kay-ROH-nee)* macaroni
  maccheroni alla chitarra, i *(mahk-kay-ROH-nee AHL-lah kee-TAHR-rah)* square pasta strands, served with sauce

maccheroni con la ricotta, i *(mahk-kay-ROH-nee kohn lah ree-KOHT-tah)* baked pasta with ricotta

macchiare *(mahk-KYAH-ray)* to stain, to spot

macchiato/a *(mahk-KYAH-toh/-tah)* with milk

macchina, la *(MAHK-kee-nah)* car, machine
  macchina fotografica, la *(MAHK-kee-nah foh-toh-GRAH-fee-kah)* (le macchine) camera

macelleria, la *(mah-chayl-lay-REE-ah)* butcher shop

madre, la *(MAH-dray)* (le madri) mother

maestro/a, il/la *(mah-ES-stroh/-trah)* teacher (grade school), instructor

magazzino, il **grande** *(GRAHN-day mah-gahd-DZEE-noh)* department store

maggio, il *(MAHD-joh)* May

maggiorana, la *(mahd-joh-RAH-nah)* marjoram

maglia, la *(MAHL-lyah)* knit shirt

maglietta, la *(mahl-LYAYT-tah)* T-shirt

maglione, il *(mahl-LYOH-nay)* (i maglioni) sweater, pullover

magnifico/a *(mahn-NYEE-fee-koh/-kah)* magnificent

magro/a *(MAH-groh/-grah)* thin, lean, low-fat

mai *(MAH-ee)* never

maiale, il *(mah-YAH-lay)* pork

maionese, la *(mah-yoh-NAY-say)* mayonnaise

mais, il *(MAH-ees)* corn

mal, il *(mahl)* pain, illness

mal di aereo, il *(mahl dee ah-EH-ray-oh)* air sickness

mal di denti, il *(mahl dee DEN-tee)* toothache

mal di macchina, il *(mahl dee MAHK-kee-nah)* car sickness

mal di mare, il *(mahl dee MAH-ray)* sea sickness

mal di testa, il *(mahl dee TES-tah)* headache

malaria, la *(mah-LAHR-yah)* malaria

malato/a *(mah-LAH-toh/-tah)* sick, unwell

malattia, la *(mah-laht-TEE-ah)* disease

male, il *(MAH-lay)* pain, harm, illness

malfatti, i *(mahl-FAHT-tee)* spinach and cheese dumplings

malloreddus *(mahl-loh-RAYD-doos)* type of wheat pasta, usually served with tomato/meat sauce

maltagliati, i *(mahl-tahl-LYAH-tee)* random shapes of pasta made from scraps of other pasta doughs

malvasia, la *(mahl-vah-ZEE-ah)* a dessert wine

mamma, la *(MAHM-mah)* mom

manager, il *(MAN-ee-juh)* manager

mancia, la *(MAHN-chah)* (le mance) tip (for service)

mandare *(mahn-DAH-ray)* to send

mandarino, il *(mahn-dah-REE-noh)* (i mandarini) tangerine

mandorla, la *(MAHN-dohr-lah)* (le mandorle) almond

mandorle, le *(MAHN-dohr-lay)* almonds

mangiare *(mahn-JAH-ray)* to eat

mangia *(MAHN-jah)* you eat (form. sing.)

mangiamo *(mahn-JAH-moh)* we eat

mangio *(MAHN-joh)* I eat

mango, il *(MAHN-goh)* (i manghi) mango

mano, la *(MAH-noh)* (le mani) hand

fatto/a a mano *(FAHT-toh/-tah ah MAH-noh)* handmade

manovale, il *(mah-noh-VAH-lay)* (i manovali) laborer, manual worker

mantellina, la *(mahn-tayl-LEE-nah)* cape

mantello, il *(mahn-TEL-loh)* cloak

mantenere *(mahn-tay-NAY-ray)* to maintain, to keep

manuale *(mah-noo-AH-lay)* manual

manubrio, il *(mah-NOO-bryoh)* handlebars

manzo, il *(MAHN-dzoh)* beef

mappa, la *(MAHP-pah)* (le mappe) map

maraschino, il *(mah-rahs-KEE-noh)* maraschino; bittersweet, clear cherry liqueur

marca, la *(MAHR-kah)* (le marche) brand

marciapiede, il *(mahr-chah-PYEH-day)* footpath

mare, il *(MAH-ray)* (i mari) sea

  al mare *(ahl MAH-ray)* seaside

  mal di mare *(mahl dee MAH-ray)* seasickness

  mare mosso *(MAH-ray MOHS-soh)* rough seas

marea, la *(mah-REH-ah)* tide

margarina, la *(mahr-gahr-EE-nah)* margarine

margherita, la *(mahr-gay-REE-tah)* (pizza) with tomato, garlic, cheese and basil

marinara, alla *(AHL-lah mah-ree-NAH-rah)* sauce of tomatoes, olives, garlic, clams and mussels

marinato/a *(mah-ree-NAH-toh/-tah)* marinated

marito, il *(mah-REE-toh)* (i mariti) husband

maritozzo, il *(mah-ree-TOHT-tsoh)* (i maritozzi) sweet bun with raisins

marmellata, la *(mahr-mayl-LAH-tah)* (le marmellate) jam

marmellata d'arance, la *(mahr-mayl-LAHT-tah dah-RAHN-chay)* marmalade

marmo, il *(MAHR-moh)* marble

marrone *(mahr-ROH-nay)* brown

marrone, il *(mahr-ROH-nay)* chestnut

marsala, la *(mahr-SAH-lah)* wine with brandy added to it

martedì, il *(mahr-tay-DEE)* Tuesday

martello, il *(mahr-TEL-loh)* hammer

martinetto, il *(mahr-tee-NAYT-toh)* jack (tech)

Martini *(mahr-TEE-nee)* vermouth, sweet or dry

marzapane, il *(mahr-tsah-PAH-nay)* marzipan

marzo, il *(MAHR-tsoh)* March

mascara, il *(mahs-KAH-rah)* mascara

mascarpone, il *(mahs-kahr-POH-nay)* a cream cheese

maschera, la *(MAHS-kay-rah)* mask

massaggio, il *(mahs-SAHD-joh)* massage

massimo/a *(MAHS-see-moh/-mah)* maximum

materassino gonfiabile, il *(mah-tayr-ahs-SEE-noh gohn-FYAH-bee-lay)* air mattress

materasso, il *(mah-tay-RAHS-soh)* mattress

matita, la *(mah-TEE-tah)* pencil

matrimoniale *(mah-tree-moh-NYAH-lay)* matrimonial, marital

  letto matrimoniale, il *(LET-toh mah-tree-moh-NYAH-lay)* (i letti) double bed

matrimonio, il *(mah-tree-MOHN-yoh)* marriage

mattina, la *(maht-TEE-nah)* (le mattine) morning

matto/a *(MAHT-toh/-tah)* crazy

maturo/a *(mah-TOO-roh/-rah)* ripe, mature

meccanico/a, il/la *(mayk-KAHN-ee-koh/-kah)* mechanic

medaglione, il *(may-dahl-LYOH-nay)* (i medaglioni) round fillet, medallion

media, la *(MED-yah)* average

mediamente *(mayd-yah-MAYN-tay)* on average

medicina, la *(may-dee-CHEE-nah)* medicine

medicinale, il *(may-dee-chee-NAH-lay)* (i medicinali) medication, drug

medico/a, il/la *(MEH-dee-koh/-kah)* doctor

medio/a *(MED-yoh/-yah)* middle, average, medium

mediocre *(may-DYOH-kray)* mediocre, second-rate

meditazione, la *(may-dee-taht-TSYOH-nay)* meditation

meglio *(MAY-lyoh)* better

mela, la *(MAY-lah)* (le mele) apple

melagrana, la *(may-lah-GRAH-nah)* pomegranate

melanzana, la *(may-lahn-DZAH-nah)* (le melanzane) eggplant

melanzane, le *(may-lahn-DZAH-nay)* eggplants

  melanzane ripiene, le *(may-lahn-DZAH-nay ree-PYEH-nay)* stuffed eggplants

melodia, la *(may-loh-DEE-ah)* tune, melody

melone, il *(may-LOH-nay)* (i meloni) (musk)melon

mendicante, il/la *(mayn-dee-KAHN-tay)* beggar

meno *(MAY-noh)* fewer, less, minus

menta, la *(MAYN-tah)* (le mente) mint

mentina, la *(mayn-TEE-nah)* peppermint

mentire *(mayn-TEE-ray)* to lie (untruth)

menù, il *(may-NOO)* (set) menu

menù a prezzo fisso, il *(may-NOO ah PRET-tsoh FEES-soh)* set-priced menu

menù turistico, il *(may-NOO too-REES-tee-koh)* tourist menu

mercato, il *(mayr-KAH-toh)* (i mercati) market, flea market

mercoledì, il *(mayr-koh-lay-DEE)* Wednesday

meringa, la *(may-REEN-gah)* (le meringhe) meringue

meringata, la *(may-reen-GAH-tah)* dessert of meringue and ice cream

merletto, il *(mayr-LAYT-toh)* lace

merluzzo, il *(mayr-LOOT-tsoh)* (i merluzzi) cod

mescita, vino alla *(VEE-noh AHL-lah MAYSH-shee-tah)* wine by the glass

mescolare *(may-skoh-LAH-ray)* to mix

mese, il *(MAY-say)* (i mesi) month

messa, la *(MAYS-sah)* mass

messa in corso *(MAYS-sah een KOHR-soh)* service in progress

messaggio, il *(mays-SAHD-joh)* (i messaggi) message

mesta e fasoi *(MAY-stah ay fah-ZOY)* polenta cooked with beans

mestiere, il *(mays-TYEH-ray)* job, trade

mestruazione, la *(mays-troo-aht-TSYOH-nay)* menstruation

metà, la *(may-TAH)* half

metallo, il *(may-TAHL-loh)* metal

metrò, il *(may-TROH)* subway

metro, il *(MET-roh)* meter

metropolitana, la *(may-troh-poh-lee-TAH-nah)* subway

mettere *(MAYT-tay-ray)* to put

mezzanotte, la *(mayd-dzah-NOHT-tay)* midnight

mezzo/a *(MED-dzoh/-dzah)* half, middle

mezzogiorno, il *(mayd-dzoh-JOHR-noh)* noon

mezz'ora, la *(mayd-DZOH-rah)* half hour

microfono, il *(mee-KROH-foh-noh)* microphone

microonda, la *(mee-kroh-OHN-dah)* microwave

mi dica *(mee DEE-kah)* tell me, = May I help you?

miele, il *(MYEH-lay)* honey

miglio, il *(MEEL-lyoh)* (le miglia) mile

migliore *(meel-LYOH-ray)* better

milanese, alla *(AHL-lah mee-lah-NAY-say)* sauced as in Milan, probably has butter

cotoletta alla milanese, la *(koh-toh-LAYT-tah AHL-lah mee-lah-NAY-say)* Wiener schnitzel

Milano *(mee-LAH-noh)* Milan

miliardo, il *(mee-LYAHR-doh)* billion

milione, il *(mee-LYOH-nay)* (i milioni) million

mille *(MEEL-lay)* (mila) thousand

millecosedde, il *(meel-lay-koh-SED-day)* mixed beans with pasta and vegetables, possibly a soup

Millefiore *(meel-lay-FYOH-ray)* liqueur flavored with herbs and alpine flowers

millimetro, il *(meel-LEE-may-troh)* (i millimetri) millimeter

minestra, la *(mee-NES-trah)* light pasta soup

minestrina, la *(mee-nays-TREE-nah)* broth

minestrone, il *(mee-nays-TROH-nay)* thick vegetable and pasta soup

minibar, il *(mee-nee-BAHR)* minibar

minibus, il *(MEE-nee-boos)* minibus

minore *(mee-NOH-ray)* less, smaller

minuto/a *(mee-NOO-toh/-tah)* minute, tiny

minuto, il *(mee-NOO-toh)* (i minuti) minute

mio/a *(MEE-oh/-ah)* my, mine

miracolo, il *(mee-RAH-koh-loh)* miracle

mirtillo, il *(meer-TEEL-loh)* (i mirtilli) blueberries

miscela, la *(meesh-SHEH-lah)* mixture, blend

miscellaneo/a *(meesh-shayl-LAH-nay-oh/-ah)* miscellaneous

miserabile *(mee-zay-RAH-bee-lay)* miserable, poor

misticanza, la *(mees-tee-KAHN-tsah)* mixed salad greens

misto/a *(MEES-toh/-tah)* mixed

misura, la *(mee-ZOO-rah)* size, measurement

misurino, il *(mee-zoo-REE-noh)* measuring cup

mitilo, il *(mee-TEE-loh)* (i mitili) mussel

mobile, il *(MOH-bee-lay)* piece of furniture

mobili, i *(MOH-bee-lee)* furniture (store)

moca, il *(MOH-kah)* mocha coffee

moda, la *(MOH-dah)* fashion

modem, il *(MOH-daym)* modem

moderno/a *(moh-DEHR-noh/-nah)* modern

modificare *(moh-dee-fee-KAH-ray)* to modify

modulo, il *(MOH-doo-loh)* (i moduli) form (paperwork)

moglie, la *(MOHL-lyay)* wife

molestia, la *(moh-LEST-yah)* harassment, annoyance

molle *(MOHL-lay)* soft

molto/a *(MOHL-toh/-tah)* a lot, (very) much, a great deal

momento, il *(moh-MAYN-toh)* (i momenti) moment

monastero, il *(moh-nahs-TEH-roh)* monastery

mondezza, la *(mohn-DAYT-tsah)* trash

mondo, il *(MOHN-doh)* world

moneta, la *(moh-NAY-tah)* (le monate) money, coins

mongolfiera, la *(mohn-gohl-FYEH-rah)* hot-air balloon

monopattino, il *(moh-noh-PAHT-tee-noh)* scooter

montagna, la *(mohn-TAHN-nyah)* mountain

montasio, il *(mohn-TAHS-yoh)* hard cow's milk cheese

montato/a *(mohn-TAH-toh/-tah)* whipped

montone, il *(mohn-TOH-nay)* mutton

monumento, il *(mohn-noo-MAYN-toh)* monument

mora, la *(MOH-rah)* (le more) blackberry, mulberry

morbido/a *(MOHR-bee-doh)* soft, tender

mordere *(MOHR-day-ray)* to bite

morire *(moh-REE-ray)* to die

mortadella, la *(mohr-tah-DEL-lah)* Bologna sausage (salted pork)

morte, la *(MOHR-tay)* death

morto/a *(MOHR-toh/-tah)* dead

mosca, la *(MOHS-kah)* (le mosche) fly

moschea, la *(mohs-KEH-ah)* mosque

mostarda, la *(mohs-TAHR-dah)* mustard

mostrare *(mohs-TRAH-ray)* to show

motel, il *(moh-TEL)* motel

motivo, il *(moh-TEE-voh)* reason, cause

moto, la *(MOH-toh)* motorcycle

motocicletta, la *(moh-toh-chee-KLAYT-tah)* (le motociclette) motorcycle

motore, il *(moh-TOH-ray)* engine, motor

motoretta, la *(moh-toh-RAYT-tah)* motor scooter

motorino, il *(moh-toh-REE-noh)* motor scooter, moped

motoscafo, il *(moh-tohs-KAH-foh)* motorboat

motorscooter, il *(MOH-oo-tuh-skoo-tuh)* motorscooter

mouse, il *(mows)* mouse (computer)

mozzarella, la *(moht-tsah-REL-lah)* a moist, mild, rubbery white cow's milk cheese

mozzarella di bufala, la *(moht-tsah-REL-lah dee BOO-fah-lah)* mozzarella made of buffalo's milk

mozzarella in carrozza, la *(moht-tsah-REL-lah een kahr-ROHT-tsah)* battered and fried mozzarella sandwich

mucca, la *(MOOK-kah)* cow

muesli, il *(MOOS-lee)* muesli

muggine, il *(MOOD-jee-nay)* mullet (fish)

multa, la *(MOOL-tah)* fine (penalty)

multare *(mool-TAH-ray)* to fine

murale, il *(moo-RAH-lay)* mural

muro, il *(MOO-roh)* (i muri) wall

muscolo, il *(MOOS-koh-loh)* (i muscoli) muscle

museo, il *(moo-ZEH-oh)* (i musei) museum

musica, la *(MOO-zee-kah)* music

musicista, il/la *(moo-zee-CHEES-tah)* (i musicisti/le musiciste) musician

musicista di strada, il/la *(moo-zee-CHEES-tah dee STRAH-dah)* busker, street musician

musulmano/a *(moo-sool-MAH-noh/-nah)* Muslim

mutande, le *(moo-TAHN-day)* underpants

muto/a *(MOO-toh/-tah)* mute

N

N, n *(EN-nay)* N, n

napoletana, la *(nah-poh-lay-TAH-nah)* (pizza) with anchovies, ham, tomatoes, capers, cheese and oregano

alla napoletana *(AHL-lah nah-poh-lay-TAH-nah)* in the style of Napoli (Naples); sauce with tomatoes, olive oil, garlic and basil

Napoli *(NAH-poh-lee)* Naples

narrativa, la *(nahr-rah-TEE-vah)* fiction

nascere *(NAHSH-shay-ray)* to be born

nascita, la *(NAHSH-shee-tah)* birth

naso, il *(NAH-soh)* nose

Natale, il *(nah-TAH-lay)* Christmas

natura, la *(nah-TOO-rah)* nature

naturale *(nah-too-RAH-lay)* non-carbonated

naturismo, il *(nah-too-REEZ-moh)* nudism

nausea, la *(NOW-zay-ah)* nausea

nausea mattutina, la *(NOW-zay-ah maht-too-TEE-nah)* morning sickness

nave, la *(NAH-vay)* ship

navetta, la *(nah-VAYT-tah)* shuttle

navigare *(nah-vee-GAH-ray)* to sail

navigazione, la *(nah-vee-gaht-TSYOH-nay)* navigation

nazionale *(naht-tsyoh-NAH-lay)* national

nazionalità, la *(naht-tsyoh-nah-lee-TAH)* nationality

nazione, la *(naht-TSYOH-nay)* nation

né ... né ... *(nay ... nay)* neither ... nor

nebbia, la *(NAYB-byah)* fog, mist

nebbioso/a *(nayb-BYOH-soh/-sah)* foggy

nebuloso/a *(nay-boo-LOH-soh/-sah)* nebulous, hazy

necessario/a *(nay-chays-SAHR-yoh/-yah)* necessary

necessità, la *(nay-chays-see-TAH)* necessity, need

negare *(nay-GAH-ray)* to deny, to refuse

negativo/a *(nay-gah-TEE-voh/-vah)* negative

negoziare *(nay-goht-TSYAH-ray)* to negotiate

negozio, il *(nay-GOHT-tsyoh)* (i negozi) shop, store

nero/a *(NAY-roh/-rah)* black

neve, la *(NAY-vay)* snow

nevica *(NAY-vee-kah)* it's snowing

niente *(NYEN-tay)* nothing

nipote (di nonni), il/la *(nee-POH-tay [dee NOHN-nee])* (i nipoti/le nipoti) grandson/granddaughter

nipote (di zii), il/la *(nee-POH-tay [dee TSEE-ee])* (i nipoti/le nipoti) nephew/niece

no *(noh)* no

nocciola, la *(noht-CHOH-lah)* (le nocciole) hazelnut

noce, la *(NOH-chay)* (le noci) nut, walnut

noce di cocco, la *(NOH-chay dee KOHK-koh)* (le noci) coconut

noce moscata, la *(NOH-chay mohs-KAH-tah)* (le noci) nutmeg

nocepesca, la *(noh-chay-PES-kah)* (le nocepesche) nectarine

nodino, il *(noh-DEE-noh)* (i nodini) veal chops

noi *(noy)* we

noioso/a *(noh-YOH-soh/-sah)* boring

noleggiare *(noh-layd-JAH-ray)* to rent

nome, il *(NOH-may)* (i nomi) name

non *(nohn)* not, doesn't

nonna, la *(NOHN-nah)* grandmother

nonni, i *(NOHN-nee)* grandparents

nonno, il *(NOHN-noh)* grandfather

non potabile *(nohn poh-TAH-bee-lay)* not safe to drink

nord, il *(nohrd)* north

Norma, alla *(AHL-lah NOHR-mah)* with spices and tomato sauce

pasta alla Norma *(PAHS-tah AHL-lah NOHR-mah)* pasta with eggplant, tomato, basil, and ricotta

normale *(nohr-MAH-lay)* regular

normalità, la *(nohr-mah-lee-TAH)* normality

nostrana *(nohs-TRAH-nah)* simple, locally made food

nostro/a *(NOHS-troh/-trah)* our

notare *(noh-TAH-ray)* to note, to write down

notifica, la *(noh-TEE-fee-kah)* (le notifiche) notification

notificare *(noh-tee-fee-KAH-ray)* to notify

notte, la *(NOHT-tay)* (le notti) night

questa notte *(KWAYS-tah NOHT-tay)* tonight

novanta *(noh-VAHN-tah)* ninety

novantacinque *(noh-vahn-tah-CHEEN-kway)* ninety-five

novantadue *(noh-vahn-tah-DOO-ay)* ninety-two

novantanove *(noh-vahn-tah-NOH-vay)* ninety-nine

novantaquattro *(noh-vahn-tah-KWAHT-troh)* ninety-four

novantasei *(noh-vahn-tah-SEH-ee)* ninety-six

novantasette *(noh-vahn-tah-SET-tay)* ninety-seven

novantatré *(noh-vahn-tah-TRAY)* ninety-three

novantotto *(noh-vahn-TOHT-toh)* ninety-eight

novantuno *(noh-vahn-TOO-noh)* ninety-one

nove *(NOH-vay)* nine

novecento *(noh-vay-CHEN-toh)* nine hundred

novembre, il *(noh-VEM-bray)* November

nubile, la *(NOO-bee-lay)* single woman

nudismo, il *(noo-DEEZ-moh)* nudism

nudista, il/la *(noo-DEES-tah)* nudist

numero, il *(NOO-may-roh)* (i numeri) number

numero di cellulare, il *(NOO-may-roh dee chayl-loo-LAH-ray)* cell phone number

numbero verde, il *(NOO-may-roh VAYR-day)* toll-free number

nuora, la *(NWOH-rah)* daughter-in-law

nuotare *(nwoh-TAH-ray)* to swim

nuoto, il *(NWOH-toh)* swimming

Nuova Zelanda, la *(NWOH-vah dzay-LAHN-dah)* New Zealand

nuovo/a *(NWOH-voh/-vah)* new

nuvola, la *(NOO-voh-lah)* cloud

nuvoloso/a *(noo-voh-LOH-soh/-sah)* cloudy

O

O, o *(oh)* O, o

o *(oh)* or

obbligare *(ohb-blee-GAH-ray)* to oblige (=to require, to force)

obbligatorio/a *(ohb-blee-gah-TOHR-yoh/yah)* required, obligatory

obelisco, l' *m (oh-bay-LEES-koh)* (gli obelischi) obelisk

oca, l' *f (OH-kah)* (le oche) goose

occhiali, gli *(ohk-KYAH-lee)* eyeglasses

occhiali da sci, gli *(ohk-KYAH-lee dah shee)* ski goggles

occhiali da sole, gli *(ohk-KYAH-lee dah SOH-lay)* sunglasses

occhio, l' *m (OHK-yoh)* (gli occhi) eye

occupare *(ohk-koo-PAH-ray)* to occupy

occupato/a *(ohk-koo-PAH-toh/-tah)* occupied, taken

oceano, l' *m (oh-CHEH-ah-noh)* ocean

odontoiatra, il/la *(oh-dohn-toh-YAHT-rah)* dentist

odore, l' *m (oh-DOH-ray)* smell

odori, gli *(oh-DOH-ree)* herbs

offelle, le *(ohf-FAYL-lay)* sweet butter cookies

offendere *(ohf-FEN-day-ray)* to offend

offerta, l' *f (ohf-FEHR-tah)* (le offerte) offer

in offerta *(een ohf-FEHR-tah)* special offer

offrire *(ohf-FREE-ray)* to offer

oggetto, l' *m (ohd-JET-toh)* (gli oggetti) object, thing

oggi *(OHD-jee)* today

olio, l' *m (OHL-yoh)* (gli oli) oil

olio d'oliva, l' *m (OHL-yoh doh-LEE-vah)* olive oil

olio solare, l' *m (OHL-yoh soh-LAH-ray)* suntan oil

oliva, l' *f (oh-LEE-vah)* (le olive) olive

ombra, l' *f (OHM-brah)* shade

ombrello, l' *m (ohm-BREL-loh)* (gli ombrelli) umbrella

ombrellone, l' *m (ohm-brayl-LOH-nay)* (gli ombrelloni) sun umbrella

ombrichelli, gli *(ohm-bree-KEL-lee)* type of pasta

omelette, l' *f (oh-muh-LET)* omelet

omeopatia, l' *f (oh-may-oh-pah-TEE-ah)* homeopathy

omosessuale, l'/l' *m/f (oh-moh-says-soo-AH-lay)* homosexual

onda, l' *f (OHN-dah)* wave

onesto/a *(oh-NES-toh/-tah)* honest, fair

opera, l' *f (OH-pay-rah)* work

opera lirica, l' *f (OH-pay-rah LEE-ree-kah)* opera

operaio/a, l'/l' *m/f (oh-pay-RAH-yoh/-yah)* factory worker

operatore/operatrice, l'/l' *m/f (oh-pay-rah-TOH-ray/-TREE-chay)* operator

opinione, l' *(oh-pee-NYOH-nay)* opinion

opulenza, la *(oh-poo-LEN-tsah)* opulence, wealth

ora, l' *f (OH-rah)* (le ore) hour

orario, l' *m (oh-RAHR-yoh)* schedule, timetable

orario continuato, l' *m (oh-RAHR-yoh kohn-tee-noo-AH-toh)* continuous hours, no pause

orario di apertura, l' *m (oh-RAHR-yoh dee ah-payr-TOO-rah)* hours of business

orata, l' *f (oh-RAH-tah)* gilthead seabream (fish)

orchestra, l' *f (ohr-KES-trah)* orchestra

ordinare *(ohr-dee-NAH-ray)* to place an order, to organize

ordinario/a *(ohr-dee-NAH-ryoh/-ryah)* ordinary

ordine, l' *m (OHR-dee-nay)* order

orecchiette, le *(oh-rayk-KYAYT-tay)* ear-shaped pasta

orecchini, gli *(oh-rayk-KEE-nee)* earrings

orecchio, l' *m (oh-RAYK-kyoh)* (le orecchie) ear

origano, l' *m (oh-REE-gah-noh)* oregano

originale *(oh-ree-jee-NAH-lay)* original

origine *(oh-REE-jee-nay)* origin, beginning

oro, l' *m (OH-roh)* gold

orologio, l' *m (oh-roh-LOH-joh)* (gli orologi) clock, watch

orologio da polso, l' *m (oh-roh-LOH-joh dah POHL-soh)* wristwatch

orrendo/a *(ohr-REN-doh/-dah)* horrendous, horrible

orzo, l' *m (OHR-dzoh)* rice-shaped pasta, barley

orzo e fagioli *(OHR-dzoh ay fah-JOH-lee)* bean and barley soup

ospedale, l' *m (ohs-pay-DAH-lay)* (gli ospedali) hospital

ospitalità, l' *f (ohs-pee-tah-lee-TAH)* hospitality

ossigeno, l' *m (ohs-SEE-jay-noh)* oxygen

osso, l' *m (OHS-soh)* (gli ossi) bone

ossobuco, l' *m (ohs-soh-BOO-koh)* veal shanks braised with vegetables, broth and white wine

ostello, l' *m* hostel *(ohs-TEL-loh)*

ostello della gioventù, l' *m*
(ohs-TEL-loh DAYL-lah joh-vayn-TOO)
youth hostel

osteria, l' *f* (ohs-tay-REE-ah) (le
osterie) inn (wine and simple
food), pub

ostrica, l' *f* (OHS-tree-kah) (le
ostriche) oyster

ottanta (oht-TAHN-tah) eighty

ottantacinque (oht-tahn-tah-
CHEEN-kway) eighty-five

ottantadue (oht-tahn-tah-DOO-ay)
eighty-two

ottantanove (oht-tan-tah-NOH-vay)
eighty-nine

ottantaquattro (oht-tahn-tah-
KWAHT-troh) eighty-four

ottantasei (oht-tahn-tah-SEH-ee)
eighty-six

ottantasette (oht-tahn-tah-SET-tay)
eighty-seven

ottantatré (oht-tahn-tah-TRAY)
eighty-three

ottantotto (oht-tahn-TOHT-toh)
eighty-eight

ottantuno (oht-tahn-TOO-noh)
eighty-one

ottenere (oht-tay-NAY-ray) to
obtain, to get

ottica, foto (FOH-toh OHT-tee-kah)
photographic supply store

ottico/a, l'/l' *m/f* (OHT-tee-koh/-
kah) optician

ottimo/a (OHT-tee-moh/-mah)
excellent

otto (OHT-toh) eight

ottobre, il (oht-TOH-bray)
October

ottocento (oht-toh-CHEN-toh)
eight hundred

ovest, il (OH-vayst) west

P

P, p (pee) P, p

pacchetto, il (pahk-KAYT-toh)
packet, parcel

pacco, il (PAHK-koh) (i pacchi)
package

pacco ordinario, il (pahk-koh
ohr-dee-NAH-ryoh) regular mail

paccocelere (pahk-koh-CHAY-lay-
ray) priority mail

padella, la (pah-DEL-lah) frying
pan

Padova (PAH-doh-vah) Padua

padre, il (PAH-dray) (i padri)
father

padrone/padrona, il/la (pah-
DROH-nay/-nah) landlord/-
lady

paese, il (pah-AY-zay) country,
nation

Paesi Bassi, i (pay-AY-zay BAHS-
see) the Netherlands

pagamento, il (pah-gah-MAYN-
toh) payment

pagare (pah-GAH-ray) to pay

pagina, la (PAH-jee-nah) page

pagina Web, la *(PAH-jee-nah web)* Web page

paio, il *(PAH-yoh)* pair

palazzo, il *(pah-LAHT-tsoh)* (i palazzi) palace

palchetto, il *(pahl-KAYT-toh)* (i palchetti) shelf

palestra, la *(pah-LES-trah)* gym

palla, la *(PAHL-lah)* (le palle) ball

palle di riso, le *(PAHL-lay dee REE-soh)* Neapolitan rice croquettes

palombo, il *(pah-LOHM-boh)* (i palombi) pigeon

palombo alla todina, il *(pah-LOHM-boh AHL-lah toh-DEE-nah)* roasted pigeon

panca, la *(PAHN-kah)* (le panche) bench

pancetta, la *(pahn-CHAYT-tah)* bacon

pancotto, il *(pahn-KOHT-toh)* bread soup, often with beaten egg or tomato

pan di Spagna, il *(pahn dee SPAHN-nyah)* honey-rum sponge cake

pandoro, il *(pahn-DOH-roh)* sponge cake topped with powdered vanilla, eaten at Christmas

pane, il *(PAH-nay)* bread

pane all'olio, il *(PAH-nay ahl-LOHL-yoh)* bread with oil

pane di segale, il *(PAH-nay dee SAY-gah-lay)* rye bread

pane integrale, il *(PAH-nay ee-tay-GRAH-lay)* whole-wheat bread

pane tostato, il *(PAH-nay tohs-TAH-toh)* toast

panelle, le *(pah-NAYL-lay)* fried chickpea fritters

panetteria, la *(pah-nayt-tay-REE-ah)* (le panetterie) bakery

panettone, il *(pah-nayt-TOH-nay)* spiced brioche, eaten at Christmas

panforte, il *(pahn-FOHR-tay)* soft Italian Christmas cake with honey, nuts, and dried fruit

panificio, il *(pah-nee-FEE-choh)* bakery

panino, il *(pah-NEE-noh)* (i panini) bread roll

panino imbottito, il *(pah-NEE-noh eem-boht-TEE-toh)* sandwich, filled roll

paninoteca, la *(pah-nee-noh-TEK-kah)* (le paninoteche) sandwich shop

panna, la *(PAHN-nah)* cream

con panna *(kohn PAHN-nah)* with steamed milk

panna acida, la *(PAHN-nah AH-cee-dah)* sour cream

panna cotta, la *(PAHN-nah KOHT-tah)* thick, creamy custard or pudding dessert

panna montata, la *(PAHN-nah mohn-TAH-tah)* whipped cream

pannolini usa-e-getta, i disposable diapers *(pahn-noh-LEE-nee oo-zah-ay-JET-tah)*

pannolino, il *(pahn-noh-LEE-noh)* (i pannolini) diaper

pannolini usa-e-getta, i disposable diapers *(pahn-noh-LEE-nee oo-zah-ay-JET-tah)*

panoramica, la *(pah-noh-RAH-mee-kah)* (le panoramiche) scenic route

panpepato, il *(pahn-pay-PAH-toh)* gingerbread; sweet dark fruit bread with honey, nuts, and spices

pantaloncini, i *(pahn-tah-lohn-CHEE-nee)* shorts

pantaloni, i *(pahn-tah-LOH-nee)* pants

panzanella, la *(pahn-tsah-NAYL-lah)* bread and tomato salad with olive oil and vinegar

panzarotti, i *(pahn-tsah-ROHT-tee)* savory filled and fried ravioli pieces (ham, cheese, tomato)

papà, il *(pah-PAH)* father, dad

paparot, il *(pah-pah-ROHT)* cornmeal and spinach soup

papassinas, i *(pah-pahs-SEE-nahs)* raisin, nut and spice cookies

pappa al pomodoro, la *(PAHP-pah ahl poh-moh-DOH-roh)* basil, tomato and bread soup

pappardella, la *(pahp-pahr-DEL-lah)* (le pappardelle) fat ribbon noodle

paprica, la *(PAHP-ree-kah)* paprika

parabrezza, il *(pah-rah-BRAYD-dzah)* windshield

paradiso, il *(pah-rah-DEE-zoh)* paradise, heaven

paralume, il *(pah-rah-LOO-may)* lampshade

paramedico/a, il/la *(pah-rah-MEH-dee-koh/-kah)* paramedic

parasole, il *(pah-rah-SOH-lay)* parasol, sunshade

paraurti, il *(pah-rah-OOR-tee)* (auto) bumper

parcella, la *(pahr-CHEL-lah)* fee

parcheggio, il *(pahr-KAYD-joh)* (i parcheggi) parking lot

parcheggio a pagamento, il *(pahr-KAYD-joh ah pah-gah-MAYN-toh)* paid parking lot

parchimetro, il *(pahr-KEE-may-troh)* (i parchimetri) parking meter

parco, il *(PAHR-koh)* (i parchi) park

parco giochi, il *(PAHR-koh JOH-kee)* playground

Parigi *(pah-REE-jee)* Paris

parlamento, il *(pahr-lah-MAYN-toh)* parliament

parlare *(pahr-LAH-ray)* to speak

parla *(PAHR-lah)* you speak (form. sing.)

parlo *(PAHR-loh)* I speak

parmigiana, alla *(AHL-lah pahr-mee-JAH-nah)* made or covered with Parmesan cheese or a cheesy sauce

parmigiana di melanzane, la *(pahr-mee-JAH-nah dee may-lahn-DZAH-nay)* eggplant parmesan

parmigiano, il *(pahr-mee-JAH-noh)* very hard, dry, sharp cheese

parola, la *(pah-ROH-lah)* word

parrozzo, il *(pahr-ROHT-tsoh)* chocolate-covered cake

parrucca, la *(pahr-ROOK-kah)* wig

parrucchiere, il *(pahr-rook-KYEH-ray)* hairdresser, barber, beauty salon

parte *(PAHR-tay)* (it) departs

parte, la *(PAHR-tay)* (le parti) part

partenopea, alla with cheese, tomato, oil, peppers, bread, olives, anchovies

partenza, la *(pahr-TEN-tsah)* (le partenze) departure

partire *(pahr-TEE-ray)* to depart, to leave

parte *(PAHR-tay)* (it) departs

partita, la *(pahr-TEE-tah)* game, match

partner, il/la *(PAHT-nuh)* partner

Pasqua, la *(PAHS-kwah)* Easter

passaggio, il *(pahs-SAHD-joh)* (i passaggi) passage

passaporto, il *(pahs-sah-POHR-toh)* (i passaporti) passport

passatempo, il *(pahs-sah-TEM-poh)* pastime, hobby

passato, il *(pahs-SAH-toh)* past

passato di verdura, il *(pahs-SAH-toh dee vayr-DOO-rah)* vegetable purèe

passeggero/a, il/la *(pahs-sayd-JEH-roh/-rah)* (i passeggeri/le passeggere) passengers

passeggiare *(pahs-sayd-JAH-ray)* to stroll

passeggiata, la *(pahs-sayd-JAH-tah)* walk

passeggino, il *(pahs-sayd-JEE-noh)* stroller

passeggio, il *(pahs-SAYD-joh)* walk, stroll

passerella, la *(pahs-say-REL-lah)* footbridge

passo, il *(PAHS-soh)* pass

passo carrabile *(PAHS-soh kahr-RAH-bee-lay)* keep clear, vehicle entrance

passo carraio *(PAHS-soh kahr-RAH-yoh)* driveway—keep clear

pasta, la *(PAHS-tah)* pasta, noodles, dough, pastry, cake, paste

pasta dentifricia, la *(PAHS-tah dayn-tee-FREE-chah)* toothpaste

pasta e fagioli *(PAHS-tah ay fah-JOH-lee)* pasta and bean soup

pasta in brodo, la *(PAHS-tah een BROH-doh)* noodle soup

pastasciutta, la *(pahs-tahsh-SHOOT-tah)* pasta (served on a plate)

pasticca per la tosse, la *(pahs-TEEK-kah payr lah TOHS-say)* (le pasticche) cough drop

pasticceria, la *(pahs-teet-chay-REE-ah)* pastry shop, with cakes and desserts

pasticcino, il *(pahs-teet-CHEE-noh)* (i pasticcini) pastries, petit four

pastiera, la *(pahs-TYEH-rah)* cream cheese, barley and candied fruit in a puff pastry

pastificio, il *(pahs-tee-FEET-choh)* pasta factory

pasti leggeri, i *(PAHS-tee layd-JEH-ree)* light meals

pastina, la *(pahs-TEE-nah)* small pasta shapes for soup

pastissada de caval, la *(pahs-tees-SAH-dah day kah-VAHL)* horsemeat stew

pasto, il *(PAHS-toh)* (i pasti) meal

pasto freddo, il *(PAHS-toh FRAYD-doh)* buffet

pastore, il *(pahs-TOH-ray)* (i pastori) minister

patata, la *(pah-TAH-tah)* (le patate) potato

patate fritte, le *(pahTAH-tah FREET-tay)* French fries

patatine fritte, le *(pah-tah-TEE-nay FREET-tay)* French fries

paté, il *(pah-TAY)* pâté

patente di guida, la *(pah-TEN-tay dee GWEE-dah)* (le patenti) driver's license

pattume, il *(paht-TOO-may)* garbage, trash

pattumiera, la *(paht-too-MYEH-rah)* garbage can, trash can

pausa, la *(POW-zah)* pause, break, lunch break

pavese, la zuppa alla *(TSOOP-pah AHL-lah pah-VAY-say)* clear soup with poached egg, croutons, cheese

pavimento, il *(pah-vee-MAYN-toh)* floor (of room)

pavone/a, il/la *(pah-VOH-nay/-nah)* peacock/peahen

paziente, il/la *(paht-TSYEN-tay)* patient (med)

pazzo/a *(PAHTS-soh/-sah)* crazy

pecan, il *(peh-KAHN)* pecan

peccato, il *(payk-KAH-toh)* sin

pecora, la *(PEH-kohr-rah)* (le pecore) sheep

pecorino, il *(pay-koh-REE-noh)* variety of cheeses made from sheep's milk

pedaggio, il *(pay-DAHD-joh)* (i pedaggi) toll

pedale, il *(pay-DAH-lay)* pedal

pedone, il/la *(pay-DOH-nay)* pedestrian

peggio *(PED-joh)* worse, worst

pelapatate, il *(pay-lah-pah-TAH-tay)* potato peeler

pelle, la *(PEL-lay)* skin

pellegrinaggio, il *(payl-lay-gree-NAHD-joh)* pilgrimage

pellicola, la *(payl-LEE-koh-lah)* film

pelo, il *(PAY-loh)* hair

pendere *(PEN-day-ray)* to hang

pene, il *(PEH-nay)* penis

penicillina, la *(pay-nee-cheel-LEE-nah)* penicillin

penisola, la *(pay-NEE-zoh-lah)* peninsula

penna, la *(PAYN-nah)* (le penne) pen, feather, pasta quill

penne, le *(PAYN-nay)* pasta tubes

pennello, il *(payn-NEL-loh)* brush

pensare *(payn-SAH-ray)* to think

  penso di no *(PAYN-soh dee noh)* I don't think so

  penso di si *(PAYN-soh dee see)* I think so

pensionato/a, il/la *(payn-syoh-NAH-toh/-tah)* retired person

pensione, la *(payn-SYOH-nay)* (le pensioni) boarding house, pension, guesthouse

  in pensione *(een payn-SYOH-nay)* retired

penso di no *(PAYN-soh dee noh)* I don't think so

penso di si *(PAYN-soh dee see)* I think so

pentola, la *(PAYN-toh-lah)* pan

pepe, il *(PAY-pay)* pepper

peperonata, la *(pay-pay-roh-NAH-tah)* stewed peppers, tomatoes, onions

peperoncino, il *(pay-pay-rohn-CHEE-noh)* (i peperoncini) chili pepper

peperone, il *(pay-pay-ROH-nay)* (i peperoni) peppers, capsicum

  paperone verde, il *(pay-pay-ROH-nay VAYR-day)* green pepper

  peperoni ripieni, i *(pay-pay-ROH-nee ree-PYEH-nee)* stuffed peppers

per *(payr)* for, to, by

  per esempio *(payr ay-ZEM-pyoh)* for example

  per favore *(payr fah-VOH-ray)* please

  per via aerea *(payr VEE-ah ah-EH-ray-ah)* by airmail

pera, la *(PAY-rah)* (le pere) pear

percentuale, la *(payr-chayn-too-AH-lay)* percentage

perché *(payr-KAY)* why, because

perdere *(PEHR-day-ray)* to lose

per favore *(payr fah-VOH-ray)* please

perfetto/a *(payr-FAYT-toh/-tah)* perfect

pericolo, il *(pay-REE-koh-loh)* (i pericoli) danger

pericolo di morte, il *(pay-REE-koh-loh dee MOHR-tay)* danger to life

pericoloso/a *(pay-ree-koh-LOH-soh/-sah)* dangerous

periodo, il *(pay-RYOH-doh)* (i periodi) (time) period

periodi brevi, i *(pay-RYOH-dee BREV-ee)* short stays

perla, la *(PEHR-lah)* (le perle) pearl

perlina, la *(payr-LEE-nah)* (le perline) bead

permanente *(payr-mah-NEN-tay)* permanent

permesso, il *(payr-MAYS-soh)* permission

permesso? *(payr-MAYS-soh)* May I get past?

permettere *(payr-MAYT-tay-ray)* to permit, to allow

pernice, la *(payr-NEE-chay)* (le pernici) partridge

pero, il *(PAY-roh)* pear (tree)

però *(pay-ROH)* yet, but

persico, il *(PEHR-see-koh)* (i persici) perch (fish)

perso/a *(PEHR-soh/-sah)* lost

persona, la *(payr-SOH-nah)* (le persone) person

personale *(payr-soh-NAH-lay)* personal

pervertito/a, il/la *(payr-vayr-TEE-toh/-tah)* pervert

per via aerea *(payr VEE-ah ah-EH-ray-ah)* by airmail

pesa, la *(PAY-sah)* weighing

pesante *(pay-SAHN-tay)* heavy

pesare *(pay-SAH-ray)* to weigh

pesca, la *(PES-kah)* (le pesche) peach

pesca, la *(PAYS-kah)* fishing

pescare *(pays-KAH-ray)* to fish

pescatora, alla *(AHL-lah pays-kah-TOH-rah)* with tomatoes and seafood

pesce, il *(PAYSH-shay)* (i pesci) fish

pesce persico, il *(PAYSH-shay PEHR-see-koh)* perch

pesce spada, il *(PAYSH-shay SPAH-dah)* swordfish

pescheria, la *(pays-kay-REE-ah)* fish shop

peso, il *(PAY-soh)* weight

peste, la *(PES-tay)* pest, nuisance

pesto, il *(PAYS-toh)* sauce of garlic, basil, pine nuts, olive oil, and Parmigiano-Reggiano cheese

pettine, il *(PET-tee-nay)* comb

petto, il *(PET-toh)* chest, breast

pettorina, la *(payt-toh-REE-nah)* bib

pezzo, il *(PET-tsoh)* (i pezzi) piece

piacciono, mi *(mee pyaht-CHOH-noh)* they are pleasing to me (=I like them)

piace, mi *(mee PYAH-chay)* it is pleasing to me (=I like it)

piacere *(pyah-CHAY-ray)* to be pleasing

  mi piace *(mee PYAH-chay)* it is pleasing to me (=I like it)

  mi piacciono *(mee pyaht-CHOH-noh)* they are pleasing to me (=I like them)

piacere, il *(pyah-CHAY-ray)* (i piaceri) pleasure, favor

  molto piacere *(MOHL-toh pyah-CHAY-ray)* pleased to meet you

  per piacere *(payr pyah-CHAY-ray)* please

piacevole *(pyah-CHAY-voh-lay)* pleasant, nice

piadina, la *(pyah-DEE-nah)* thin flatbread of white flour, lard, salt, and water

piaga, la *(PYAH-gah)* (le piaghe) sore, wound

piangere *(PYAHN-jay-ray)* to weep, to cry

piano/a *(PYAH-noh/-nah)* softly, slowly

piano, il *(PYAH-noh)* floor, story

pianta, la *(PYAHN-tah)* map, plant

piantina, la *(pyahn-TEE-nah)* map

piattino, il *(pyaht-TEE-noh)* saucer

piatto/a *(PYAHT-toh/-tah)* flat

piatto, il *(PYAHT-toh)* (i piatti) dish, plate, course, meal

  piatto del giorno, il *(PYAHT-toh dayl JOHR-noh)* specialty of the day

  piatto di carne, il *(PYAHT-toh dee KAHR-nay)* meat dish

  piatto fondo, il *(PYAHT-toh FOHN-doh)* bowl

piazza, la *(PYAHT-tsah)* (le piazze) town square

  piazza principale, la *(PYAHT-tsah preen-chee-PAH-lay)* large public square

piazzale, il *(pyaht-TSAH-lay)* large public square

piazza principale, la *(PYAHT-tsah preen-chee-PAH-lay)* main square, town square

piccante *(peek-KAHN-tay)* sharp (flavor), spicy

piccata alla marsala, la *(peek-KAH-tah AHL-lah mahr-SAHL-lah)* veal sautéed in marsala sauce

picchetto, il *(peek-KAYT-toh)* (i picchetti) peg, stake

piccione, il *(peet-CHOH-nay)* (i piccioni) pigeon

piccolo/a *(PEEK-koh-loh/-lah)* small, little

piccone, il *(peek-KOH-nay)* pickax

pici, i *(PEE-chee)* fat, hand-rolled, spaghetti-like pasta

picnic, il *(PEEK-neek)* picnic

piede, il *(PYEH-day)* (i piedi) foot

piegare *(pyay-GAH-ray)* to fold (up), to bend

Piemonte *(pyay-MOHN-tay)* Piedmont

pieno/a *(PYEH-noh/-nah)* full, full-bodied (wine)

pietà, la *(pyay-TAH)* Mary with body of Christ

pietra, la *(PYEH-trah)* stone

pigiama, il *(pee-JAH-mah)* (i pigiami) pajamas

pigione, la *(pee-JOH-nay)* rent

pila, la *(PEE-lah)* (le pile) battery

pillola, la *(PEEL-loh-lah)* (le pillole) pill

  pillola del giorno dopo, la *(PEEL-loh-lah dayl JOHR-noh DOH-poh)* morning-after pill

pilota, il/la *(pee-LOH-tah)* pilot

ping-pong, il *(peeng-PONG)* table tennis

pinolo, il *(pee-NOH-loh)* (i pinoli) pine nut

pinza, la *(PEEN-tsah)* pliers

pinzette, le *(peen-TSAYT-tay)* tweezers

pioggia, il *(PYOHD-jah)* rain

piombo, il *(PYOHM-boh)* lead

piove *(PYOH-vay)* it's raining

piovoso/a *(pyoh-VOH-soh/-sah)* rainy

pisarei e fasó, i *(pee-sah-RAY-ee ay fah-SOH)* bread dumplings with beans

piscina, la *(peesh-SHEE-nah)* swimming pool

piselli, i *(pee-SEL-lee)* peas

pisello, il *(pee-SEL-loh)* (i piselli) pea, dick (vulgar)

pista, la *(PEES-tah)* trail

pistacchio, il *(pees-TAHK-kyoh)* (i pistacchi) pistachio

pistola, la *(pees-TOH-lah)* pistol, nozzle

pitta, la *(PEET-tah)* pita bread

pittore/pittrice, il/la *(peet-TOH-ray/-TREE-chay)* painter

pittura, la *(peet-TOO-rah)* painting

più *(pyoo)* more

pizza, la *(PEET-tsah)* (le pizze) pizza

  pizza al taglio, la *(PEET-tsah ahl TAHL-lyoh)* pizza by the slice

  pizza bianca, la *(PEET-tsah BYAHN-kah)* tomato-less pizza with olive oil and rosemary

  pizza d'asporto, la *(PEET-tsah dahs-POHR-toh)* pizza to go

pizza Margherita, la *(PEET-tsah mahr-gay-REE-tah)* pizza with tomato, mozzarella, basil, and olive oil

pizza quattro formaggi, la *(PEET-tsah KWAHT-troh fohr-MAHD-jee)* pizza with tomatoes, mozzarella, and other cheeses, usually including gorgonzola

pizza quattro stagioni, la *(PEET-tsah KWAHT-troh stah-JOH-nee)* pizza with mozzarella, tomatoes, mushrooms, artichokes, ham, olives

pizza Siciliana, la *(PEET-tsah see-chee-LYAH-nah)* thick-crust pizza with lots of toppings and cheese

plastica, la *(PLAHS-tee-kah)* plastic

pneumatico, lo *(pnay-oo-MAH-tee-koh)* (gli pneumatici) tire

po' (di), un *(oon poh [dee])* a little (of)

poco/a *(POH-koh/-kah)* few

poco, un *(oon POH-koh)* a little

podista, il/la *(poh-DEES-tah)* walker, runner

poesia, la *(poh-ay-ZEE-ah)* poetry

poggiolo, il *(pohd-JOH-loh)* balcony

poi *(poy)* then, later

E poi? *(ay poy?)* Anything else?

polenta, la *(poh-LEN-tah)* cornmeal mush, cornmeal pasta

polenta alla piemontese, la *(poh-LEN-tah AHL-lah pyay-mohn-TAY-say)* cornmeal mush layered with meat

polenta concia, la *(poh-LEN-tah KOHN-chah)* polenta and cheese

polenta e coniglio, la *(poh-LEN-tah ay koh-NEEL-lyoh)* cornmeal mush and rabbit stew

polipo, il *(POH-lee-poh)* (i polipi) octopus

politica, la *(poh-LEE-tee-kah)* politics

politico/a, il/la *(poh-LEE-tee-koh/-kah)* politician

polizia, la *(poh-leet-TSEE-ah)* police

pollame, il *(pohl-LAH-may)* poultry, fowl

polleria, la *(pohl-lay-REE-ah)* poultry shop

pollice, il *(POHL-lee-chay)* thumb

polline, il *(POHL-lee-nay)* pollen

pollo, il *(POHL-loh)* (i polli) chicken

pollo all'abruzzese, il *(POHL-loh ahl-lah-broot-TSAY-say)* chicken with sweet peppers

pollo alla diavola, il *(POHL-loh AHL-lah dee-AH-voh-lah)* spicy grilled chicken

pollo alla romana, il *(POHL-loh AHL-lah roh-MAH-nah)*

chicken, tomato sauce, sweet peppers

pollo novello, il *(POHL-loh noh-VEL-loh)* spring chicken

polmone, il *(pohl-MOH-nay)* (i polmoni) lung

polmonite, la *(pohl-moh-NEE-tay)* pneumonia

polpetta di carne, la *(pohl-PAYT-tah dee KAHR-nay)* (le polpette) meatball

polpettina, la *(pohl-payt-TEE-nah)* (le polpettine) tiny meatball

polpettone, il *(pohl-payt-TOH-nay)* meatloaf

polpo, il *(POHL-poh)* (i polpi) octopus

polso, il *(POHL-soh)* wrist

polvere, la *(POHL-vay-ray)* powder

pomeriggio, il *(pohm-may-REED-joh)* (i pomeriggi) afternoon

pommarola, la *(pohm-mah-ROH-lah)* tomato, garlic, basil sauce

pomodori, i *(poh-moh-DOH-ree)* tomatoes

pomodori secchi, i *(poh-moh-DOH-ree SAYK-kee)* sun-dried tomatoes

pomodorino, il *(poh-moh-dohr-EE-noh)* (i pomodorini) cherry tomato

pomodoro, il *(pohm-moh-DOH-roh)* (i pomodori) tomato

pompa, la *(POHM-pah)* pump

pompiere, il *(pohm-PYEH-ray)* (i pompieri) fireman

ponte, il *(POHN-tay)* (i ponti) bridge

popcorn, il *(POHP-kohn)* popcorn

popolare *(poh-poh-LAH-ray)* popular

popolo, il *(POH-poh-loh)* people

popone, il *(poh-POH-nay)* melon

porcellino, il *(pohr-chayl-LEE-noh)* piglet

porchetta, la *(pohr-KAYT-tah)* roast suckling pig

porcini, i *(pohr-CHEE-nee)* type of mushroom

porco/a, il/la *(POHR-koh/-kah)* pig

porpora *(POHR-poh-rah)* purple

porro, il *(POHR-roh)* (i porri) leek

porta, la *(POHR-tah)* (le porte) door

portacenere, il *(pohr-tah-CHAY-nay-ray)* (i portaceneri) ashtray

portadocumenti, il *(pohr-tah-doh-koo-MAYN-tee)* file folder

portafoglio, il *(pohr-tah-FOHL-lyoh)* wallet

portare *(pohr-TAH-ray)* to bring, to carry, to wear

portatile *(pohr-TAH-tee-lay)* portable

portatile, il *(pohr-TAH-tee-lay)* laptop

portico, il *(POHR-tee-koh)* covered walkway

porto, il *(POHR-toh)* (i porti) port, harbor

portobagagli, i *(pohr-toh-bah-GAHL-lyee)* baggage porters

possedere *(pohs-say-DAY-ray)* to possess, to have

possiamo *(pohs-SYAH-moh)* we can, we are able to, we may

possibile *(pohs-SEE-bee-lay)* possible

posso *(POHS-soh)* I can, I am able to, I may

posta, la *(POHS-tah)* mail

posta assicurata, la *(POHS-tah ahs-see-koo-RAH-tah)* insured mail

posta elettronica, la *(POHS-tah ay-layt-TROH-nee-kah)* e-mail

posta ordinaria, la *(POHS-tah ohr-dee-NAHR-yah)* surface mail

posta prioritaria, la *(POHS-tah pree-oh-ree-TAHR-yah)* airmail, priority mail

posta raccomandata, la *(POHS-tah rahk-koh-mahn-DAH-tah)* airmail with receipt, registered mail

postale, l'ufficio *m (oof-FEE-choh pohs-TAH-lay)* post office

posteggio di tassi, il *(pohs-TAYD-joh dee TAHS-see)* taxi stand

postino/a, il/la *(pohs-TEE-noh/-nah)* mailman/mailwoman

posto, a *(ah POHS-toh)* that's it
 a tutto posto? *(TOOT-toh ah POHS-toh?)* everything all right?

posto, il *(POHS-toh)* place, seat

potabile *(poh-TAH-bee-lay)* drinkable, safe to drink

potenza, la *(poh-TEN-tsah)* power, strength

potere *(poh-TAY-ray)* to be able to, can, may
 possiamo *(pohs-SYAH-moh)* we can
 posso *(POHS-soh)* I can
 potrebbe *(POH-tray-bay)* you could, you might be able to (form. sing.)
 potrei *(poh-TREH-ee)* I could, I might be able to, could I?
 può *(pwoh)* you can (form. sing.)

povero/a *(POH-vay-roh/-rah)* poor

povertà, la *(poh-vayr-TAH)* poverty

pozza, la *(POHT-tsah)* puddle

pozzanghera, la *(poht-TSAHN-gay-rah)* puddle

Praga *(PRAH-gah)* Prague

pranzo, il *(PRAHN-dzoh)* (i pranzi) lunch

ora di pranzo, l' *(LOH-rah dee PRAHN-dzoh)* lunch hour

prataiolo, il *(prah-tah-YOH-loh)* type of mushroom

pratica, la *(PRAH-tee-kah)* practice

precauzione, la *(pray-kowt-TSYOH-nay)* caution

precendente *(pray-chay-DEN-tay)* previous

precisamente *(pray-chee-zah-MAYN-tay)* precisely, exactly

preferenza, la *(pray-fay-REN-tsah)* preference

preferire *(pray-fay-REE-ray)* to prefer

pregare *(pray-GAH-ray)* to pray

preghiera, la *(pray-GYEH-rah)* prayer

prego *(PREH-goh)* you're welcome

premere *(PREM-ay-ray)* to press

prenda! *(PREN-dah)* take!

prendere *(PREN-day-ray)* to take
prenda! *(PREN-dah)* take!
prendo *(PREN-doh)* I take
lo prendo *(loh PREN-doh)* I'll have
prendere in affitto *(PREN-day-ray een ahf-FEET-toh)* to rent

prenotare *(pray-noh-TAH-ray)* to reserve

prenotato *(pray-noh-TAH-toh)* reserved

prenotazione, la *(pray-noh-taht-TSYOH-nay)* (le prenotazioni) reservation

preoccupato/a *(pray-ohk-koo-PAH-toh/-tah)* worried

prepagato/a *(pray-pah-GAH-toh/-tah)* prepaid

preparare *(pray-pah-RAH-ray)* to prepare

preservativo, il *(pray-sayr-vah-TEE-voh)* (i preservativi) condom

presidente/tessa, il/la *(pray-see-DEN-tay/dayn-TAYS-sah)* president

pressione, la *(prays-SYOH-nay)* pressure
pressione alta, la *(prays-SYOH-nay AHL-tah)* high blood pressure
pressione del sangue, la *(prays-SYOH-nay dayl SAHN-gway)* blood pressure

prestare *(prays-TAH-ray)* to lend

presto *(PRES-toh)* early, soon

prete, il *(PREH-tay)* (i preti) priest

prezioso/a *(prayt-TSYOH-soh/-sah)* precious, valuable

prezzemolo, il *(prayt-TSAY-moh-loh)* parsley

prezzo, il *(PRET-tsoh)* (i prezzi) price

menù a prezzo fisso, il *(may-NOO ah PRET-tsoh FEES-soh)* set-priced menu

prigione, la *(pree-JOH-nay)* prison

prima, la *(PREE-mah)* the first

prima classe, la *(PREE-mah KLAHS-say)* first class

prima colazione, la *(PREE-mah koh-laht-TSYOH-nay)* breakfast

prima di *(PREE-mah dee)* before

primavera, la *(pree-mah-VEHR-ah)* (le primavere) spring (season)

primi, i *(PREE-mee)* entrees

primo/a *(PREE-moh/-mah)* first

primo ministro, il/la *(PREE-moh mee-NEES-troh)* prime minister

primo piatto, il *(PREE-moh PYAHT-toh)* first course

principale *(preen-chee-PAH-lay)* main

privato/a *(pree-VAH-toh/-tah)* private

probabile *(proh-BAH-bee-lay)* probably, likely

probabilità, la *(proh-bah-bee-lee-TAH)* probability

problema, il *(proh-BLEH-mah)* problem

produrre *(proh-DOOR-ray)* to produce

professione, la *(proh-fays-SYOH-nay)* profession, occupation

professore/essa, il/la *(proh-fays-SOH-ray/-soh-RAYS-sah)* professor, teacher (=high school or university teacher)

profitto, il *(proh-FEET-toh)* (i profitti) profit

profondo/a *(proh-FOHN-doh/-dah)* deep

profumeria, la *(proh-foo-may-REE-ah)* perfumery

profumo, il *(proh-FOO-moh)* (i profumi) perfume

programma, il *(proh-GRAHM-mah)* (i programmi) program

programmatore/trice di computer, il/la *(proh-grahm-mah-TOH-ray/-TREE-chay dee kom-PYOO-tur)* computer programmer

proibire *(proh-ee-BEE-ray)* to forbid, to prohibit

proibito/a *(proh-ee-BEE-toh/-tah)* prohibited, forbidden

proiettore, il *(proh-yayt-TOH-ray)* projector

promessa, la *(proh-MAYS-sah)* promise

promettere *(proh-MAYT-tay-ray)* to promise

pronto/a *(PROHN-toh/-tah)* ready, quick, "Hello" (phone)

pronto soccorso, il *(PROHN-toh sohk-KOHR-soh)* first aid

pronunciare *(proh-noon-CHAH-ray)* to pronounce

propano, il *(proh-PAH-noh)* propane

proprietario/a, il/la *(proh-pryay-TAHR-yoh/-yah)* owner

prosciutto, il *(prohsh-SHOOT-toh)* ham

  prosciutto affumicato, il *(prohsh-SHOOT-toh ahf-foo-mee-KAH-toh)* smoked ham

  prosciutto cotto, il *(prohsh-SHOOT-toh KOHT-toh)* ham, cooked or boiled

  prosciutto crudo, il *(prohsh-SHOOT-toh KROO-doh)* cured ham

prossimo/a *(PROHS-see-moh/-mah)* next

prostituta, la *(prohs-tee-TOO-tah)* (le prostitute) prostitute (female)

prostituto, il *(prohs-tee-TOO–toh)* (i prostituti) prostitute (male)

proteina, la *(proh-tay-EE-nah)* protein

protetto/a *(proh-TET-toh/-tah)* protected

provare *(proh-VAH-ray)* to attempt, to try something on

provolone, il *(proh-voh-LOH-nay)* firm, often smoked cheese

provviste, la *(prohv-VEES-tah)* provisions, supply, stock

prugna, la *(PROON-nyah)* (le prugne) plum

prugna secca, la *(PROON-nyah SAYK-kah)* prune

pub, il *(poob)* pub

pubblico, il *(POOB-blee-koh)* public, audience

pugilato, il *(poo-jee-LAH-toh)* boxing

pulce, la *(POOL-chay)* (le pulci) flea

pulire *(poo-LEE-ray)* to clean

pulito/a *(poo-LEE-toh/-tah)* clean, tidy, neat

pulizia, la *(poo-leet-TSEE-ah)* cleaning

pullman, il *(POOL-mahn)* (i pullman) town-to-town bus, motor coach

pullover, il *(pool-LOH-vayr)* pullover, sweater

pulmino, il *(pool-MEE-noh)* minibus

pulpito, il *(POOL-pee-toh)* pulpit

punire *(poo-NEE-ray)* to punish

puntino/a *(poon-TEE-noh/-nah)* medium (meat)

punto, il *(POON-toh)* point, dot (e.g., .com)

  punto d'Internet, il *(POON-toh DEEN-tayr-nayt)* Internet point

  punto di vendita, il *(POON-toh dee VAYN-dee-tah)* point of sale

puntuale *(poon-too-AH-lay)* punctual

puntura, la *(poon-TOO-rah)* bite (e.g., mosquito), sting

può *(pwoh)* you are able to (form. sing.)

purè, in *(een poo-REH)* creamed

puro/a *(POO-roh/rah)* pure, clear

puttanesca, alla *(AHL-lah poot-tah-NAYS-kah)* sauce of anchovies, capers, black olives, tomatoes, olive oil, garlic

putto, il *(POOT-tah)* (i putti) cherub, cupid

Q

Q, q *(koo)* Q, q

qua *(kwah)* here

quaderno, il *(kwah-DEHR-noh)* notebook

quadrato, il *(kwah-DRAH-toh)* square

quaglia, la *(KWAHL-lyah)* (le quaglie) quail

qualche *(KWAHL-kay)* a few

qualcosa *(kwahl-KOH-sah)* something

qualcuno/a *(kwahl-KOO-noh/-nah)* someone

quale *(KWAH-lay)* what

qualifica, la *(kwah-LEE-fee-kah)* (le qualifiche) qualification

qualità, la *(kwah-lee-TAH)* quality

quando *(KWAHN-doh)* when

quante *f pl (KWAHN-tay)* how many

quanti *m pl (KWAHN-tee)* how many

quantità, la *(kwahn-tee-TAH)* quantity, amount

quanto/a *(KWAHN-toh/-tah)* how much, how long

quaranta *(kwah-RAHN-tah)* forty

quarantacinque *(kwah-rahn-tah-CHEEN-kway)* forty-five

quarantadue *(kwah-rahn-tah-DOO-ay)* forty-two

quarantanove *(kwah-rahn-tah-NOH-vay)* forty-nine

quarantaquattro *(kwah-rahn-tah-KWAHT-troh)* forty-four

quarantasei *(kwah-rahn-tah-SEH-ee)* forty-six

quarantasette *(kwah-rahn-tah-SET-tay)* forty-seven

quarantatré *(kwah-rahn-tah-TRAY)* forty-three

quarantotto *(kwah-rahn-TOHT-toh)* forty-eight

quarantuno *(kwah-rahn-TOO-noh)* forty-one

quaresima, la *(kwah-RAY-see-mah)* Lent

quartiere, il *(kwahr-TYEH-ray)* suburb, district, area

quartirolo, il *(kwahr-tee-ROH-loh)* creamy, soft, cow's milk cheese

quarto, il *(KWAHR-toh)* (i quarti) quarter

quasi crudo/a *(KWAH-zee KROO-doh/-dah)* very rare (meat)

quattordici *(kwaht-TOHR-dee-chee)* fourteen

quattro *(KWAHT-troh)* four

quattro formaggi *(KWAHT-troh fohr-MAHD-jee)* four types of cheese (pizza)

quattro stagioni *(KWAHT-troh stah-JOH-nee)* vegetables, cheese, ham, bacon (pizza)

quattrocento *(kwaht-troh-CHEN-toh)* four hundred

quello/a *(KWAY-loh/-lah)* that (thing)

questa notte *(KWAYS-tah NOHT-tay)* tonight

questi/queste *(KWAYS-tee/KWAYS-tay)* these

questo/a *(KWAYS-toh/-tah)* this

qui *(kwee)* here

quieto/a *(KWYAY-toh/-tah)* quiet, still

quindici *(KWEEN-dee-chee)* fifteen

quota, la *(KWOH-tah)* quota, share; altitude, height

R

R, r *(EHR-ray)* R, r

rabarbaro, il *(rah-BAHR-bah-roh)* rhubarb

rabbino, il *(rahb-BEE-noh)* rabbi

racchetta, la *(rahk-KAYT-tah)* racket

raccomandare *(rah-koh-mahn-DAH-ray)* to recommend

raccomandata, la *(rahk-koh-mahn-DAH-tah)* registered mail, certified mail

rada, la *(RAH-dah)* harbor

radar, il *(RAH-dahr)* radar

radiatore, il *(rahd-yah-TOH-ray)* radiatore

radicchio, il *(rah-DEEK-kyoh)* red lettuce, type of chicory

radio, la *(RAHD-yoh)* radio

radiocomando, il *(rahd-yoh-koh-MAHN-doh)* remote control

rafano, il *(RAH-fah-noh)* horseradish

raffreddore, il *(rahf-frayd-DOH-ray)* cold (illness)

raffreddore da fieno, il *(rahf-frayd-DOH-ray dah FYEH-noh)* hay fever

ragazza, la *(rah-GAHT-tsah)* (le ragazze) girl, young woman, girlfriend

ragazzo, il *(rah-GAHT-tsoh)* (i ragazzi) boy, young man, boyfriend

ragione, la *(rah-JOH-nay)* reason

ragioniere/a, il/la *(rah-joh-NYEH-ray/-rah)* accountant

ragno, il *(RAHN-yoh)* (i ragni) spider

ragù, al *(ahl rah-GOO)* meat sauce for pasta

rallentare *(rah-layn-TAH-ray)* to slow down

rapa, la *(RAH-pah)* (le rape) turnip

rapido/a *(RAH-pee-doh/-dah)* quick
 rapido *(RAH-pee-doh)* (train) express train connecting large towns and cities (must pay supplement)

rapinare *(rah-pee-NAH-ray)* to rob

rapporto, il *(rah-POHR-toh)* relationship, connection

rappresentante di commercio, il/la *(rahp-pray-zayn-TAHN-tay dee kohm-MEHR-choh)* sales representative

rappresentare *(rahp-pray-zayn-TAH-ray)* to represent

raramente *(rah-rah-MAYN-tay)* rarely, seldom

raro/a *(RAH-roh/-rah)* rare, uncommon

rasoio, il *(rah-SOH-yoh)* razor
 rasoio elettrico, il *(rah-SOH-yoh ay-LET-tree-koh)* electric razor

raspo, il *(RAHS-poh)* grape stalk

ravanello, il *(rah-vah-NEL-loh)* (i ravanelli) radish

ravioli, i *(rah-vee-OH-lee)* stuffed pasta squares
 ravioli alla piemontese, i *(rah-vee-OH-lee AHL-lah pyay-mohn-TAY-say)* ravioli filled with beef and vegetables

raviolini, i *(rah-vyoh-LEE-nee)* small ravioli

re, il *(ray)* king

reale *(ray-AH-lay)* real, genuine

realistico/a *(ray-ah-LEES-tee-koh/-kah)* realistic

recente *(ray-CHEN-tay)* recent

recessione, la *(ray-chays-SYOH-nay)* recession

recipiente, il *(ray-chee-PYEN-tay)* container

reciprocità, la *(ray-chee-proh-chee-TAH)* reciprocity

reclamo, il *(ray-KLAH-moh)* (i reclami) complaint

redditto, il *(RED-deet-toh)* income

redini, le *(REH-dee-nee)* reins

refe, il *(RAY-fay)* thread, yarn

refrigeratore, il *(ray-free-jay-rah-TOH-ray)* refrigerator

regalo, il *(ray-GAH-loh)* (i regali) gift
 negozio di regali, il *(nay-GOHT-tsyoh dee ray-GAH-lee)* gift shop

reggia, la *(RED-jah)* (le regge) (royal) palace

reggipetto, il *(rayd-jee-PET-toh)* bra

reggiseno, il *(rayd-jee-SAY-noh)* (i reggiseni) bra

regina, la *(ray-JEE-nah)* queen

regionale *(ray-joh-NAH-lay)* regional; slow train

regione, la *(ray-JOH-nay)* region

registrare *(ray-jees-TAH-ray)* to register

registro, il *(ray-JEES-troh)* register, registry

regola, la *(REH-goh-lah)* (le regole) rule

regolare *(ray-goh-LAH-ray)* regular, medium

regolare *(ray-goh-LAH-ray)* to regulare, to control

relazione, la *(ray-laht-TSYOH-nay)* relationship

religione, la *(ray-lee-JOH-nay)* religion

religioso/a *(ray-lee-JOH-soh/-sah)* religious, sacred

reliquia, la *(ray-LEE-kwyah)* relic

rene, il *(REH-nay)* (i reni) kidney

respirare *(rays-pee-RAH-ray)* to breathe

resto, il *(RES-toh)* return change (money)

  non da resto *(nohn dah RES-toh)* doesn't give change

rete, la *(RAY-tay)* net

  in rete *(een RAY-tay)* on the Internet

  rete fissa, la *(RAY-tay FEES-sah)* land line (phone)

riagganciare *(ree-ahg-gahn-CHAH-ray)* to hang up (phone)

ribes, il *(REE-bays)* current

  ribes nero, il *(REE-bays NAY-roh)* black currant

  ribes rosso, il *(REE-bays ROHS-soh)* red currant

ribollita, la *(ree-bohl-LEE-tah)* thick Tuscan soup made with bread and vegetables

ricamo, il *(ree-KAH-moh)* embroidery

ricciarelli, i *(reet-chyah-RAYL-lee)* Sienese almond cookies

ricco/a *(REEK-koh/-kah)* rich

ricetta, la *(ree-CHET-tah)* (le ricette) prescription

ricevere *(ree-CHAY-vay-ray)* to receive

ricevuta, la *(ree-chay-VOO-tah)* (le ricevute) receipt

richiesta (di) *(ree-KYES-tah [dee])* request (for)

  richiesta di intervento, la *(ree-KYES-tah dee een-tayr-VEN-toh)* request for help

riciclabile *(ree-chee-KLAH-bee-lay)* recyclable

riciclaggio, il *(ree-chee-KLAHD-joh)* recycling

riciclare *(ree-chee-KLAH-ray)* to recycle

ricordino, il *(ree-kohr-DEE-noh)* souvenir

ricotta, la *(ree-KOHT-tah)* a white, unripened cheese similar to cottage cheese

ridere *(REE-day-ray)* to laugh

rifiutare *(ree-fyoo-TAH-ray)* to refuse

rifiuto, il *(ree-FYOO-toh)* refusal

rifondere *(ree-FOHN-day-ray)* to refund, to reimburse

refugio, il *(ree-FOO-joh)* (i rifugi) shelter, refuge

rigaglie, le *(ree-GAHL-lyay)* giblets

rigatoni, i *(ree-gah-TOH-nee)* stubby pasta tubes

rilassamento, il *(ree-lahs-sah-MAYN-toh)* relaxation

rilievo, il *(ree-LYEH-voh)* relief (e.g., art)

rimborso, il *(reem-BOHR-soh)* reimbursement, refund

rimedio, il *(ree-MED-yoh)* (i rimedi) remedy, cure

rimmel, il *(REEM-mayl)* mascara

rimozione forzata, la *(ree-moht-TSYOH-nay fohr-TSAH-tah)* tow-away zone

ringraziare *(reen-graht-TSYAH-ray)* to thank

riparare *(ree-pah-RAH-ray)* to repair

ripetere *(ree-PEH-tay-ray)* to repeat

ripido/a *(REE-pee-doh/-dah)* steep

ripieno/a *(ree-PYEH-noh/-nah)* stuffed, filled

ripieno, il *(ree-PYEH-noh)* stuffing

riposare *(ree-poh-SAH-ray)* to rest

riposo, il *(ree-POH-soh)* rest

riprodure *(ree-proh-DOO-ray)* to reproduce

riscaldamento, il *(rees-kahl-dah-MYAN-toh)* heating

riscaldamento centrale, il *(rees-kahl-dah-MAYN-toh chayn-TRAH-lay)* central heating

riscaldare *(rees-kahl-DAH-ray)* to heat, to warm up

rischo, il *(REES-koh)* (i rischi) risk

riservato/a *(ree-sayr-VAH-toh/-tah)* reserved

riservato ai disabili *(ree-sayr-VAH-toh AH-ee dee-ZAH-bee-lee)* reserved for the disabled

risi e bisi, i *(REE-see ay BEE-see)* rice with beans and bacon

riso, il *(REE-soh)* rice

riso in cagnon, il *(REE-soh een KAHN-nyohn)* rice with sage and parmesan

riso integrale, il *(REE-soh een-tay-GRAH-lay)* brown rice

risotto, il *(ree-SOHT-toh)* rice cooked in a meat, fish or vegetable broth until creamy

rispetto, il *(rees-PET-toh)* respect

rispondere *(rees-POHN-day-ray)* to answer, to respond

risposta, la *(rees-POHS-tah)* response, answer

ristorante, il *(rees-toh-RAHN-tay)* (i ristoranti) restaurant (more formal)

ristoro, il *(rees-TOH-roh)*
refreshment

ritardo, il *(ree-TAHR-doh)* (i ritardi)
delay

ritiro bagagli, il *(ree-TEE-roh bah-GAHL-lyee)* baggage claim

ritornare *(ree-tohr-NAH-ray)* to
return

ritorno, il *(ree-TOHR-noh)* (i ritorni)
return trip, return

riva, la *(REE-vah)* shore, bank

riviera, la *(ree-VYEH-rah)* coast

rivista, la *(ree-VEES-tah)* (le riviste)
magazine

roba, la *(ROH-bah)* things, stuff,
belongings

robiola, la *(roh-BYOH-lah)* type of
creamy cheese made of cow's
and sheep milk

rocca, la *(ROHK-kah)* (le rocche)
fortress

roccia, la *(ROHT-chah)* (le rocce)
rock

  fare roccia *(FAH-ray ROHT-chah)*
to go rock climing

rock, il *(rohk)* rock (music)

rognone, il *(rohn-NYOH-nay)* (i
rognoni) kidney

rollino, il *(rohl-LEE-noh)* (i rollini)
roll of film

Roma *(ROH-mah)* Rome

romantico/a *(roh-MAHN-tee-koh/-kah)* romantic

romanzo, il *(roh-MAHN-dzoh)* novel

rompere *(ROHM-pay-ray)* to
break

rondò, il *(rohn-DOH)* traffic
circle

rosa *(ROH-zah)* pink

rosatello, il *(roh-zah-TEL-loh)*
rosé (wine)

rosato, il *(roh-ZAH-toh)* rosé
(wine)

rosbif, il *(ROHZ-beef)* roast beef

rosé, il *(roh-ZAY)* rosé (wine)

rosmarino, il *(rohz-mah-REE-noh)*
rosemary

rossetto, il *(rohs-SAYT-toh)*
lipstick

rosso/a *(ROHS-soh/-sah)* red

rosticceria, la *(rohs-teet-chay-REE-ah)* take-away shop for
roast meat and other
prepared food

rosumada, la *(roh-soo-MAH-dah)*
Milanese eggnog with red
wine

rotatoria, la *(roh-tah-TOHR-yah)*
traffic circle

rotonda, il *(roh-TOHN-dah)*
rotunda

rotondo/a *(roh-TOHN-doh/-dah)*
round, full

rotto/a *(ROHT-toh/-tah)* broken

rotula, la *(ROH-too-lah)* kneecap

roulotte, la *(roo-LET)* roulette

rovina, la *(roh-VEE-nah)* ruin

rubato/a *(roo-BAH-toh/-tah)* stolen

rubinetto, il *(roo-bee-NAYT-toh)* faucet

acqua dal rubinetto, l' *f (AHK-kwah dahl roo-bee-NAYT-toh)* tap water

ruchetta, la *(roo-KAYT-tah)* arugula

rucola, la *(ROO-koh-lah)* arugula

rugby, il *(ROOG-bee)* rugby

rullino, il *(rool-LEE-noh)* (i rullini) roll of film

rum-babà, il *(room-bah-BAH)* rum-soaked cake

rumoroso/a *(roo-moh-ROH-soh/-sah)* noisy

ruota, la *(RWOH-tah)* (le ruote) wheel

rurale *(roo-RAH-lay)* rural, country

ruscello, il *(roosh-SHEL-loh)* stream

ruspante *(roos-PAHN-tay)* free-range

russare *(roos-SAH-ray)* to snore

rustico/a *(ROOS-tee-koh/-kah)* rustic, country, rural

alla rustica *(AHL-lah ROOS-tee-kah)* with garlic, anchovies, oregano

S

S, s *(EHS-say)* S, s

sabato, il *(SAH-bah-toh)* Saturday

sabbia, la *(SAHB-byah)* sand

sabbie mobili, le *(SAHB-byay MOH-bee-lee)* quicksand

sabbioso/a *(sahb-BYOH-soh/-sah)* sandy

saccarina, la *(sahk-kah-REE-nah)* saccharin(e)

sacchetto, il *(sahk-KAYT-toh)* shopping bag

sacco, il *(SAHK-koh)* (i sacchi) sack

sacco a pelo, il *(SAHK-koh ah PAY-loh)* sleeping bag

sala, la *(SAH-lah)* hall, room

sala d'aspetto, la *(SAH-lah dahs-PET-toh)* waiting room

salama da sugo ferrarese, la *(sah-LAH-mah dah SOO-goh fayr-rah-RAY-say)* pork sausage

salame, il *(sah-LAH-may)* salami

salamino, il *(sah-lah-MEE-noh)* small salami

salario, il *(sah-LAHR-yoh)* pay, wage

salato/a *(sah-LAH-toh/-tah)* salty

saldi, i *(SAHL-dee)* sale(s)

saldo, il *(SAHL-doh)* account balance, payment, settlement

sale, il *(SAH-lay)* salt

salire *(sah-LEE-ray)* to board, to climb

salgo *(SAHL-goh)* I climb/go up

sale *(SAH-lay)* you climb/go up (form. sing.)

saliamo *(sahl-YAH-moh)* we climb/go up

salmone, il *(sahl-MOH-nay)* salmon

salmonella, la *(sahl-moh-NEL-lah)* salmonella

salone, il *(sah-LOH-nay)* living room, sitting room

salotto, il *(sah-LOHT-toh)* living room, sitting room

salsa, la *(SAHL-sah)* (le salse) sauce

salsiccia, la *(sahl-SEET-chah)* (le salsicce) pork sausage

saltato/a *(sahl-TAH-toh/-tah)* sautéed

saltimbocca, il *(sahl-teem-BOHK-kah)* rolled veal and ham with sage, served in a wine sauce

salume, il *(sah-LOO-may)* salami, cured pork

salumeria, la *(sah-loo-may-REE-ah)* delicatessen

salumi, i *(sah-LOO-mee)* cured pork products, cold cuts

salute *(sah-LOO-tay)* toast: "to your health," "cheers"

salva slip, i *(SAHL-vah sleep)* panty liners

salve *(SAHL-vay)* hello, hi

salvia, la *(SAHL-vyah)* sage
  burro e salvia *(BOOR-roh ay SAHL-vyah)* (pizza) with sage and butter, no tomato sauce

salviettine detergenti per bambini, le *(sahl-vyayt-TEE-nay day-tayr-JAYN-tee payr bahm-BEE-nee)* baby wipes

sambuca, la *(sahm-BOO-kah)* anise-flavored liqueur

sandali, i *(SAHN-dah-lee)* sandals

sandalo, il *(SAHN-dah-loh)* (i sandali) sandal

sangue, il *(SAHN-gway)* blood
  al sangue *(ahl SAHN-gway)* rare (meat)
  pressione del sangue, il *(prays-SYOH-nay dayl SAHN-gway)* blood pressure

sanguinaccio, il *(sahn-gwee-NAHT-choh)* chocolate blood pudding, black pudding

san Silvestro, il *(sahn seel-VES-troh)* New Year's Eve

santo/a, il/la *(SAHN-toh/-tah)* saint

santuario, il *(sahn-too-AHR-yoh)* shrine, sanctuary

sapere *(sah-PAY-ray)* to know
  sa *(sah)* you know (form. sing.)
  so *(soh)* I know
  sappiamo *(sahp-PYAH-moh)* we know

sapone, il *(sah-POH-nay)* soap

saponetta, la *(sah-poh-NAYT-tah)* (le saponette) bar of soap

sapore, il *(sah-POH-ray)* flavor

saporoso/a *(sah-poh-ROH-soh/-sah)* tasty

sarde, le *(SAHR-day)* sardines

Sardegna, la *(sahr-DAYN-nyah)* Sardinia

sardina, la *(sahr-DEE-nah)* (le sardine) sardine

sardine, le *(sahr-DEE-nay)* sardines

sarta, la *(SAHR-tah)* dressmaker

sarto, il *(SAHR-toh)* tailor

satellite, il *(sah-TEL-lee-tay)* satellite

sauna, la *(SOW-nah)* sauna

savoiardi, i *(sah-voh-YAHR-dee)* ladyfinger cookies

sbadato/a *(zbah-DAH-toh/-tah)* careless, inattentive

sbagliato/a *(zbahl-LYAH-toh/-tah)* wrong

sbaglio, lo *(ZBAHL-lyoh)* (gli sbagli) mistake

sbarco, lo *(ZBAHR-koh)* unloading, disembarkation

sbucciapatate, lo *(zboot-chah-pah-TAH-tay)* potato peeler

scacchi, gli *(SKAHK-kee)* chess

scadenza, la *(skah-DEN-tsah)* expiration, sell-by date

scaduto/a *(skah-DOO-toh/-tah)* expired, out of date

scala, la *(SKAH-lah)* stairs, staircase

scala mobile, la *(SKAH-lah MOH-bee-lay)* escalator

scalare *(skah-LAH-ray)* to climb

scaldaacqua, lo *(skahl-dah-AHK-kwah)* water heater

scaldabagno, lo *(skahl-dah-BAHN-nyoh)* water heater

scaldare *(skahl-DAH-ray)* to heat (up)

scaldato/a *(skahl-DAH-toh/-tah)* heated

scale, le *(SKAH-lay)* stairs, stairway

scalinata, la *(skah-lee-NAH-tah)* stairway, staircase, flight of stairs

scalogno, lo *(skah-LOHN-nyoh)* (gli scalogni) shallot

scaloppina, la *(skah-lohp-PEE-nah)* (le scaloppine) veal cutlet

scaloppina alla Valdostana, la *(skah-lohp-PEE-nah AHL-lah vahl-doh-STAH-nah)* veal cutlet filled with ham and cheese

scamorza, la *(skah-MOHR-tsah)* cow's milk cheese similar to mozzarella

scampi, gli *(SKAHM-pee)* type of small lobster, prawns

scampo, lo *(SKAHM-poh)* (gli scampi) prawn

scanner, lo *(SKAHN-ner)* scanner

scarafaggio, lo *(skah-rah-FAHD-joh)* (gli scarafaggi) cockroach

scaricare *(skah-ree-KAH-ray)* to download

scarole, lo *(skah-ROH-lay)* endive

scarpa, la *(SKAHR-pah)* (le scarpe) shoe

scarpe, le *(SKAHR-pay)* shoes

scarpone, lo *(skahr-POH-nay)* (gli scarponi) hiking or ski boot

scatola, la *(SKAH-toh-lah)* (le scatole) box, can

scatoletta, la *(skah-toh-LAYT-tah)* small can or box

scavo, lo *(SKAH-voh)* (gli scavi) excavation

scegliere *(SHAY-lyay-ray)* to choose, to select

scelta, la *(SHAYL-tah)* (le scelte) choice, selection

scendere *(SHAYN-day-ray)* to go down, to descend, to get off

scheda internazionale, la *(SKEH-dah een-tayr-naht-tsyoh-NAH-lay)* international phone card

scheda telefonica, la *(SKEH-dah tay-lay-FOH-nee-kah)* phone card

schermo, lo *(SKAYR-moh)* screen

schiena, la *(SKYEH-nah)* back

schmorbraten *(shmohr-BRAH-ten)* braised beef or pork roast

sci, lo *(shee)* skiing

sci nautico, lo *(shee NOW-tee-koh)* waterskiing

sciarpa, la *(SHAHR-pah)* (le sciarpe) scarf

scienza, la *(SHEN-tsah)* science

scienziato/a, lo/la *(shen-TSYAH-toh/-tah)* scientist

sciopero, lo *(SHOH-pay-roh)* strike

sciovia, la *(shoh-VEE-ah)* ski lift, ski tow

sciroppo, lo *(shee-ROHP-poh)* syrup

sciroppo per la tosse, lo *(shee-ROHP-poh payr lah TOHS-say)* cough syrup

scogliera, la *(skohl-LYEH-rah)* cliff

scomodo/a *(SKOH-moh-doh/-dah)* uncomfortable

scontato/a *(skohn-TAH-toh/-tah)* at a discount

scontento/a *(skohn-TEN-toh/-tah)* dissatisfied, displeased

sconto, lo *(SKOHN-toh)* discount

scontrino, lo *(skohn-TREE-noh)* (gli scontrini) receipt (when prepaying for item, e.g., at a bar)

scotch, lo *(skohch)* Scotch whiskey

scottatura, la *(skoht-tah-TOO-rah)* sunburn

scottiglia, la *(skoht-TEEL-lyah)* hearty stew using a variety of meats

scotto/a *(SKOHT-toh/-tah)* overcooked

Scozia, la *(SKOHT-tsyah)* Scotland

scrittore/scrittrice, lo/la *(skree-TOH-ray/-TREE-chay)* writer

scrivere *(SKREE-vay-ray)* to write

scultura, la *(skool-TOO-rah)* sculpture

scuola, la *(SKWOH-lah)* school

scuola superiore, la *(SKWOH-lah soo-pay-RYOH-ray)* high school

scuro/a *(SKOO-roh/-rah)* dark

scusa, la *(SKOO-zah)* apology

scusi, (mi) *([mee] SKOO-zee)* Excuse me, I apologize

se *(say)* if

secchio, il *(SAYK-kyoh)* (i secchi) bucket

secco/a *(SAYK-koh/-kah)* dry (wine)

secondo/a *(say-KOHN-doh/-dah)* second

seconda classe, la *(say-KOHN-dah KLAHS-say)* second class

secondo piatto, il *(say-KOHN-doh PYAHT-toh)* main (second) course

secondo, il *(say-KOHN-doh)* (i secondi) second

sedano, il *(SED-ah-noh)* (i sedani) celery

sedativo, il *(say-dah-TEE-voh)* sedative

sedere *(say-DAY-ray)* to sit

sedia, la *(SED-yah)* (le sedie) chair, seat

sedia a rotelle, la *(SED-yah ah roh-TEL-lay)* wheelchair

sedici *(SAY-dee-chee)* sixteen

seggiolino, il *(sayd-joh-LEE-noh)* child seat

seggiolino di sicurezza, il *(sayd-joh-LEE-noh dee see-koo-RAYT-tsah)* child's car seat

seggiolone, il *(sayd-joh-LOH-nay)* highchair

seggiovia, la *(sayd-joh-VEE-ah)* chairlift

segnale, il *(sayn-NYAH-lay)* signal, dial tone

segnare *(sayn-NYAH-ray)* to score

segno, il *(SAYN-nyoh)* sign

segretario/a, il/la *(say-gray-TAHR-yoh/-yah)* secretary

segreteria telefonica, la *(say-gray-tay-REE-ah tay-lay-FOH-nee-kah)* voice mail

segreto/a *(say-GRAY-toh/-tah)* secret, confidential

seguire *(say-GWEE-ray)* to follow

sei *(SEH-ee)* six

seicento *(say-ee-CHEN-toh)* six hundred

seimila *(say-ee-MEE-lah)* six thousand

selciato, il *(sayl-CHAH-toh)* cobbled surface

self-service cafeteria, self-service

selvaggina, la *(sayl-vahd-JEE-nah)* game (food)

semaforo, il *(say-MAH-foh-roh)* traffic light

semifreddo, il *(say-mee-FRAYD-doh)* chilled dessert made with ice cream

seminario, il *(say-mee-NAHR-yoh)* (i seminari) seminary, seminar

semi secco/a *(say-mee-SAYK-koh/-kah)* medium-dry

semola, la *(SAY-moh-lah)* bran

semolino, il *(say-moh-LEE-noh)* semolina

semplice *(SAYM-plee-chay)* simple

sempre *(SEM-pray)* always

senape, la *(SEH-nah-pay)* mustard

seno, il *(SAY-noh)* breast

senso unico, il *(SEN-soh OO-nee-koh)* one-way

sentiero, il *(sayn-TYEH-roh)* path

sentire *(sayn-TEE-ray)* to feel

senza *(SEN-tsah)* without

senza piombo *(SEN-tsah PYOHM-boh)* unleaded

separatamente *(say-pah-rah-tah-MAYN-tay)* separately

separato/a *(say-pah-RAH-toh/-tah)* separate, separated

seppia, la *(SAYP-pyah)* cuttlefish (similar to squid)

sera, la *(SAY-rah)* (le sere) evening

serio/a *(SEHR-yoh/-yah)* serious

serpente, il *(sayr-PEN-tay)* snake

serrato/a *(sayr-RAH-toh/-tah)* closed

serratura, la *(sayr-rah-TOO-rah)* lock

servire *(sayr-VEE-ray)* to serve

servizi, i *(sayr-VEET-tsee)* services

servizi igienici, i *(sayr-VEET-tsee ee-JEH-nee-chee)* toilets

servizi privati esterni, i *(sayr-VEET-tsee pree-VAH-tee ays-TEHR-nee)* private toilet, but outside the room

servizi pubblici, i *(sayr-VEET-tsee POOB-blee-chee)* toilets

servizio, il *(sayr-VEET-tsyoh)* (i servizi) service, service charge

sessanta *(says-SAHN-tah)* sixty

sessantadue *(says-sahn-tah-DOO-ay)* sixty-two

sessantacinque *(says-sahn-tah-CHEEN-kway)* sixty-five

sessantanove *(says-sahn-tah-NOH-vay)* sixty-nine

sessantaquattro *(says-sahn-tah-KWAHT-troh)* sixty-four

sessantasei *(says-sahn-tah-SEH-ee)* sixty-six

sessantasette *(says-sahn-tah-SET-tay)* sixty-seven

sessantatré *(says-sahn-tah-TRAY)* sixty-three

sessantotto *(says-sahn-TOHT-toh)* sixty-eight

sessantuno *(says-sahn-TOO-noh)* sixty-one

sesso, il *(SES-soh)* sex

seta, la *(SAY-tah)* silk

sete, la *(SAY-tay)* thirst

  Ho sete *(oh SAY-tay)* I'm thirsty

settanta *(sayt-TAHN-tah)* seventy

  settantacinque *(sayt-tahn-tah-CHEEN-kway)* seventy-five

  settantadue *(sayt-tahn-tah-DOO-ay)* seventy-two

  sessantanove *(sayt-tahn-tah-NOH-vay)* seventy-nine

  settantaquattro *(sayt-tahn-tah-KWAHT-troh)* seventy-four

  settantasei *(sayt-tahn-tah-SEH-ee)* seventy-six

  settantasette *(sayt-tahn-tah-SET-tay)* seventy-seven

  settantatré *(sayt-tahn-tah-TRAY)* seventy-three

  settantotto *(sayt-tahn-TOHT-toh)* seventy-eight

  settantuno *(sayt-tahn-TOO-noh)* seventy-one

sette *(SET-tay)* seven

settecento *(sayt-tay-CHEN-toh)* seven hundred

settembre, il *(sayt-TEM-bray)* September

settimana, la *(sayt-tee-MAH-nah)* (le settimane) week

  fine settimana, il *(FEE-nay sayt-tee-MAH-nah)* weekend

  settimana santa, la *(sayt-tee-MAH-nah SAHN-tah)* Holy Week

sfogliatelle, le *(sfohl-lyah-TEL-lay)* shell-shaped pastries stuffed with ricotta, almond paste, candied fruit or other sweets

sfogo, lo *(SFOH-goh)* rash

  sfogo da pannolino, lo *(SFOH-goh dah pahn-noh-LEE-noh)* diaper rash

sformato, lo *(sfohr-MAH-toh)* quiche-like, savory baked custard; type of soufflé

sfortuna, la *(sfohr-TOO-nah)* misfortune, bad luck

sfuso, lo *(SFOO-soh)* carafe (of wine)

S.G.C. *(ES-say jee chee)* (Strada di Grande Communicazione) non-toll expressway indicated by blue sign, can be more scenic and take longer than the autostrada

sgombro, lo *(ZGOHM-broh)* mackerel

shampoo, lo *(SHAHM-poo)* shampoo

sherry, lo *(SHAY-ree)* sherry

shorts, gli *(shohts)* shorts

sì *(see)* yes

si effettua *(see ayf-fayt-TOO-ah)* in effect (=operates)

siamo *(SYAH-moh)* we are

Sicilia, la *(see-CHEE-lyah)* Sicily

siciliana *(see-chee-LYAH-nah)* (pizza) with capers, black olives and cheese

sicurezza, la *(see-koo-RAYT-tsah)* security, safety

sicuro/a *(see-KOO-roh/-rah)* safe, secure

sigaretta, la *(see-gah-RAYT-tah)* (le sigarette) cigarette

sigaro, il *(SEE-gah-roh)* (i sigare) cigar

signora, la *(seen-NYOH-rah)* (le signore) lady

signore, il *(seen-NYOH-ray)* (i signori) gentleman

signorina, la *(seen-nyoh-REE-nah)* (le signorine) miss, young woman

Silvestro *(seel-VES-troh)* herb/nut liqueur

simile *(SEE-mee-lay)* similar

simpatico/a *(seem-PAH-tee-koh/-kah)* nice, likable

simposio, il *(seem-POHZ-yoh)* (i simposi) symposium

sinagoga, la *(see-nah-GOH-gah)* synagogue

sincero/a *(seen-CHEH-roh/-rah)* sincere, honest

sindaco, il *(SEEN-dah-koh)* mayor

singolo/a *(SEEN-goh-loh/-lah)* single

sinistra, la *(see-NEES-trah)* left

sintetico/a *(seen-TEH-tee-koh/-kah)* synthetic

sintomo, il *(SEEN-toh-moh)* (i sintomi) symptom

sinusite, la *(see-noo-ZEE-tay)* sinusitis, sinus infection

sirena, la *(see-REH-nah)* siren

siringa, la *(see-REEN-gah)* (le siringhe) syringe, piping bag (cooking)

sisma, il *(SEEZ-mah)* (i sismi) earthquake

sismico/a *(SEEZ-mee-koh/-kah)* seismic, earthquake (e.g., zone)

situazione, la *(see-too-aht-TSYOH-nay)* situation

slavina, la *(zlah-VEE-nah)* snowslide

slip, lo *(zleep)* (gli slip) briefs, swim trunks, bikini underwear

smeraldo, lo *(zmay-RAHL-doh)* emerald

smog, lo *(zmohg)* smog

smoking, lo *(SMOH-oo-keeng)* tuxedo

smottamento, lo *(zmoht-tah-MAYN-toh)* landslide

snack-bar, lo *(SNEK-bahr)* snack bar

so, Non lo *(nohn loh soh)* I don't know.

sobborgo il *(sohb-BOHR-goh)* (i sobborghi) suburb

soccorso, il *(sohk-KOHR-soh)* help

sociale *(soh-CHAH-lay)* social

società, la *(soh-chay-TAH)* society

sodo/a *(SOH-doh/-dah)* hard, firm

soffitto, il *(sohf-FEET-toh)* (i soffitti) ceiling

soffriggere *(sohf-FREED-jay-ray)* to fry lightly

software, il *(SOHFT-weh-uh)* software

sogliola, la *(SOHL-lyoh-lah)* (le sogliole) sole

sogliole alla mugnaia, le *(SOHL-lyoh-lay AHL-lah moon-NYAH-yah)* sole cooked in butter and served with parsley and lemon

soia, la *(SOH-yah)* soy

solamente *(soh-lah-MAYN-tay)* only, just

solare *(soh-LAH-ray)* solar, sun

soldato, il *(sohl-DAH-toh)* (i soldati) soldier

soldi, i *(SOHL-dee)* money, cash

soldo, il *(SOHL-doh)* (i soldi) penny, cent

sole, il *(SOH-lay)* sun

soleggiato/a *(soh-layd-JAH-toh/-tah)* sunny

solo/a *(SOH-loh/-lah)* only

solo andata *(SOH-loh ahn-DAH-tah)* one-way (ticket)

solstizio, il *(sohl-STEET-tsyoh)* solstice

solubile *(soo-LOO-bee-lay)* instant (coffee)

somaro, il *(soh-MAH-roh)* (i somari) donkey

somma, la *(SOHM-mah)* addition, sum

sommelier, il *(soh-muh-LYAY)* wine steward, wine waiter

sonnellino, il *(sohn-nayl-LEE-noh)* nap

sonno, il *(SOHN-noh)* sleep

sono *(SOH-noh)* I am

soppressa, la *(sohp-PRES-sah)* a pork salami

sopra *(SOH-prah)* on, over, above

sopracciglio, il *(sohp-praht-CHEEL-lyoh)* (i sopraccigli) eyebrow

sorbetto, il *(sohr-BAYT-toh)* sorbet

sordo/a *(SOHR-doh/-dah)* deaf

sorella, la *(soh-REL-lah)* (le sorelle) sister

sorpassare *(sohr-pahs-SAH-ray)* to pass

sorpresa, la *(soh-PRAY-sah)* surprise

sospeso/a *(sohs-PAY-soh/-sah)* suspended

sosta *(SOHS-tah)* stop, park

sottaceto, il *(soht-tah-CHAY-toh)* (i sottaceti) pickle

sotto *(SOHT-toh)* under, below, beneath

sottolio, il *(soht-TOHL-yoh)* (stored) in oil

sottopassaggio, il *(soht-toh-pahs-SAHD-joh)* (i sottopassaggi) underpass

sottotetto, il *(soht-toh-TAYT-toh)* attic

sottotitoli, i *(soh-toh-TEE-toh-lee)* subtitles

sottoveste, la *(soht-toh-VES-tay)* slip

sottrarre *(soht-TRAHR-ray)* to subtract

spaghetti, gli *(spah-GAYT-tee)* spaghetti

spaghetti all'amatriciana, gli *(spah-GAYT-tee AHL-lah-mah-tree-CHAH-nah)* spaghetti with sauce of tomato, bacon and Pecorino cheese

Spagna, la *(SPAHN-nyah)* Spain

spago, lo *(SPAH-goh)* string, twine

spalla, la *(SPAHL-lah)* (le spalle) shoulder

spasmo, lo *(SPAHZ-moh)* spasm

spasso, lo *(SPAHS-soh)* enjoyment, amusement

spátzle, lo *(SPAH-tslay)* type of egg noodle or small dumpling

spazio, lo *(SPAHT-tsyoh)* space, room

spazzatura, la *(spaht-tsah-TOO-rah)* garbage, trash

spazzolino da denti, lo *(spaht-tsoh-LEE-noh dah DEN-tee)* toothbrush

specchio, lo *(SPEK-kyoh)* mirror

speciale *(spay-CHAH-lay)* special

specialista, lo/la *(spay-chah-LEES-tah)* specialist

specialità, la *(spay-chah-lee-TAH)* speciality

specialità della casa, la *(spay-chah-lee-TAH DAYL-lah KAH-sah)* house specialty

speck, lo *(spek)* type of smoked ham similar to bacon

spedire *(spay-DEE-ray)* to send, to mail

spedirlo *(spay-DEER-loh)* to ship it "È possibile spedirlo?" = Is it possible to ship it?

spelonca, la *(spay-LOHN-kah)* (le spelonche) cave, cavern

spendere *(SPEN-day-ray)* to spend

spesa, la *(SPAY-sah)* expense, cost

spesso *(SPAYS-soh)* often

spesso/a *(SPAYS-soh/-sah)* thick, dense, heavy

spettacolo, lo *(spayt-TAH-koh-loh)* performance, show

spettacoloso/a *(spayt-tah-koh-LOH-soh/-sah)* spectacular

speziato/a *(spayt-TSYAH-toh/-tah)* spicy

spezie, le *(SPET-tsyay)* spices

spezzatino, lo *(spayt-tsah-TEE-noh)* stew

spiacente *(spyah-CHEN-tay)* sorry

spiaggia, la *(SPYAHD-jah)* beach

spicciolo, lo *(SPEET-choh-loh)* (gli spiccioli) small change, coin

spiedino, lo *(spyay-DEE-noh)* (gli spiedini) kebab

spiedo, allo *(AHL-loh SPYEH-doh)* broiled, roasted on spit

spigola, la *(SPEE-goh-lah)* European seabass

spilla, la *(SPEEL-lah)* brooch, pin

spina, la *(SPEE-nah)* electrical plug

alla spina *(AHL-lah SPEE-nah)* draft (beer), on tap

spina multipla, la *(SPEE-nah MOOL-tee-plah)* adaptor

spinaci, gli *(spee-NAH-chee)* spinach

spingere *(SPEEN-jay-ray)* to press, to push

splendido/a *(SPLEN-dee-doh/-dah)* splendid

sporco/a *(SPOHR-koh/-kah)* dirty

sport, lo *(spohrt)* sport

sportello, lo *(spohr-TEL-loh)* counter, window

sportello automatico, lo *(spohr-TEL-loh ow-toh-MAH-tee-koh)* ATM

sposalizio, lo *(spoh-zah-LEET-tsyoh)* wedding

sposare *(spoh-ZAH-ray)* to marry

sposato/a *(spoh-ZAH-toh/-tah)* married

SPQR the Senate and the People of Rome

spray, lo *(SPRAH-ee)* spray

spremuta, la *(spray-MOO-tah)* fresh fruit juice

spugnola, la *(spoon-NYOH-lah)* morel mushroom

spumante, lo *(spoo-MAHN-tay)* sparkling (wine)

spumone, lo *(spoo-MOH-nay)* whipped-cream ice cream, frothy egg-white-and-cream dessert

spuntino, lo *(spoon-TEE-noh)* (gli spuntini) snack

squadra, la *(SKWAH-drah)* team

stabile *(STAH-bee-lay)* stable, steady

stadio, lo *(STAHD-yoh)* stadium

stagionale *(stah-joh-NAH-lay)* seasonal

aperta stagionale *(ah-PEHR-tah stah-joh-NAH-lay)* open during tourist season

stagionato/a *(stah-joh-NAH-toh/-tah)* aged, seasoned

stagione, la *(stah-JOH-nah)* (le stagioni) season

quattro stagioni *(KWAHT-troh stah-JOH-nee)* (pizza) with various vegetables, cheese, ham and bacon

stampa, la *(STAHM-pah)* printing, print

stampante, la *(stahm-PAHN-tay)* printer

stampare *(stahm-PAH-ray)* to print

stanco/a, *(STAHN-koh/-kah)* tired

stanza, la *(STAHN-tsah)* room

stare *(STAH-ray)* to be, to stay, to remain

  sta *(stah)* you are (form. sing.), he/she/it is

  stanno *(STAHN-noh)* they are

  stiamo *(STYAH-moh)* we are

  sto *(stoh)* I am

stasera *(stah-SAY-rah)* tonight, this evening

Stati Uniti, gli *(STAH-tee oo-NEE-tee)* the United States

stato civile, lo *(STAH-toh chee-VEE-lay)* marital status

statua, la *(STAH-too-ah)* (le statue) statue

stazione, la *(staht-TSYOH-nay)* station

  stazione d'autobus, la *(staht-TSYOH-nay DOW-toh-boos)* bus station

  stazione di servizio, la *(staht-TSYOH-nay dee sayr-VEET-tsyoh)* gas station

  stazione ferroviaria, la *(staht-TSYOH-nay fayr-roh-VYAHR-yah)* train station

stecca di cioccolato, la *(STAYK-kah dee chohk-koh-LAH-toh)* (le stecche) chocolate bar

stecchino, lo *(stayk-KEE-noh)* (gli stecchini) toothpick

stella, la *(STAY-lah)* (le stelle) star

stelline, le *(stayl-LEE-nay)* little pasta stars

stesso/a *(STAYS-soh/-sah)* same

stile, lo *(STEE-lay)* style

stinco, lo *(STEEN-koh)* (gli stinchi) shanks (e.g., veal or ham)

stipendio, lo *(stee-PEND-yoh)* salary

stiramento, lo *(stee-rah-MAYN-toh)* sprain

stitichezza, la *(stee-tee-KAYT-tsah)* constipation

stivale, lo *(stee-VAH-lay)* (gli stivali) boot

Sto bene. *(stoh BEH-nay)* I'm fine/well.

stoccafisso, lo *(stohk-kah-FEES-soh)* dried cod

Stoccolma *(stohk-KOHL-mah)* Stockholm

stoffa, la *(STOHF-fah)* fabric

stomaco, lo *(STOH-mah-koh)* stomach

  mal di stomaco, il *(mahl dee STOH-mah-koh)* stomachache

stordito/a *(stohr-DEE-toh/-tah)* dizzy, dazed

storia, la *(STOHR-yah)* history

storico/a *(STOH-ree-koh/-kah)* historical

storione, lo *(stoh-RYOH-nay)* sturgeon

storta, la *(STOHR-tah)* sprain

stoviglie, le *(stoh-VEEL-lyay)* dishes

stracchino, lo *(strahk-KEE-noh)* semi-soft, mild, cow's milk cheese

stracciatella, la *(straht-chah-TEL-lah)* clear soup of egg, cheese and semolina; vanilla ice cream with chocolate chips

stracotto, lo *(strah-KOHT-toh)* beef stew or pot roast

strada, la *(STRAH-dah)* (le strade) road, street

Strada di Grande Communicazione *(STRAH-dah dee GRAHN-day kohm-moo-nee-kaht-TSYOH-nay)* non-toll expressway indicated by blue sign, can be more scenic and take longer than the autostrada

strame, lo *(STRAH-may)* hay, straw

straniero/a *(strah-NYEH-roh/-rah)* foreign

strano/a *(STRAH-noh/-nah)* strange

strapazzate *(strah-paht-TSAH-tay)* scrambled (eggs)

strato, lo *(STRAH-toh)* (gli strati) layer, stratum

strega, la *(STRAY-gah)* (le streghe) witch

Strega *(STRAY-gah)* sweet herb liqueur

stress, lo *(stress)* stress

stretto/a *(STRAYT-toh/-tah)* tight

stringozzi, gli *(streen-GOHT-tzee)* shoelace-like wheat pasta, usually served with a meat or tomato sauce

strutto, lo *(STROOT-toh)* lard

stucco, lo *(STOOK-koh)* stucco, plaster, putty

studente/studentessa, lo/la *(stoo-DEN-tay/stoo-den-TES-sah)* (gli studenti/le studentesse) student

studiare *(stoo-DYAH-ray)* to study, to learn

stufa, la *(STOO-fah)* stove, heater

stufatino, lo *(stoo-fah-TEE-noh)* beef stew

stufato/a *(stoo-FAH-toh/-tah)* braised

stufato, lo *(stoo-FAH-toh)* (gli stufati) stew

stupendo/a *(stoo-PEN-doh/-dah)* stupendous, wonderful

stupido/a *(STOO-pee-doh/-dah)* stupid

stupro, lo *(STOO-proh)* rape

stuzzicadenti, lo *(stoot-tsee-kah-DEN-tee)* (gli stuzzicadenti) toothpick

su *(soo)* on, up

su ordinazione *(soo ohr-dee-naht-TSYOH-nay)* make to order

subito *(SOO-bee-toh)* right away, immediately

suburbana, la *(soo-boor-BAH-nah)* suburban bus line

succo, il *(SOOK-koh)* (i succhi) juice

succo d'arancia, il *(SOOK-koh dah-RAHN-chah)* orange juice

succo di frutta, il *(SOOK-koh dee FROOT-tah)* fruit juice

succo di mela, il *(SOOK-koh dee MAY-lah)* apple juice

sud, il *(sood)* south

suggerire *(sood-jay-REE-ray)* to suggest

sugo, il *(SOO-goh)* (i sughi) sauce

suino/a *(soo-EE-noh/-nah)* swine

suo/a *(SOO-oh/-ah)* your/s

suocero/a, il/la *(SWOH-chay-roh/-rah)* father-/mother-in-law

suonare *(swoh-NAH-ray)* to play (e.g., an instrument)

suora, la *(SWOH-rah)* (le suore) nun

supermercato, il *(soo-payr-mayr-KAH-toh)* (i supermercati) supermarket

superstizione, la *(soo-payr-steet-TSYOH-nay)* superstition

Superstrada, la *(soo-payr-STRAH-dah)* non-toll expressway indicated by blue sign, can be more scenic and take longer than the autostrada

suppa, la *(SOO-pah)* soup

supplemento/a *(soop-play-MAYN-toh/-tah)* extra, supplementary

supplì, i *(soop-PLEE)* fried rice croquettes

surf da neve, il *(soorf dah NAY-vay)* snow boarding

susina, la *(soo-SEE-nah)* (le susine) plum

svanire *(zvah-NEE-ray)* to disappear, to vanish

sveglia, la *(ZVAYL-lyah)* alarm clock

svenire *(zvay-NEE-ray)* to faint

Svizzera, la *(ZVEET-tsay-rah)* Switzerland

T

T, t *(tee)* T, t

tabaccaio, il *(tah-bah-KAH-yoh)* tobacconist

tabaccheria, la *(tah-bahk-kay-REE-ah)* tobacconist's shop

tabacchi, il *(tah-BAHK-kee)* tobacconist

tabacco, il *(tah-BAHK-koh)* tobacco

tabulato, il *(tah-boo-LAH-toh)* printout

tabulatrice, la *(tah-boo-lah-TREE-chay)* computer printer

tacchino, il *(tahk-KEE-noh)* (i tacchini) turkey

taccuino, il *(tahk-koo-EE-noh)* notebook

tachimetro, il *(tah-KEE-may-troh)* speedometer

taglia, la *(TAHL-lyah)* size, cut

tagliare *(tahl-LYAH-ray)* to cut (up), to slice

tagliatelle, le *(tahl-lyah-TEL-lay)* pasta ribbons, similar to fettucine

tagliato/a a cubetti *(tahl-LYAH-toh/-tah ah coo-BAYT-tee)* diced

tagliaunghie, il *(tahl-lyah-OON-gyay)* nail clippers

taglierini, i *(tahl-lyay-REE-nee)* thinner version of tagliatelle (pasta)

taglio, il *(TAHL-lyoh)* (i tagli) cut
  al taglio *(ahl TAHL-lyoh)* (pizza) by the slice
  taglio di capelli, il *(TAHL-lyoh dee kah-PAYL-lee)* haircut

tajarin, i *(tah-yah-REEN)* thin pasta similar to tagliatelle

tampone, il *(tahm-POH-nay)* (i tamponi) tampon

tanto *(TAHN-toh)* a lot of, so much, so many

tappeto, il *(tahp-PAY-toh)* rug, carpet

tappo, il *(TAHP-poh)* (i tappi) plug
  tappi per le orecchie, i *(TAHP-pee payr lay oh-RAYK-kyay)* earplugs

tardi *(TAHR-dee)* late
  più tardi *(pyoo TAHR-dee)* later

tardo/a *(TAHR-doh/-dah)* slow

targa, la *(TAHR-gah)* (le targhe) license plate

numero di targa, il *(NOO-may-roh dee TAHR-gah)* license plate number

tariffa, la *(tah-REEF-fah)* fare
  tariffa postale, la *(tah-REEF-fah pohs-TAH-lay)* postage

tartufo, il *(tahr-TOO-foh)* (i tartufi) truffle
  tartufi di cioccolata, i *(tahr-TOO-fee dee chohk-koh-LAH-tah)* chocolate truffles

tasca, la *(TAHS-kah)* pocket

tassa, la *(TAHS-sah)* tax

tassì, il *(tahs-SEE)* (i tassì) taxi

tasso di cambio, il *(TAHS-soh dee KAHM-byoh)* exchange rate

tastiera, la *(tahs-TYEH-rah)* keyboard

tasto, il *(TAHS-toh)* (i tasti) button, key (not for lock)

tatto, il *(TAHT-toh)* touch

taverna, la *(tah-VEHR-nah)* (le taverne) tavern; modest, simple restaurant

tavola, la *(TAH-voh-lah)* (le tavole) table
  tavola calda, la *(TAH-voh-lah KAHL-dah)* warm snack bar
  tavola fredda, la *(TAH-voh-lah FRAYD-dah)* cold snack bar

taxi, il *(TAHK-see)* (i taxi) taxi

tazza, la *(TAHT-tsah)* (le tazze) cup

tazzina, la *(taht-TSEE-nah)* coffee cup

tè, il *(tay)* tea

tè alla pesca, il *(tay AHL-lah PES-skah)* peach-flavored tea

tè al limone, il *(tay ahl lee-MOH-nay)* lemon-flavored tea

tè caldo, il *(tay KAHL-doh)* hot tea

tè freddo, il *(tay FRAYD-doh)* iced tea

teatro, il *(tay-AH-troh)* theater

teatro dell'opera, il *(tah-AH-troh dayl-LOH-pay-roh)* opera house

teiera, la *(tay-YEH-rah)* teapot

telecomando, il *(tay-lay-koh-MAHN-doh)* remote control

teleconferenza, la *(tay-lay-kohn-fay-REN-tsah)* teleconference

telefonare *(tay-lay-fohn-NAH-ray)* to telephone

telefonata, la *(tay-lay-foh-NAH-tah)* phone call

telefonino, il *(tay-lay-foh-NEE-noh)* (i telefonini) cell phone

telefono, il *(tay-LEH-foh-noh)* (i telefoni) telephone

telefono cellulare, il *(tay-LEH-foh-noh chayl-loo-LAH-ray)* cell phone

telefono pubblico, il *(tay-LEH-foh-noh POOB-blee-koh)* public telephone

telegramma, il *(tay-lay-GRAHM-mah)* telegram

televisione, la *(tay-lay-vee-SYOH-nay)* television

tema, il *(TEH-mah)* (i temi) theme, topic

temperamatite, il *(taym-pay-rah-mah-TEE-tay)* pencil sharpener

temperatura, la *(taym-pay-rah-TOO-rah)* temperature

temperino, il *(taym-pay-REE-noh)* penknife

tempio, il *(TEM-pyoh)* temple

tempo, il *(TEM-poh)* time, weather

temporale, il *(taym-poh-RAH-lay)* storm

tenda, la *(TEN-dah)* tent

tendina, la *(ten-DEE-nah)* curtain

tenere *(tay-NAY-ray)* to hold, to keep

tennis, il *(TEN-nees)* tennis

tensione, la *(tayn-SYOH-nay)* tension

tensione premestruale, la *(tayns-SYOH-nay pray-mays-troo-AH-lay)* PMS

tergicristallo, il *(tayr-jee-krees-TAHL-loh)* (i tergicristalli) windshield wiper

termine, il *(TEHR-mee-nay)* (i termini) end

Terra, la *(TEHR-rah)* Earth

terra, la *(TEHR-rah)* land, ground

terracotta, la *(tayr-rah-KOHT-tah)* terracotta

terrazzo, il *(tayr-RAHT-tsoh)* terrace, balcony

terremoto, il *(tayr-ray-MOH-toh)* (i terremoti) earthquake

terribile *(tayr-REE-bee-lay)* terrible

terzo/a *(TEHR-tsoh/tsah)* third

tesi, la *(TEH-see)* thesis

tessera, la *(TES-say-rah)* (membership) card, pass, ticket

testa, la *(TES-tah)* head

testarolo, il *(tays-tah-ROH-loh)* (i testaroli) crepe

testicolo, il *(tays-TEE-koh-loh)* (i testicoli) testicle

Tevere, il *(TAY-vay-ray)* Tiber

tiepido/a *(TYEH-pee-doh/-dah)* tepid, warm

timbrare *(teem-BRAH-ray)* to stamp, to postmark

timido/a *(TEE-mee-doh/-dah)* timid, shy

timo, il *(TEE-moh)* thyme

tipico/a *(TEE-pee-koh/-kah)* typical

tipo, il *(TEE-poh)* type

tiramisù, il *(tee-rah-mee-SOO)* sponge cake soaked in coffee, topped with mascarpone, eggs, chocolate/coffee powders

tirare *(tee-RAH-ray)* to pull

Tirreno, il mar *(mahr teer-REN-noh)* Tyrrhenian Sea

tisana, la *(tee-ZAH-nah)* (le tisane) herb tea

titolo, il *(TEE-toh-loh)* title

toast, il *(TOH-oost)* toasted sandwich

toccare *(tohk-KAH-ray)* to touch
non toccare! *(nohn tohk-KAH-ray)* don't touch!

toeletta, la *(toh-ay-LET-tah)* (le toelette) restroom, toilet, WC

tofu, il *(TOH-foo)* tofu

toilette, la *(twah-LET)* restroom, toilet, WC

tomaxelle, le *(toh-mah-KSAYL-lay)* stuffed veal rolls

tomba, la *(TOHM-bah)* grave, tomb

tondo, il *(TOHN-doh)* round painting

tonno, il *(TOHN-noh)* tuna

tonsilla, la *(tohn-SEEL-lah)* (le tonsille) tonsil

topo, il *(TOH-poh)* (i topi) mouse, rat

torace, il *(toh-RAH-chay)* chest

torcia elettrica, la *(TOHR-chah ay-LET-tree-kah)* flashlight

tordo, il *(TOHR-doh)* (i tordi) thrush (bird)

Torino *(toh-REE-noh)* Turin

tornare *(tohr-NAH-ray)* to return

torre, il *(TOHR-ray)* tower

torrone, il *(tohr-ROH-nay)* nougat

torta, la *(TOHR-tah)* (le torte) cake, pie, tart

torta manfreda, la *(TOHR-tah mahn-FRAY-dah)* liver pate with Parmesan and Marsala

torta Margherita, la *(TOHR-tah mahr-gay-REE-tah)* cake with meringue, fruit, whipped cream

tortelli, i *(tohr-TEL-lee)* stuffed pasta, variety of shapes

tortellini, i *(tohr-tel-LEE-nee)* small filled dough rings with sauce or in soup

tortino, il *(tohr-TEE-noh)* (i tortini) savory pie

Toscana, la *(tohs-KAH-nah)* Tuscany

tossire *(tohs-SEE-ray)* to cough

tostapane, il *(tohs-tah-PAH-nay)* toaster

tostato/a *(tohs-TAH-toh/-tah)* toasted

totale *(toh-TAH-lay)* total

totano, il *(TOH-tah-noh)* squid

tovaglia, la *(toh-VAHL-lyah)* tablecloth

tovagliolo, il *(toh-vahl-LYOH-loh)* (i tovaglioli) napkin

tra *(trah)* between, among

tradurre *(trah-DOOR-ray)* to translate

traduzione, la *(trah-doot-TSYOH-nay)* translation

traffico, il *(TRAHF-fee-koh)* traffic

traghetto, il *(trah-GAYT-toh)* (i traghetti) ferry

tragicità, la *(trah-jee-chee-TAH)* tragedy

tragico/a *(TRAH-jee-koh/-kah)* tragic

tram, il *(trahm)* (i tram) streetcar, tram

tramezzino, il *(trah-mayd-DZEE-noh)* (i tramezzini) sandwich

tramonto, il *(trah-MOHN-toh)* sunset

tranquillo/a *(trahn-KWEEL-loh/-lah)* quiet

trasferire *(trahs-fay-REE-ray)* to transfer

trasporto, il *(trahs-POHR-toh)* transport

trattoria, la *(traht-toh-REE-ah)* (le trattorie) usually inexpensive restaurant serving simple food, local dishes

tre *(tray)* three

trecento *(tray-CHEN-toh)* three hundred

tredici *(TRAY-dee-chee)* thirteen

treno, il *(TREN-oh)* (i treni) train

trenta *(TRAYN-tah)* thirty

trentacinque *(trayn-tah-CHEEN-kway)* thirty-five

trentadue *(trayn-tah-DOO-ay)* thirty-two

trentanove *(trayn-tah-NOH-vay)* thirty-nine

trentaquattro *(trayn-tah-KWAHT-troh)* thirty-four

trentasei *(trayn-tah-SEH-ee)* thirty-six

trentasette *(trayn-tah-SET-tay)* thirty-seven

trentatré *(trayn-tah-TRAY)* thirty-three

trentotto *(trayn-TOHT-toh)* thirty-eight

trentuno *(trayn-TOO-noh)* thirty-one

trifola, la *(TREE-foh-lah)* (le trifole) truffle

triglia, la *(TREEL-lyah)* (le triglie) mullet

trilione *(tree-LYOH-nay)* trillion

trina, la *(TREE-nah)* lace

triplo/a *(TREE-ploh/-plah)* triple

trippa, la *(TREEP-pah)* tripe

triste *(TREES-tay)* sad

troppo *(TROHP-poh)* too, too much, too many

trota, la *(TROH-tah)* (le trote) trout

trovare *(troh-VAH-ray)* to find

trucco, il *(TROOK-koh)* make-up

tu *(too)* you (informal, singular)

tubetto, il *(too-BAYT-toh)* (i tubetti) tube

tubetti, i *(too-BAYT-tee)* small, tubular pasta

turismo, il *(too-REEZ-moh)* tourism

turista, il/la *(too-REES-tah)* (i turisti/le turiste) tourist

turistico/a *(too-REES-tee-koh/-kah)* tourist

tutte direzioni *(TOOT-tay dee-rayt-TSYOH-nee)* all directions

tutti/tutte *(TOOT-tee/-tay)* all (plural)

tutto/a *(TOOT-toh/-tah)* all, the whole, everything

TV, la *(tee-VOO)* TV

U

U, u *(oo)* U, u

ubriaco/a *(oo-bree-AH-koh/-kah)* inebriated, drunk

uccello, l' *m* *(oot-CHEL-loh)* (gli uccelli) bird

uccidere *(oot-CHEE-day-ray)* to kill

udire *(oo-DEE-ray)* to hear

ufficio, l' *m* *(oof-FEE-choh)* (gli uffici) office

ufficio del turismo, l' *m* *(oof-FEE-choh dayl too-REES-moh)* tourist office

ufficio postale, l' *m* *(oof-FEE-choh pohs-TAH-lay)* post office

uguale *(oo-GWAH-lay)* equal, the same

ultimo/a *(OOL-tee-moh/-mah)* last

umbrici, gli *(oom-BREE-chee)* type of long noodle

umido, in *(een OO-mee-doh)* stewed

undici *(OON-dee-chee)* eleven

unico/a *(OO-nee-koh/-kah)* combined

a senso unico *(ah SEN-soh OO-nee-koh)* one-way traffic

università, l' *f (oo-nee-vayr-see-TAH)* university

universo, l' *m (oo-nee-VEHR-soh)* universe

uno *(OO-noh)* one

uomini, gli *(WOH-mee-nee)* men

uomo, l' *m (WOH-moh)* (gli uomini) man

uomo d'affari, l' *m (WOH-moh dahf-FAH-ree)* businessman

uova, le *(WOH-vah)* eggs

uova alla romana, le *(WOH-vah AHL-lah roh-MAH-nah)* omelet with beans, onions, herbs

uovo, l' *m (WOH-voh)* (le uova) egg

urbana *(oor-BAH-nah)* urban bus line

urbano/a *(oor-BAH-noh/-nah)* urban, town

urgente *(oor-JEN-tay)* urgent

urina, l' *f (oo-REE-nah)* urine

usa e getta *(oo-zah-ay-JET-tah)* disposable

usare *(oo-ZAH-ray)* to use

usa e getta *(oo-zah-ay-JET-tah)* disposable

uscire *(oosh-SHEE-ray)* to exit

uscita, l' *f (oosh-SHEE-tah)* (le uscite) exit

uscita di sicurezza, l' *f (oosh-SHEE-tah dee see-koo-RAYT-tsah)* emergency exit

uso, l' *m (OO-zoh)* usage

utile *(OO-tee-lay)* useful

uva, l' *f (OO-vah)* (le uva) grape

uva bianca, l' *f (OO-vah BYAHN-kah)* green grapes

uva nera, l' *f (OO-vah NAY-rah)* red grapes

uva passa, l' *f (OO-vah PAHS-sah)* raisin

uva spina, l' *f (OO-vah SPEE-nah)* gooseberry

V

V, v *(voo)* V, v

va *(vah)* you go (form. sing.)

vacante *(vah-KAHN-tay)* vacant

vacanza, la *(vah-KAHN-tsah)* (le vacanze) vacation

vaccinazione, la *(vaht-chee-naht-TSYOH-nay)* vaccination

vada! *(VAH-dah)* go!

vado *(VAH-doh)* I go

vagina, la *(vah-JEE-nah)* vagine

vagone, il *(vah-GOH-nay)* wagon, train car

vagone letto, il *(vah-GOH-nay LET-toh)* sleeping car

vai via! *(VAH-ee VEE-ah)* go away!

valanga, la *(vah-LAHN-gah)* (le valanghe) avalance

validità, la *(vah-lee-dee-TAH)* validity

valido/a *(VAH-lee-doh/-dah)* valid

valigetta, la *(vah-lee-JAYT-tah)* briefcase

valigia, la *(vah-LEE-jah)* (le valige) bag, suitcase

valle, la *(VAHL-lay)* valley

valore, il *(vah-LOH-ray)* value

valuta, la *(vah-LOO-tah)* currency

vandalismo, il *(vahn-dah-LEEZ-moh)* vandalism

vaniglia, la *(vah-NEEL-lyah)* vanilla

vapore, al/a *(ahl/ah vah-POH-ray)* steamed

vaporetto, il *(vah-poh-RAYT-toh)* (i vaporetti) waterbus

vaso, il *(VAH-zoh)* vase

Vaticano, il *(vah-tee-KAH-noh)* the Vatican

vecchio/a *(VAYK-kyoh/-kyah)* old, aged

vedere *(vay-DAY-ray)* to see

vedovo/a *(VAY-doh-voh/-vah)* widowed

vedovo/a, il/la *(VAY-doh-voh/-vah)* widower/widow

vegetaliano/a *(vay-jay-tah-LYAH-noh/-nah)* vegan

vegetariano/a *(vay-jay-tah-RYAH-noh/nah)* vegetarian

velenoso/a *(vay-lay-NOH-soh/-sah)* poisonous

veloce *(vay-LOH-chay)* fast

velocità, la *(vay-loh-chee-TAH)* speed

vena, la *(VAY-nah)* (le vene) vein

vendere *(VEN-day-ray)* to sell

vendita, la *(VAYN-dee-tah)* sale

venerdì, il *(vay-nayr-DEE)* Friday

Venezia *(vay-NAYT-tsyah)* Venice

venire *(vay-NEE-ray)* to come

venti *(VAYN-tee)* twenty

venticinque *(vayn-tee-CHEEN-kway)* twenty-five

ventidue *(vayn-tee-DOO-ay)* twenty-two

ventinove *(vayn-tee-NOH-vay)* twenty-nine

ventiquattro *(vayn-tee-KWAHT-troh)* twenty-four

ventisei *(vayn-tee-SEH-ee)* twenty-six

ventisette *(vayn-tee-SET-tay)* twenty-seven

ventitré *(vayn-tee-TRAY)* twenty-three

ventotto *(vayn-TOHT-toh)* twenty-eight

ventuno *(vayn-TOO-noh)* twenty-one

ventilare *(vayn-tee-LAH-ray)* to ventilate

ventilatore, il *(vayn-tee-lah-TOH-ray)* fan

vento, il *(VEN-toh)* wind
tira vento *(TEE-rah VEN-toh)* it's windy

ventoso/a *(vayn-TOH-soh/-sah)* windy

ventotto *(vayn-TOHT-toh)* twenty-eight

ventre, il *(VEN-tray)* stomach
dolori al ventre, i *(doh-LOH-ree ahl VEN-tray)* stomach ache

ventuno *(vayn-TOO-noh)* twenty-one

verde *(VAYR-day)* green, creamed green vegetables

verdura, la *(vayr-DOO-rah)* (le verdure) vegetables
verdura mista, la *(vayr-DOO-rah MEES-tah)* mixed vegetables
verdure di stagione, le *(vayr-DOO-ray dee stah-JOH-nay)* vegetables in season

venduto/a *(vayn-DOO-toh/-tah)* sold

ventura, la *(vayn-TOO-rah)* luck, chance

verità, la *(vay-ree-TAH)* truth

verme, il *(VEHR-may)* (i vermi) worm

vermicelli, i *(vayr-mee-CHEL-lee)* very thin spaghetti

vero/a *(VAY-roh/-rah)* true

versamento, il *(vayr-sah-MAYN-toh)* payment

verza, la *(VAYR-dzah)* (le verze) green cabbage

vescica, la *(vaysh-SHEE-kah)* (le vesciche) blister, bladder

vespa, la *(VES-pah)* (le vespe) wasp

vespasiano, il *(vays-pah-ZYAH-noh)* urinal

vespro, il *(VES-proh)* vespers

vestito, il *(vays-TEE-toh)* (i vestiti) dress

vetrata, la *(vay-TRAH-tah)* stained-glass window

vetro, il *(VAY-troh)* glass
vetro soffiato, il *(VAY-troh sohf-FYAH-toh)* blown glass

via, la *(VEE-ah)* street, road, way
via aerea *(VEE-ah ah-EH-ray-ah)* air mail

Viacard, la *(vee-ah-KAHRD)* self-service toll payment lane that accepts credit cards (Caution: card may need chip to work)

viaggiare *(vee-ahd-JAH-ray)* to travel

viaggio, il *(vee-AHD-joh)* (i viaggi) trip, travel, voyage
viaggio d'affari, il *(vee-AHD-joh dahf-FAH-ree)* business trip

viale, il *(vee-AH-lay)* street, avenue, boulevard

vialone nano, il *(vee-ah-LOH-nay NAH-noh)* squat, absorbent rice

vicinato, il *(vee-chee-NAH-toh)* neighborhood

vicino/a *(vee-CHEE-noh/-nah)* nearby, close

vicino a *(vee-CHEE-noh ah)* near to

vicolo, il *(VEE-koh-loh)* alley, lane

videocamera, la *(vee-day-oh-KAH-may-rah)* videocamera

vietare *(vyay-TAH-ray)* to forbid, to prohibit

vietato/a *(vyay-TAH-toh/-tah)* forbidden, prohibited

vietato consumare cibi o bevande *(vyay-TAH-toh kohn-soo-MAH-ray CHEE-boh oh bay-VAHN-day)* no eating or drinking allowed

vietato entrare *(vyay-TAH-toh ayn-TRAH-ray)* no entry

vietato fotografare *(vyay-TAH-toh fot-toh-grah-FAH-ray)* no photographs

vietato fumare *(vyay-TAH-toh foo-MAH-ray)* no smoking

vietato l'ingresso *(vyay-TAH-toh leen-GREHS-soh)* no admittance

vietato toccare *(vyay-TAH-toh tohk-KAH-ray)* do not touch

vietato usare flash *(vyay-TAH-toh oo-ZAH-ray flesh)* no flash

vigna, la *(VEEN-nyah)* vineyard, wine cellar

vigneto, il *(veen-NYAY-toh)* vineyard

villaggio, il *(veel-LAHD-joh)* (le villaggi) village

vincere *(VEEN-chay-ray)* to win

vino, il *(VEE-noh)* (i vini) wine

lista dei vino, la *(LEES-tah DAY-ee VEE-noh)* wine list

vino bianco, il *(VEE-noh BYAHN-koh)* white wine

vino della casa, il *(VEE-noh DAYL-lah KAH-sah)* house wine

vino rosso, il *(VEE-noh ROHS-soh)* red wine

vino spumante, il *(VEE-noh spoo-MAHN-tay)* sparkling wine

viola *(vee-OH-lah)* purple

viola, la *(vee-OH-lah)* viola

violenza, la *(vee-oh-LEN-tsah)* violence

violinista, il/la *(vee-oh-lee-NEES-tah)* violinist

violino, il *(vee-oh-LEE-noh)* violin

VIP *(veep)* V.I.P.

virus, il *(VEE-roos)* virus

visciola, la *(VEESH-shoh-lah)* sour cherry

visibile *(vee-ZEE-bee-lay)* visible

visione, la *(vee-ZYOH-nay)* vision

visita, la *(VEE-zee-tah)* visit

visita guidata, la *(VEE-zee-tah gwee-DAH-tah)* guided tour

visitare *(vee-zee-TAH-ray)* to visit

viso, il *(VEE-zoh)* face

vista, la *(VEES-tah)* view, sight

vita, la *(VEE-tah)* life

vitamina, la *(vee-tah-MEE-nah)* (le vitamine) vitamin

vitello, il *(vee-TEL-loh)* veal

vitello alla bolognese, il *(vee-TEL-loh AHL-lah boh-lohn-NYAY-say)* veal cutlet with Parma ham and cheese

vitello tonnato, il *(vee-TEL-loh tohn-NAH-toh)* chilled veal slices in a creamy tuna sauce

vitto, il *(VEET-toh)* food

vivanda, la *(vee-VAHN-dah)* food

vivere *(VEE-vay-ray)* to live

vocabolarietto, il *(voh-kah-boh-lah-RYET-toh)* phrasebook

vocabolario, il *(voh-kah-boh-LAHR-yoh)* dictionary

voce, il *(VOH-chay)* voice

vodka, la *(VOHD-kah)* vodka

voglia, la *(VOHL-lyah)* wish, desire

volare *(voh-LAH-ray)* to fly

volere *(voh-LAY-ray)* to want

volo, il *(VOH-loh)* (i voli) flight

volta, la *(VOHL-tah)* (le volte) time, turn

  a volte *(ah VOHL-tay)* at times, sometimes

  una volta *(OO-nah VOHL-tah)* once

vomito, il *(VOH-mee-toh)* vomit

vongola, la *(VOHN-goh-lah)* (le vongole) clams

alla vongole *(AHL-lah VOHN-goh-lay)* sauce of clams, garlic, pepper, olive oil, parsley, possibly tomatoes

zuppa di vongole, la *(TSOOP-pah dee VOHN-goh-lay)* clam, white-wine soup

vorrei *(vohr-REH-ee)* I would like

vorremmo *(vohr-REM-moh)* we would like

vuoto/a *(VWOH-toh/-tah)* empty

W

W, w *(DOHP-pyoh voo)* W, w

wafer, il *(VAH-fayr)* wafer

WC, il *(vee-CHEE)* bathroom

weekend, il *(wee-KEND)* weekend

whisky, il *(WEES-kee)* whisky

würstel, il *(VUR-stul)* hot dog, wiener

X

X, x *(eeks)* X, x

Y

Y, y *(EEP-see-lohn)* Y, y

yoga, il *(YOH-gah)* yoga

yogurt, il *(YOH-goort)* yogurt

Z

Z, z *(DZEH-tah)* Z, z

zabaglione, lo *(dzah-bahl-LYOH-nay)* dessert custard of egg yolks, sugar, and Marsala wine

zabaione, lo *(dzah-bah-YOH-nay)* dessert custard of egg yolks, sugar, and Marsala wine

zafferano, lo *(dzahf-fay-RAH-noh)* saffron

zaffiro, lo *(dzahf-FEE-roh)* sapphire

zaino, lo *(DZAH-ee-noh)* (gli zaini) backpack

zampirone, lo *(dzahm-pee-ROH-nay)* mosquito repellent

zanzara, la *(dzahn-DZAH-rah)* (le zanzanre) mosquito

zecca, la *(TSAYK-kah)* (le zecche) tick (insect)

zenzero, lo *(DZAYN-dzay-roh)* ginger

zero, lo *(DZEH-roh)* zero

zeta *(DZEH-tah)* zee

zia, la *(TSEE-ah)* (le zie) aunt

zingaro/a, lo/la *(TSEEN-gah-roh/-rah)* gypsy

zio, lo *(TSEE-oh)* (gli zii) uncle

ziti, gli *(DZEE-tee)* medium-sized pasta tubes

zona, la *(DZOH-nah)* zone

zona disco, la *(DZOH-nah DEES-koh)* paid parking zone

zona pedonale, la *(DZOH-nah pay-doh-NAH-lay)* pedestrian zone

zucca, la *(TSOOK-kah)* pumpkin, gourd

zucchero, lo *(TSOOK-kay-roh)* sugar

zucchina, la *(tsook-KEE-nah)* (le zucchine) zucchini

zucchini ripieni, gli *(tsook-KEE-noh ree-PYEH-nee)* stuffed zucchini

zucchino, lo *(tsook-KEE-noh)* (gli zucchini) zucchini

zucchini ripieni, gli *(tsook-KEE-noh ree-PYEH-nee)* stuffed zucchini

zuccotto, lo *(tsook-KOHT-toh)* frozen or semi-frozen dessert of ice cream, cake and brandy

zuppa, la *(TSOOP-pah)* (le zuppe) soup

zuppa del giorno, la *(TSOOP-pah dayl JOHR-noh)* soup of the day

zuppa di ceci, la *(TSOOP-pah dee CHAY-chee)* hearty chickpea soup

zuppa inglese, la *(TSOOP-pah een-GLAY-say)* rum-soaked sponge cake filled with cream and chocolate or candied fruit

zuppo/a (di) *(TSOOP-poh/pah)* soaked (with)

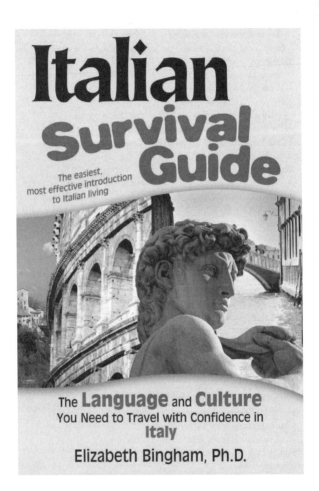

Italian
Survival Guide

The easiest, most effective introduction to Italian living

The **Language** and **Culture**
You Need to Travel with Confidence in
Italy

Elizabeth Bingham, Ph.D.

About *Italian Survival Guide:*
The Language and Culture You Need to Travel with Confidence in Italy

Italian Survival Guide is a no-frills course that gets down to the nitty-gritty from the start. It's a forthright view of what really helps when traveling in Italy, with a realistic understanding of how much time most travelers have to prepare.

Three Survival Books in One!

Phrasebook/dictionary—survival vocabulary
"Learn Italian" book—survival grammar
Everyday culture book—survival social
knowledge

All you need for a confident trip.

Important travel vocabulary and cultural information, easy explanations of grammar (and what you can ignore), exercises for practice, study tips, travel hints, reality checks, compact dictionaries.

Don't just visit a country. Experience it.
Use a Survival Guide!

Having

I have ___.	ho ___	*oh ___*
Do you have __?	Ha ___?	*ah ___?*
We have ___.	Abbiamo ___.	*ahb-BYAH-moh ___*
He/she/it has __.	Ha ___.	*ah ___*

Existence and Identifying

I am ___.	Sono ___	*SOH-noh ___*
You are/Are you?	È ___.	*eh ___*
He/she/it is ___.	È ___.	*eh ___*
There is ___.	C'è ___.	*cheh ___*
There are ___.	Ci sono ___.	*chee SOH-noh ___*
Here it is! / Here you are!	Ecco!	*EK-koh!*
What is that?	Che cos'è quello?	*kay KOH-say KWAYL-loh?*
That is ___.	È ___.	*eh ___*

Want, Need, and Must

I would like ___.	Vorrei ___. / Desidero ___.	*vohr-REH-ee ___ / day-ZEE-day-roh ___*
Would you like __?	Desidera ___?	*day-ZEE-day-rah __?*
I need ___.	Ho bisogno di __.	*oh bee-ZOHN-nyoh dee__*
I need something for __.	Ho bisogno di qualcosa per ___	*oh bee-ZOHN-nyoh dee kwahl-KOH-sah payr ___*
Do I need to/ have to __? Must I __?	Devo (verb)?	*DAY-voh ___?*
You have to/ need to/must ___.	Deve (verb).	*DAY-vay ___*